Bright, Brilliant Days

Douglas Gageby and
The Irish Times

Edited by
Andrew Whittaker

A. & A. Farmar

British Library Cataloguing in Publication Data
A CIP catalogue record for this book is available from the British
Library

ISBN-10: 1-899047-66-2
ISBN-13: 978-1-899047-66-6

First published in 2006
by
A. & A. Farmar Ltd
78 Ranelagh Village, Dublin 6, Ireland
Tel +353-1-496 3625 Fax +353-1-497 0107
Email afarmar@iol.ie

Photographs courtesy of the Gageby family,
except for p 90, courtesy Mary Maher.
Drawing on p 158 by Michael Viney.

Printed and bound by ColourBooks
Typeset and designed by A. & A. Farmar
Cover designed by Kevin Gurry

Preface

Andrew Whittaker

This book covers much ground but I hope reads lightly. The authors are interested in the transformation of modern Ireland, *The Irish Times*'s part in it, and its reforming and internationally renowned editor Douglas Gageby. No more talented authors could have been found and none more diverse. They co-operated in order to stimulate, inform and entertain readers interested in some remarkable personalities and events of the recent past.

The principle I adopted was not to accept the first story that came my way, nor even to be guided by my own general impressions. Either I was present myself at the events, or else they are described by people who were there or who have particular expertise to analyse them, and whose reports I have checked with as much thoroughness as possible. Where accounts clash, that is part of the historical evidence.

The book was conceived at a memorial meeting for Gageby, organised by *The Irish Times* in July 2004. It struck me as I looked around the gathering that the recollections and judgments of Gageby's colleagues and rivals should be collected while we still had our wits about us. I consulted the Gageby family and some former colleagues. Old friends Anna and Tony Farmar of A. & A. Farmar, book publishers, encouraged me and offered to publish the result—if there was a result. Well, here it is.

I did not invite or reject essayists according to whether they were likely to be favourable or unfavourable to Gageby. I chose writers whom I knew or who I believed would write interestingly. I cast the net widely, but another book could be put together from those who had already published their own books, or whose talents I passed over for lack of space, or who declined to write, or who agreed but had to drop out, or whom I did not know well enough to ask, or whom I did not have the wit to think of, or who died too soon. When I found that some people had suffered a bad time under Gageby, I did not withdraw the invitation to write but encouraged them to give forthright accounts of their experiences and opinions.

This is no hagiography nor is it intentionally revisionist, though I see that time revises us all. It is not an official history of *The Irish Times* during the era nor an authorised biography of Gageby: for while most of the authors were eye-witnesses or have a special skill in reviewing events, they have had no access to family or company papers.

The views of the authors are their own and do not attach to any institutions or organisations with which they may be connected.

Douglas Gageby's articles from Germany of 60 years ago, with which he burst upon Irish journalism, are reprinted here. They are classics of 'I was there' reporting.

I thank Geraldine Kennedy, the editor of *The Irish Times*, and her predecessor Conor Brady for their permissions to reprint biographical material and reminiscences. Brady's autobiography *Up with The Times* (Dublin 2005) is essential reading for the commercial and personnel ups and downs of the last 30 years of the newspaper. I also thank the editor of *The Times* of London for permission to reprint its obituary of Gageby, and its author for his advice, though I may not name him.

I am grateful to my wife Rosalind, who for the second time in four years has suffered her life being tormented by a book (books keep strange hours) and who read drafts and suggested many improvements.

I thank Dermot James, former company secretary of *The Irish Times*, and Mary Maher for assistance in identifying people in photographs.

Other *Irish Times* colleagues whom I consulted helped greatly but wish to be anonymous.

Alan Bestic, the author (and a remarkable raconteur), who was then a reporter on the *Irish Press*, reported from Germany and Eastern Europe about four months before Gageby's visit of autumn 1946. He has helped with descriptions of how the *Irish Press* was managed then.

Drafts of several chapters were read by William Kingston and Antoin Murphy as well as by various of the authors, to the benefit of the book.

William Scally selected and loaned to me political and historical works about the relevant period from his personal collection.

Evelyn McGovern and Dermot Sherlock of the Alumni Office in Trinity College, Dublin, dug up the academic records of Douglas and Dorothy Gageby for me.

The staff of the Gilbert Library in Pearse Street, Dublin, where newspapers are kept, were cheery and helpful, as always.

I thank the librarians at Dublin City University who gave Senator Martin Mansergh access to the copies of Gageby's leading articles, lodged there by his family.

As after a war there is a memorial to the unknown soldier, I gratefully thank any helpers whom I have ungratefully failed by haste or inadvertence to mention above.

Additional reading
Below are some other works relating to the subject readers might like to know about:

Robert Fisk, *In Time of War,* Gill & Macmillan, Dublin, 1983, recounts *inter alia* Gageby's service in translating documents washed up from a German submarine.
Donal Foley, *Three Villages,* Egotist Press, Dublin, 1977, his autobiography, with introductions by Maeve Binchy and Mary Maher.
Tony Gray, *Mr Smyllie, Sir,* Gill & Macmillan, Dublin, 1991. This, the classic account of the famous editor, is broader than its title suggests. It is a useful history of *The Irish Times* commercially, particularly from the 1930s to the 1950s, explaining the changing ownership and the evolution of editorial attitudes.
John Healy, *Healy, Reporter,* House of Healy, Achill, 1991, on his life as a reporter including working for Gageby in the Irish News Agency and the *Evening Press.*
John Healy, *The Death of an Irish Town,* House of Healy, Achill, 1988: the preface tells how Gageby made him write this famous book, previously published as *No One Shouted Stop.*
John Horgan, *Irish Media, A Critical History Since 1922,* Routledge, London, 2001, is essential.
Ivor Kenny, *In Good Company,* Gill & Macmillan, Dublin, 1987. This includes an excellent 24-page interview with Gageby illuminating his upbringing and opinions.
The Liberal Ethic . . ., a compilation of correspondence carried in *The Irish Times* in January to March 1950, and published by the newspaper as a pamphlet.

Contents

Contents

The contributors

Bruce Arnold is chief critic of the *Irish Independent*. He has written 14 books including a history of Irish art, biographies of William Orpen, Mainie Jellett and Jack Yeats, a tetralogy of novels, and most recently *The Spire and Other Essays on Modern Irish Culture*. He has written political biographies of Jack Lynch, Charles Haughey and Margaret Thatcher. In 2003 he was made an OBE. On leaving Trinity College Dublin he joined *The Irish Times*, as he relates in his contribution here, but has spent the greater part of his career in journalism with the *Irish Independent*.

Maeve Binchy is the author of 18 books. Her novels have been immensely popular and have appeared in many languages. She was a school teacher before she became women's editor of *The Irish Times* and, as related in her contribution here, frustrated Douglas Gageby into calling her 'Mrs Snell' because . . . well, read her essay to find out why.

Dr John Bowman is an historian, political scientist and broadcaster. He presents current affairs and historical programmes for RTÉ radio and television. His book *De Valera and the Ulster Question: 1917–1973* won the Ewart-Biggs literary prize for its contribution to North-South understanding. He won the television documentary of the year award for his 'John Charles McQuaid: What the Papers Say', a two-part exploration of the archives of the late Roman Catholic Archbishop of Dublin, Dr John Charles McQuaid.

Wesley Boyd was born in Co. Fermanagh in 1933 and spent most of his early life in Belfast. He entered journalism at the age of 18 and worked on a number of weekly papers before joining the Belfast daily, the *Northern Whig*. In 1956 he became the paper's London editor and lobby correspondent at Westminster at the age of 23. When the *Northern Whig* closed he worked as a sub-editor in the BBC's London newsroom. He returned to Ireland in 1963 as diplomatic correspondent of *The Irish Times*. In 1969 he joined RTÉ News as a senior editor and was head of news from 1974 to 1990.

James Downey is a leader writer and political columnist for the *Irish Independent*. He worked as a journalist on the *Evening Press* before joining *The Irish Times*, where he became London editor and later deputy editor to Douglas Gageby. He won the Liam Hourican Award in 1996 as Ireland's European Journalist of the Year.

Colonel Ned Doyle retired from the Army as Director of Signals. He is a chartered engineer. He trained as a soldier, NCO and officer during the 1939–45 Emergency, doing officer training with Douglas Gageby. He became the military writer for *The Irish Times*. He contributed to the anthology, *An Irish Childhood*, edited by A. Norman Jeffares and Antony Kamm (London, 1987, Dublin 1992). He has lectured and written on UN peacekeeping in *International Peacekeeping* and on military history for *The Irish Sword*. He was on the staff of the International Peace Academy, Vienna, for 19 years.

John Horgan, former Professor of Journalism at Dublin City University, worked for *The Irish Times* as general and foreign reporter, education correspondent and religious affairs correspondent between 1963 and 1973, when he became editor of *The Irish Times* weekly publication, *The Education Times* (1973–6). He was a member of Seanad Éireann (1969–77), Dáil Éireann (1977–81) and the European Parliament (1981–3).

Nicholas Leonard entered journalism at Oxford where he was editor of the university newspaper, *Cherwell*. After working for the *Investor's Chronicle* and the *Evening Standard* in London, he became the first financial editor of *The Irish Times* in 1963, leaving in 1964 to become the launch editor of the Irish weekly magazine, *Business and Finance*. Later in his journalistic career he was London editor of the *Irish Independent* and worked for LBC Radio and the *Financial Times* group. He now lives in the UK and contributes a weekly column of Westminster political comment to the *Irish Independent*.

Sam McAughtry was born in 1921. He served as an RAF officer in the Second World War, 1940–46, and in the Northern Ireland civil service until 1977 He was a trade unionist and NI Labour Party member. He joined *The Irish Times* as a columnist in 1981 at Douglas Gageby's invitation and continued until 1986 when he was Irish Columnist of the Year. His publications include short stories. memoirs, travel books and a novel. He has broadcast on the BBC and RTÉ. He was conferred with an honorary doctorate by NUI Maynooth in 1998. He was a member of Seanad Éireann from 1996 to 1998.

Derek McCullagh was appointed the accountant of *The Irish Times* in 1968. He was appointed to the board of *The Irish Times* in 1978 and was production director from 1996, holding both posts until he retired in 2002. He is a past chairman of the Financial Executives Association.

Patsy McGarry has been religious affairs correspondent with *The Irish*

Times since 1997 having joined the paper in 1994. He has worked for Independent Newspapers, the Irish Press group, *Magill* magazine, RTÉ and also worked for many years on pirate radio in Dublin. He received a national media award for articles on the fall of Charles Haughey and was awarded the 1998 Templeton European Religion Writer of the Year. He is the editor of *Christianity*, (Veritas, Dublin, 2001) and author of *The Book of Jesus Reports* (The Irish Times, Dublin 2001).

Senator Martin Mansergh, elected on the Agricultural Panel, since 2002, was appointed member of the Council of State in 2004. He was an *Irish Times* columnist from 2003 to 2006. He is a former special advisor on Northern Ireland to Taoisigh Charles Haughey, Albert Reynolds and Bertie Ahern. Author of *The Legacy of History for Making Peace in Ireland* he received the 1994 Tipperary Peace Prize with Fr Alex Reid and Rev. Roy Magee for mediation work leading to the paramilitary ceasefires. He was a member of the Department of Foreign Affairs from 1974 to 1981.

Kevin Myers, writer, broadcaster and novelist (*Banks of Green Willow*, 2001), is author of the best-selling *Kevin Myers* (2002), a gathering of his celebrated and provocative 'Irishman's Diary' in *The Irish Times*, for which he wrote for over 25 years (another collection will appear from The Lilliput Press in 2007.) His memoir *Watching the Door* on his period working as a journalist in Belfast in the 1970s was published in 2006. He is now a columnist with the *Irish Independent*.

Conor O'Clery is a journalist and author and lives in Dublin. He worked for *The Irish Times* from 1972 to 2005. He was assistant editor from 1978 to 1981 and news editor from 1981 to 1985, following which he served as foreign correspondent in Russia, China and the United States.

Fionnuala O Connor, born in Belfast, has reported from Northern Ireland for more than 30 years. She profiled the main players in the 'peace process' in a recent book, *Breaking the Bonds*, and has written a history of the integrated education sector, *A Shared Childhood*. Her 1993 analysis of northern Catholics, *In Search of a State*, won the Ewart-Biggs award and Orwell prize. She is an *Irish Times* columnist and writes for the *Economist*.

Donal O'Donovan was born in Dublin in 1928 and educated at Blackrock College and University College Dublin. He joined the *Sunday Independent* in 1950 and *The Irish Times* in 1954. He was assistant editor when he left to become public relations manager of the Bank of Ireland in 1970. He returned to newspapers in 1981. He is author of biographies of Kevin Barry (1985) and Raymond McGrath (1989). He is married to Jenny McGrath and they have four children.

Olivia O'Leary is an author and broadcaster and has presented TV and radio current affairs programmes in Ireland and the UK, including RTÉ's 'Questions & Answers', 'Today Tonight', 'Prime Time', and the BBC's 'Newsnight'. She was a political journalist for *The Irish Times* and then the *Sunday Tribune*. She has won Jacob's awards in Ireland and a Sony award in the UK for her BBC Radio 4 series, 'Between Ourselves'. *Party Animals*, a second collection of her RTÉ Radio 1 political sketches, was published in 2006 by O'Brien Press, Dublin.

Andrew O'Rorke is the chairman of Hayes Solicitors, the longest-established firm of solicitors in Dublin. He was previously managing partner. He has represented clients in all Irish courts and in the European Court of Justice. He has served as vice-chairman of the Employment Appeals Tribunal. His main practice area is in defamation, on which he has advised *The Irish Times* for many years.

Paul Tansey is a former economics correspondent and assistant editor of *The Irish Times*. He was also deputy editor of the *Sunday Tribune*. He has published two books on the Irish labour market: *Making the Irish Labour Market Work* (Gill & Macmillan, Dublin, 1991) and *Ireland at Work* (Oaktree Press, Dublin, 1998). He now works as an economic consultant.

Michael Viney, a migrant from London's Fleet Street, joined *The Irish Times* in 1962, aged 29, and left the staff in 1975. In 1977 he moved to west Mayo with his family and began the column 'Another Life', which continues as a commentary on nature and ecology, themes also of his books and films for television.

Andrew Whittaker was London editor, business editor and assistant general manager of *The Irish Times*, 1962–78. He is editor of the business law journal *Competition*. He is author of *The Church of Ireland in the Age of Louis XIV*, Dublin, 2004.

Bright, brilliant days

Andrew Whittaker

He was self-deprecating. It was a strange characteristic for a man from whom such confidence, even passion, flowed to his readers. He made them feel leaders of liberalism in illiberal times and contemporaries in the creation of a new Ireland out of a ham-fisted or even shameful old one. I think he honed a natural trait into a management tool, and it certainly helped him with his staff.

When he was a junior and soon an editor in the *Irish Press* after the Second World War he demurred at praise and said his seniors had the bright idea. When he was senior in *The Irish Times* he praised his staff and said it was their idea. When he was in between, I don't know what he did, for his closest colleagues never seemed to have caught him in that mode. He didn't seem to do in-betweens, he was a very definite man. Eventually, I suppose, the writers in this book are trying, in all our own ways, to find what he was in-between about, what he and our times were really made of.

Douglas Gageby was among the finest editors and most ingenious creators and most successful proprietors of a serious newspaper in English in the 20th century. Indeed in more than English, for his view extended around the world. He had opinions and curiosity about classical liberal papers such as the post-war duo, *Le Monde* of Paris and the *Frankfurter Allgemeine Zeitung*, both of which he could read, but also about many that he couldn't. He was fascinated by how papers became influential organs of their society. He reprinted with avidity a series of long articles written in the mid-1960s by the foreign correspondents of *The Times* of London, who evaluated quality papers around the world, and also Moscow's *Pravda*, Peking's *People's Daily*, and the semi-official organ (as it was always curiously described) of President Nasser's dictatorship in Cairo, *Al Ahram*. He was trying to learn from them all.

Some of them have since fallen or been transformed with their regimes, including *Le Monde*, whose founding director after the Second World War, Hubert Beuve-Méry, he particularly cherished. But his *Irish Times* sails on. Not always happily or serenely, but so far fortunately, although chastened by recurring bouts of management folly. It can still be admired for showing brio and courage in crass and ignorant times, as his successor-but-one, Geraldine Kennedy did in the autumn of 2006 by printing revelations about his private finances that rocked the government of Taoiseach Bertie Ahern.

Gageby did not much like America or its newspapers, except the *New York Times* and—definitely his favourite—the *Christian Science Monitor*, which in the 1960s was a cultivated New England paper deploying a modest network of foreign correspondents with unusual writing ability. (I did not know then that he had quit the Church of Ireland beliefs of his County Westmeath mother for the even more arcane observances of the Christian Scientists.) Once, after a long tour around America, I enthused to him about the *Rocky Mountain News*, a gem of a newspaper that I had happened upon and which I declared suitable even for Europeans and, indeed, the only readable paper between the Mohave desert and the headwaters of the Potomac. He grunted. As to English papers, he took the news service of *The Times*, with its outstanding Washington correspondent Louis Heren, and the *Guardian*, which provided the laconic American essays of Alistair Cooke and the Kremlinology of the finest master of that trade among a generation of brilliant ex-communist exiles from Eastern Europe, Isaac Deutscher. The cost of such services was not only the syndication fees they charged to a small, poor, but growing newspaper like us, but the manpower cost of re-typing their articles in London for telexing to Dublin, and then putting a young, poor but growing staff, including me, to work with scissors and paste to reduce the flood to a small number of shimmering, transparent reports on one page of our paper—or if there were some international crisis, such as Chairman Mao's Cultural Revolution or the Vietnam war, another half page.

Combining challenges was Gageby's strength. Compared one by one with his contemporaries as editors or innovators or owners he was excellent, or better than average, or at least highly interesting. If he was not always and necessarily top dog, the quintessential boss, the finest, yet when all challenges were taken together he was by the consent of his contemporaries and in particular *Irish Times* readers outstanding, remarkable, exceptional. Nor were those judges cannon fodder for any editor, even him; no, instead they were Clausewitzs, every one, and their 'Letters to the Editor' showed it. They and their successors will judge Gageby and our descriptions of him by the highest standard there is: their educated own.

His work was regarded with enthusiasm by foreigners who discovered it, whether as travellers or because of the flux of reporters and interviewers through Belfast and Dublin during the long years of the

Troubles in Northern Ireland. Many came from organisations whose readers or viewers could no doubt sign their American Express credit cards but were otherwise scarcely literate and (for the two things go together) were incurious about politics unless shooting was involved. They were not prepared for a writers' paper like *The Irish Times* with its writers' freely attentive audience. They streamed into Gageby's office to talk to him, and he was patient and good humoured with them.

This book aims at a narrow but one of the most entertaining niches in literature, that of unputdownable recollections of a formative journalist at the top of his era. I think of three whose talents remind me of Gageby. In the 19th century was the discontented Scot, James Gordon Bennett, who founded the revolutionary *New York Herald* in 1835 and built it up on the back of a new middle-class readership interested, among other things, in his innovative 'money article'. Its circulation came to equal that of *The Times* of London and a dim gleam of its title remains in the Paris-based *New York Herald Tribune*. Before launching the *Herald* he wrote from Washington for another paper and in 1827–8 invented for it the modern 'news story' about politicians. He did not scruple to describe his despatches as being sent 'From the Court of John Q. Adams', just as in our age *Le Canard enchaîné* reported the activities of President Charles de Gaulle as from the court of Versailles under le Roi Soleil. When Bennett had his own paper, his competitors were vexed at his initiative in hiring paid reporters not only to discover the price of the wheat crop in up-state New York but to report politics from Washington in the manner he had done. They were outraged that those reporters got exclusive briefings from the sons of President John Tyler. There, surely, is a true precursor of John Healy's and Douglas Gageby's 'Backbencher' column in *The Irish Times* in the 1960s?

The 20th-century editors I had in mind were Harold Ross, first editor of the *New Yorker*, and Henry Luce, the inventor of *Time* and *Life* and *Fortune*, but I must move on.

Gageby passed from being utterly junior to middling senior while quite young, as with battlefield promotions. In 1959 when he accepted his second and pressing invitation from *The Irish Times*'s managing director, George Hetherington, to join the board and own shares and be joint managing director, he was 39. Already he had been an exceptional student, a happy soldier, a suitor whose beautiful, bicycling girl friend, Dorothy Lester, had said 'Yes' and turned him into an adoring young husband, then a journalist learning his trade as sub-editor, then rapidly deputy editor of the new *Sunday Press* and after that editor of a briefly contentious national news agency launched by an anti-Fianna Fáil coalition government, and then in 1954 the editor brought back to launch what after a halting start became Dublin's vividly successful *Evening Press*—though by his own account it nearly died in its first year until a scoop by his subordinates John Healy and James Downey turned it around.

When Hetherington first approached him it was to become editorial director of *The Irish Times* for the purpose of rescuing the company's audacious new tabloid, the *Sunday Review*, which needed more readers and advertisers. Gageby said no, but astutely added that if they wanted to come back and ask him to become a full board director, and if the board was truly 'national' in its interests (meaning not west-British) as Hetherington claimed, then he would listen. Hetherington was back to him within the year.

Why did Gageby leave the *Irish Press* for *The Irish Times*? I think for two usual reasons: the challenge and the money. He must have seen that ownership and management of the *Irish Press* would continue within the de Valera family. There was no future for him except as a waged employee. Hetherington offered him a new challenge together with financial influence as joint managing director. He could aspire to do even better some day, while acknowledging that no director of *The Irish Times* in the last half century had made money from his shares except by selling them. But the shares were bankable. One might have to borrow to buy them, but one could also borrow against them.

That year Dorothy's father died. Gageby was 39 and she and he had four young children. What man in that circumstance doesn't need a new job with more money? He told his young colleague and later editorial rival, Tim Pat Coogan, that he had secured from *The Irish Times* a contract that would mean 'they'd have to sell the building to get rid of me' (memorial by Coogan in *Irish Independent*, 29 June 2004).

His mother-in-law, Elsie Lester, sold the Station House in Recess, Co. Galway, and a family arrangement was made whereby Dorothy and Douglas bought Riversdale House, off Bushy Park Road, Rathgar—a large house and gardens standing above the river Dodder, previously occupied by international horse woman Iris Kellet and long on the market. An extension was built for Elsie. Riversdale was in the only part of Dublin that Gageby knew, the lawned suburb of Rathgar. It was fifteen minutes' walk from the Lesters' large and stylish Fairfield House on Highfield Road (between the Rathgar and Dartry trams) that Dorothy had left on 12 July 1944 to marry him when he was a 25-year-old lieutenant with no obvious career. (His address on their marriage certificate is McKee Barracks; her age is 22.) Once married they moved nearby, to live in Winton Avenue, Rathgar, scarcely eight minutes' walk from her mother's house. It was a remarkable address for a lieutenant.

Fifteen years later, in 1959, moving into Riversdale House and holding a directorship in the Irish Times, Douglas provided Dorothy with an equivalent place to that she left in 1944 to marry him.

When they married some aspects of life were simple. There was only one 'French' restaurant in Dublin in 1944. It was owned by Louis Jammet and his sculptress wife Yvonne. The staple fare of Dublin's traditional dining rooms in the Shelbourne, Russell and Hibernian hotels near St Stephen's Green, or in the Dolphin in Essex Street (now Temple Bar) were straightforward seafood like prawns, lobster or sole, and prime meat like Rumsteak Henri IV with Béarnaise or Colbert sauces. The anticipation of these would cheer, welcome and warm those returning from the races at Leopardstown, the Phoenix Park or the Curragh—who, on arrival, were fortified in the front lounge and bar of all hotels by blazing fires with brandies and whiskeys. It was to Jammet's on Nassau Street that the young Gagebys went for their wedding reception with Dorothy's sister Patricia and their mother Elsie (their father being sequestered in Geneva by the war) and Douglas's aunts Elizabeth and Margaret, for both his parents were dead. Thousands of restaurants in French provincial towns before, after and even during the war, could provide for lunch six or more gutsy courses such as *rillettes, pâté de lièvre, jambon cru du pays, andouilles, tripes à la mode de Caen, bifteck* with soufflé potatoes, maybe a pheasant in season or a partridge in cream and Calvados, or a leg of lamb larded with anchovies, or skewered larks. At Jammet's the Gagebys had duck with peas, followed by fresh raspberries. It was not Cistercian fare but it was austere—I suspect rather from the tastes of the party than from wartime privation.

We can assume that M. Jammet's managers knew that the bride, their guest at the table for six, was the daughter of Mr Seán Lester, the esteemed Irish diplomat and secretary-general of the League of Nations in Geneva. They probably knew that she was marrying an unknown army officer on a short leave, for good managers know such things.

Reviewed in 1959 when he went to *The Irish Times*, Gageby was a man with a conspicuously fine education from the Belfast Royal Academy (he said his children received nothing like so good an education in Dublin) and from Trinity College, Dublin, where—he never mentioned it—at the end of his second year he had carried off one of the handful of Scholarships awarded by competitive examination and so could aspire to a career as a professor of French or German. He gave that prospect up for Ireland, the Army and journalism, I think in that order.

In 1946 Gageby demonstrated precocious maturity and humanity as well as writing talent during an extended tour of devastated Germany, initiated at his own expense using the gratuity that he got on resigning from the Army. He made an expedition with Dorothy and their toddler, Susan, to visit her father in Geneva, then crossed into Germany and called in that ghastly autumn on people whom he had known as a schoolboy and an undergraduate when he attended German courses in Heidelberg before the war. His reports were splashed on the front page of the *Irish Press* and were gripping, passionate, superb. They are reproduced in this book. His humanity shines through them, as it did later through his advice to an old army colleague, Ned Doyle (who also writes in this book) whom he asked to write for *The Irish Times* about military affairs: 'We have often discussed wars' real victims. Young men can run when things get rough. Women are tied to their children's pace.'

In the post-war world Gageby had a meteoric career as a manager of journalists. He was assistant editor of the new *Sunday Press*. He was editor of the new and contentious Irish News Agency. He was launch editor of the *Evening Press*. He was a hot property. He had a loving and bright, wordly-wise but modest wife to support him. Fuelled by his passion for the political but peaceful unification of Ireland he developed a steely ambition. I sense that Dorothy suppressed whatever doubts she had about his leaving the *Irish Press*, which from his teenage years had formed and expressed his political opinions; and that they agreed that he should jump to *The Irish Times*—exactly, but only—when it confessed its journalistic desperation for him and showed thereby that he was vital to its future.

Gageby was never, ever an entrepreneur. He fronted ventures by established managers who were cautious, although occasionally adventurous, but who in the long run were to disapppoint. When they put their money behind him they had already evaluated the risks so far as they could. They invited him to risk himself as their manager and to drive beyond their ability. What *The Irish Times* board acquired in him was a decade and a half of success in newspaper development and his evident ability in 'man management' as the Army called it. He was their last hope for the future of their 'hind tit' Dublin newspaper group—I use the natural Mayo farming vocabulary of John Healy, one of his star writers both before and after his switch from *Press* to *Times*, whose talents Gageby described as those of an 18th-century pamphleteer and who became a friend.

Gageby delivered for the board of *The Irish Times* all right, but not in the way it expected. Since early in the 20th century the owners of the paper, the Arnotts of the Dublin department store and the baronetcy, and their successors of the Dublin mercantile class (who eventually included Major Tom McDowell), had bought or bred a small stable of what they hoped would be thoroughbreds, innovative papers with speed and good wind: the racing paper the *Irish Field*, bought for £250 about 1903, the *Weekly Irish Times*, re-launched in 1941 as the *Times Pictorial Weekly*, the *Radio Review*, bought for its coverage of an increasingly popular phenomenon, the *Sunday Review*, started from scratch in 1957, and the *Evening Mail*, bought in 1960 as a spavined flat racer that they tried to turn into a jumper. Their stud policy belied the company's reputation at every stage (at least as it was put about later) for being in terminal decline, incorrigibly Protestant, covertly unionist, and haughty withal.

As it turned out, the board invested in Gageby just too late. One by one he had to advise or consent as four of the five junior titles were shut down. Only the oldest, the *Field*, survived but has been sold since. The company was over-stretched. Its finances could support no more failure. Even worse, they could not support successful growth, which requires even more capital than failure. They retrenched.

From the pruning, Gageby rescued some ideas and writers. With their help and as the world turned round and round (Fidel Castro, Nikita Khrushchev, Grace Kelly, Jack Kennedy, Pope John XXIII, the EEC, television, the Pill, the Beatles) and the Irish economy lurched into life in the mid 1960s he began a triumphant reform. It was not of the broad but shallow publishing group that he had joined: it was, instead and by inadvertence, of the already liberal-minded and long since ex-unionist daily newspaper where he was now in effect editorial director.

The title 'editorial director' was not known then. Gageby was among the early ones to prise up from outside the defensive portcullis, then about three quarters of a century in existence, that Fleet Street editors in London and Dublin had lowered behind themselves to keep out their directors, subject only to the sanction of dismissal. He interfered with his first two editors, Alec Newman (see the essays by Donal O'Donovan and Bruce Arnold in this book) and Alan Montgomery, who is usually reported as having sat on an interview board to find a public relations man for Guinness's and, finding that he was better qualified and worse paid than the applicants, took the job himself. Only the newspaper historian Hugh Oram has reported that 'he [Montgomery] says it didn't happen like that and that the main, immediate cause of him leaving the paper was the refusal of the board to give him a car' (Hugh Oram *The Newspaper Book,* Dublin 1983, page 294). That rings like a true coin. When made editor in 1963 Gageby clanged down the portcullis of editorial inviolability again and paraded the editorial floor without contradiction by directors or managers from downstairs.

Journalist Patsy Dyke gave a scarce glimpse of him at work in his shadowy management period in *The Irish Times* after 1959 but before he was made editor in 1963. She was writing about the group's adventurous tabloid *Sunday Review*, trained by Ted Nealon (who was to become a member of the Dáil) and then John Healy, who had worked with Gageby in the Irish News Agency and then the *Evening Press*:

> 'I went into *The Irish Times* newsroom to collect my husband, Cathal O'Shannon, and John Healy and Douglas Gageby were sitting over in the corner. John had the idea that he wanted a girl to do the social column in the *Sunday Review*. I just walked in and they said, "There she is" .
> . . . Well, it started just as a Saturday night diary and I had to go around and get into hotels, 21st-birthday parties, weddings, and if there were any names in town or any personalities, to cover them as well. It developed into two diaries, with one for the country. John had this idea that it should be upmarket, so I had a lovely Mercedes car to travel around in and I was told to stay in the best hotels. That was really tough!' (Hugh Oram *Paper Tigers,* Belfast 1993, page 79).

Clearly Healy was pushing the gossip column and the Mercedes and Gageby was authorising his budget. The Merc, the grand hotels, reeked of the newfound wealth and celebration with which the mohair-suited business class and second generation of Fianna Fáil parliamentarians charged out of the shadows of the civil and economic wars of the 1920s to 1940s into moneyed notoriety. They buried the idealism and austerity of the formative de Valera era, which had attracted Gageby as a schoolboy, in champagne, brandy, boasting and gossip.

Gageby already knew about women readers and the utility of gossip. When he launched the *Evening Press* in September 1954—with an elephant from Dublin Zoo leading a razmataz procession along O'Connell Street—he did so with the advice, as he self-deprecatingly claimed, of the *Irish Press*'s general manager Jack Dempsey ringing in his ears: 'Half the people on this island are women and our papers are too political and too stuffed with sport. We want a newer paper, we want a paper that will interest women and not just cookery and things like that.' (Hugh Oram *Paper Tigers* page 124).

Once the *Evening Press* got established, convent educated girls-about-town liked appearing in Terry O'Sullivan's social column, pictured in their dance dresses. These young women were now going out to work and the world spun gorgeously with them. A decade later Gageby tried to incorporate that journalism of social columns and pretty girls into *The Irish Times* but he hit a problem. The girls now wanted to write.

And even if they did not want to write themselves, they wanted to read about themselves and their contemporary lives—accompanied by pictures that their mothers could still approve.

The central puzzle of Gageby's career was his symbiosis with Major Tom McDowell. McDowell invented the Irish Times Trust of 1974, which borrowed from the Bank of Ireland to buy them both out, along with three other owner-directors. It made them millionaires in our terms of three decades later. It also redeemed the preference shareholders, who had been long years without a dividend. It gave any of them who had purchased below face value not only an unanticipated profit but one that was largely tax-free when capital gains tax was soon imposed. For 38 years McDowell was chief executive under one title or another—from 1963 when he succeeded Gageby until he quit in 2001 after a financial crisis too many. Not until a full-blown biography of either man is written, with access to personal and company documents and preferably with the cooperation of McDowell's long-time, talented but frustrated commercial number two, Louis O'Neill, can their relationship be described in the round. I offer only a sketch.

Both Gageby and McDowell were brought up and schooled in Belfast, a desperate and bitter city. Both were bright, scholarship boys. They had close families and rather few friends. Gageby was a private man, McDowell I think a lonely one. Both stood sideways to the norms of post-war Irish society. Gageby was trying to enlarge its boundaries, McDowell's manner aped the recent colonial past. They had short military careers, one in Ireland the other in England. Gageby, while intensely proud of his, cherished it in his bloodstream. McDowell flaunted his in his mustachios and fob watches and faux-English carry-on, as if imitating Colonel Mahon of the Munster Fusiliers, who was important in Intelligence and who captivated the salons in journalist Claud Cockburn's autobiography of his time in Budapest in the 1920s, *In Time of Trouble*.

> Colonel Mahon used, on his occasional visits, to get around a good deal among the Hungarian aristocrats, such as the Esterhazys and the Andrassys and would talk to them knowledgeably about horses. He told me once that his sole desire was to retire as soon as possible to his considerable estates in Tipperary——'limestone country, my boy, only country for raising horses'.

McDowell effortlessly overtopped Mahon by his autumn 1969 approach to No. 10 Downing Street and a lunch in the British embassy in Dublin. He asked for 'guidance' from London for himself and one or two other directors in respect of 'lines' that might be helpful about policy towards Northern Ireland. In language not quite achieving Cockburn's lapidary style, the embassy reported to London that McDowell had called Gageby 'a very fine journalist, an excellent man, but on Northern questions a renegade or white nigger'. This was only revealed 30 years later when a letter marked 'Secret & Personal' was released from the archives in London—and missed by *The Irish Times*, a piquant blunder.

I don't know what Gageby, then in his second retirement, thought of his old friend after that, but I bet he stood by him, for Gageby was a man at ease in his world. His good humour kept him so, insulating him from the intensities and jealousies that distracted those around him, for whom there was no man so awe inspiring as their calm and cheerful captain steering into a rising storm.

Calm captains conceal their troubles. In 1963 Gageby bolted, I think with relief, to the editorship of *The Irish Times* and blessed McDowell for lifting from his shoulders the business and financial responsibilities that he had suffered, indeed which he had been hired by Hetherington to suffer. He disliked management when separated from daily contact with the journalists and the product. He had become a captain promoted away from his ship and fretting in the head office of his Line. The deal was this: McDowell would run the company and leave Gageby to run the journalists; and Gageby would leave McDowell alone to manage the business. It was a devil's pact but it let Gageby put out to sea again on spectacular voyages like the Odysseus he was. For one who had scored in single figures in mathematics in his Trinity College entrance scholarship examination (out of 200) it must have been a blessed release from profit and loss accounts and balance sheets and I think he was forever grateful to McDowell for it.

Gageby was a top-class manager, an intuitive one, not a figures one. He applied himself to the essentials of his beloved product just as an engineer may perfect the chassis of a car without being responsible for the advertising budget of the marque or the capital financing of the distribution chain. He was suited by character and education to running a 'knowledge business' (the phrase comes from his contemporary, the management writer Peter Drucker) such as a high-quality newspaper. He would have been right if he felt that commercial managers could never do his job; but he did not give time to understanding theirs, and that was a mistake, given the narrow management resources otherwise available in *The Irish Times*. Drucker was a confidant of the American magazine tycoon Henry Luce and was consulted in the early 1940s about a proposed newspaper venture; he glanced over the invitation and wrote:

'The first thing to look at in any kind of publication is not the financial projections. First comes editorial. Does the publication make editorial sense? And if so, are the people who propose it competent to do the editorial job? Only then does one even look at the figures.' (Drucker *Adventures of a Bystander,* New York 1978, page 235). Of course Drucker was right, but he assumed that competent people would be there to look at the figures and manage the project. In New York that may have been so, but in Europe even 20 years later there was a dearth of such expertise. That was why the Canadian media mogul Roy Thomson became so notorious and cut such a swathe though post-war newspaper businesses in Britain and Ireland. He did not worry about the editorial coming first, for he knew that a local or provincial paper had a franchise with its readers that could last for decades; he wished for nothing more devoutly than that the editors and writers would stick around. What he wanted was more management of more advertisements as post-war economies grew and matured, delivering enlarged importance to the roles of consumers, retailers and advertisers.

The person who applied Thomson's Canadian and British lessons best, who had the ambition and a mastery of financial innovation in order to acquire old Irish newspapers from their owners and make a fortune from them, was the young marketing tycoon Tony O'Reilly. He aimed high and bought the largest-circulation Dublin morning newspaper, the *Irish Independent* cheaply in 1973 by a clever piece of financial engineering and the help of Nicholas Leonard (who also writes in this book). In Ireland he also bought the *Belfast Telegraph,* which Thomson acquired first but which his empire later sold to O'Reilly's. He developed his group into a multinational empire with predictable and rising profits. He has made it many times larger than *The Irish Times.* Being acquired by a tycoon may terrify the workers but it need not be bad for a newspaper's readers. Nor is ownership by a trust necessarily beneficial to either staff or readers. *The Irish Times* staff has had to be culled in the three decades since the trust was formed and the paper continues to charge a high daily price to readers.

Why did readers of *The Irish Times* not fly to O'Reilly's welcoming pages? I have heard various conjectures but they sound thin and inadequate. Overall, I think, the *Irish Independent* was just not good enough for readers of *The Irish Times* to switch to. It did not invest in sustained and subtle inducements that might have attracted them while avoiding driving its existing readers into the arms of the *Irish Press* or of English dailies. But O'Reilly may not mind that; he stuck to his market, or rather, he drifted with his readers as they changed. Gageby used to do that. Maybe O'Reilly is right for the *Independent* as Gageby was for the *Times.*

The characters and styles of newspapers are slow to develop.

I come back to the primacy of editorial and attitude, the attitude of readers. As it were in the distance and proverbially I hear an old, murmured complaint that switchers from *The Irish Times* had O'Reilly's unacceptable social vanities to contend with: photographs or column inches chronicling his visits to the races or his international guests or his colleagues and managers with their wives. Such vanity vexed readers with less to be vain about, or with different qualities to be vain about, or who had a more challenging attitude to their newspaper and wanted such stuff kept for Sundays. They were acclimatised to the thinner air of D'Olier Street, where Gageby's photograph never appeared in his pages, where the imagined music in the background was an adventurous mixture of Monteverdi and *Je ne regrette rien* and where embattled liberals could breathe deeply of the intoxicating air in which everything was lightness, expressing the almost inexpressible, the magical, those inexhaustible bright, brilliant days.

Something magical

Maeve Binchy

Douglas Gageby wouldn't have been at all surprised to see today's women running *The Irish Times*. He would have seen it coming and not before its time. Women could do anything else in the paper. Why shouldn't one of them end up in the editor's chair?

I went for an interview to be *The Irish Times* women's editor in 1968. I was aching to get the job but fearful that at the age of 28 I was too old and hadn't ever worked in a newspaper. Years of bellowing in a classroom were a useful training for life but maybe not for journalism.

News editor Donal Foley and editor Douglas Gageby sat like the friends they were, chatting about the world, and I thought it would be wonderful to work here at the heart of the universe and maybe get to say things that readers out there would agree or disagree with. Mr Gageby asked me what kind of things would I put in a Women's Page that week and I chatted on happily about my own hobby horses and then came to a halt.

'No mention of fashion or cookery at all?' he asked me over his glasses.

This had been an omission.

I assured him that these topics would be brilliantly covered by Experts.

It seemed to work and I got the job. I spent the first day hiring the Experts. Gabrielle Williams was already doing fashion so I gave her a special slot for it and then got Theodora Fitzgibbon, Irwin Stewart and T. P. Whelehan on board for the cookery and wine. Then I did my own piece.

Exhausted, I asked my colleagues where did I go to get somebody to type my own work? There was a dead silence. Apparently we typed it ourselves. At no time in the interview was I asked could I type. I thought it took a year to learn typing.

In fact it takes a weekend. The good kind men and women at other desks in *The Irish Times* took a page each of my handwriting to type for that first day then I was on my own. Four fingers and a thumb they said. And now nearly 40 years later that's the way I still type, like the wind and with few pauses for punctuation. Other people are better qualified to punctuate than I am, and I wouldn't ever want to take another person's job.

From the very start Douglas Gageby seemed to regard women as equal to men. I never heard him say that this or that wasn't really a girl's job, a lady's job or a woman's job. Women were sent to the North to the Troubles, women could do banking stories, industry disputes, sports coverage.

There were never any jokes about women, even on the occasion when I did a report of an All Ireland final at Croke Park and didn't put in the score. I said truthfully that I thought someone else would put it in the heading, and I said it with such a sense of outrage at the injustice of it all that I was forgiven and told to write a nice letter of apology to the winning team. And of course to remember to my dying day that you always put in the score.

This was long before political correctness. If Douglas Gageby felt that women were equal to men it was because he really thought it, it had nothing to do with how it looked or how it would make him appear. He made one concession only, he didn't use any colourful language when women were present. He had a huge vocabulary of abuse for politicians north and south of the border and across the Irish Sea, he could be alliterative and graphic describing them but never in front of women. And if he did by accident let the soldier's word (as he used to call it) escape, he would apologise as if he had stood on your foot, for letting his own legendary politeness down.

When Douglas Gageby died in 2004 I wrote a piece about his temper in the office and how he never bore grudges or let things escalate. A thunderous row could be over in minutes and he would be sunny and optimistic again. His family was astounded at this information. Never in their combined memories had he lost his temper at all. There had been no dramatic confrontations or flinging of a newspaper to the ground in disgust. They had just never seen him like this. It sounded like a different person entirely.

And I thought to myself yet again what a wise man he was. Keep all that kind of thing for the office, reserve the bad temper for the staff who had got something wrong, not for the family at home.

II

If you were responsible for a page you had to attend the midday conference where *yesterday's* paper was discussed and analysed and then *tomorrow's* paper was planned. There was no such thing as *today's* paper. There was a huge solidarity amongst those who attended this daily conference. I never reported outside those walls how Mr Gageby had become apoplectic about a sports editor who had described a soccer match as a nip and tuck affair.

'Completely, totally and utterly meaningless,' he said over and over. 'Why don't you use the words from the Jabberwocky song next time, they make a lot more sense. Nip and tuck indeed!'

Or when he was incandescent with rage with a financial report which he said had achieved the impossible and made the already incomprehensible world of banking even more opaque than before.

Always when these tirades were being delivered I stared at the floor, told nobody at all and hoped they had the same high standards when it was my turn.

My turn wasn't long coming.

On a Friday I had an apology on the Women's Page for Thursday's article which should have said 1–1½ lbs of split peas, not 11½ lbs of split peas.

On the Thursday I had an apology for Wednesday's page which said that some dress in fashionable Richard Alan's shop had been reduced to £5 when we should have said £50.

On the Wednesday the telephone number for the brand new Gay Switchboard in Belfast had turned out to be a greengrocer in the Shankhill Road who wasn't amused.

Neither was Mr Gageby. He said that my page had now become a collector's item it was so bad. That nowhere in the world had anyone edited such a collection of rubbish and—worse—such inaccurate rubbish. He had once seen a very poor women's page in the *Straits Times* in Singapore but mine was way worse.

I saw the others looking at the floor too and no one ever made a joke about the *Straits Times*, so I think the unspoken *omerta* might have worked. But as I went back out to Dalkey that day on the train there were salt tears on my face. They were probably in there grooming my successor already. I remember having supper with my father that night realising that I would be unemployed and unemployable in a week's time and obviously radiating such a sense of gloom that he had to ask what happened?

He thought about it for a while. 'Was the nip and tuck man sacked?' he asked. It turned out he hadn't been. And neither had the man who had achieved the impossible and made the incomprehensible world of banking even more opaque. 'I think you're in with a chance,' my father said.

He was right. Next day Mr Gageby had totally forgotten it. My successor was not groomed for another five years, when I wanted to move anyway.

III

Young women writing theses on the women's movement often ask me about the patriarchal attitudes in *The Irish Times* back in the late 1960s and early 1970s. It must have been terrible, they say sympathetically, as if we had chained ourselves to some railing in D'Olier Street, been denied a voice or an equal salary or had received several pats on the head to keep us quiet.

I don't think I am being unduly sunny and Pollyanna-ish when I say things weren't that bad at all. I can't hand on heart say that we came into a nest of chauvinist pigs doing everything in their power to resist change.

The Irish Times I joined in 1968 was a very fine place where women were already highly regarded. Mary Maher, a journalist from Chicago, was here already making her voice heard. She had come in with her remarkably fresh eye on the customs and traditions which we had all grown up immersed in and had forgotten to question. She was fearless at describing both the aspirations of middle-class Dublin as seen from a rugby club dance and of a different Ireland as experienced barefoot in a pilgrimage to Lough Derg.

Suddenly we began to see ourselves as others saw us.

The paper had a brilliant woman journalist, Eileen O'Brien, who wrote 'A Social Sort of Column'. As a document of the Ireland of its time it was without parallel, cataloguing not the clothes of those who attended embassy functions or smart dinner dances, which some publications thought were part of a world that readers wanted to peer at through a keyhole. Instead, Eileen recorded the many examples of social deprivations that could be seen all around us in a nation which was far from cherishing its children equally. There was now no hiding place. Once 'A Social Sort of Column' was published we could no longer claim that we didn't know such things existed.

Shortly after this Nell McCafferty's column 'In the Eyes of the Law' opened up the children's courts to those of us whose lives had never brought us there.

And all through the paper there were women dotted around as sub-editors, librarians, photographers, reporters and writers. Renagh Holohan and Caroline Walsh, who had both been pupils of mine in the classroom, joined the paper and outstripped me. There were Averil Douglas, Mary Cummins, Maeve Donnellan, Ella Shanahan, Elgy Gillespie, Maev Kennedy, Olivia O'Leary and, of course, Geraldine Kennedy—who became editor—the list goes on and on.

My memory of the time was that every one of us felt that we were there by right because someone thought we were good enough to hire, and not because there was some niche that a woman could fill.

It was a lovely time , of course it was. We could get to meet anyone we wanted to in Ireland. We didn't have to go home to our tea at six o'clock because there were always press receptions offering us drink and canapés. We had power, huge power to get things out into the open.

Mary Maher and I wrote the first articles in Ireland acknowledging the presence and plight in our country of the 'Female Homosexual'. We were watched with some amusement by Nell McCafferty who hadn't yet come out as a lesbian.

When the women's movement took shape and gained power it had a ready platform in *The Irish Times*. In our minds we did not have to restrict ourselves to talking about righting wrongs: we could get out and right them.

IV

I used to object to the word 'spinster' being used as a description in the newspaper because it seemed wrong. There was a sense of blame about it.

'ELDERLY SPINSTER FOUND DEAD'

'SPINSTER INJURED BY BUS'

It made it appear that it was the very spinsterhood or singleness of the woman that somehow contributed to her fate. If she had been married it wouldn't have happened.

Mr Gageby said he thought this was far fetched, the word spinster had an honourable tradition in meaning a person who did the spinning. I saw nothing particularly glorious to commemorate in that and it became a matter of contention. My point was that if they said 'bachelor' in similar circumstances then I would think it was fair.

One day, weary of it all, he announced that as a matter of house style the word 'spinster' was not to be used unless a corresponding 'bachelor' was to be found in the same issue of the paper.

It was a tiny victory and probably I think largely ignored but I was delighted with it and organised a celebration lunch which went on all afternoon. At this lunch the spinsters and married women toasted the gigantic success we had achieved over the mighty *Irish Times*, while the men stayed at their desks and wrote the paper.

Nowadays when women in all branches of the media are seen as men's equals it's hard to remember a time back then when *The Irish Times* stood out like a shining beacon in treating both sexes exactly the same.

V

And we all, men or women, dreaded equally Mr Gageby getting some new enthusiasm.

He went to a function where he had been bored witless by people talking about golf. They apparently never stopped re-enacting golf games they had played, doing practice swings

'There's nothing about golf in your page this week, not one single thing,' he glared at me over his glasses, looking at the schedule. Mildly, I said I thought that was a matter for sports. Nonsense, apparently it was the single most important thing in the lifeblood of the whole country.

I was off interviewing famous women golfers before the day was over and next day on the train to Sligo and the bus to Rosse's Point with a borrowed set of clubs taking swipes at the air on the Atlantic. Then there was the driving range, then golf gadgets and accessories, and finally mercifully he forgot about golf for a while.

Some months later he met people who said that it was strange *The Irish Times* never wrote about etiquette. 'Try and do something about it,' he said and I genuinely misunderstood him. I thought that like myself he regarded etiquette books as an abhorrence. The very notion of telling innocent vulnerable people that there was one way to speak that made you acceptable and one which put you outside the Pale was destructive nonsense.

So I found a new book by a lovely elegant woman called Jean Begley and spent half a page of *The Irish Times* tearing it and its ethic to shreds. Mrs Begley and I were invited onto RTÉ's 'Late Late Show' to discuss the matter further. She was gentle and restrained and full of dignity and I was increasingly loud and red faced and awful. Even my nearest and dearest were hard pushed to support me. They all wanted to be like her. No one wanted to be like me. She won hands down. I was humbled at the thought of facing Mr Gageby on Monday.

He was generous and sympathetic. 'You see the thing is that you already have confidence. You don't need a book,' he consoled me.

'Not much confidence today,' I said, full of self pity.

The others at the conference, the important people who looked after finance, the news desk, sports, features, advertising, circulation, looked from one to the other, not knowing what we were talking about. It wasn't one of those terrifying diatribes where they would have to look at the floor. But they didn't know what it was.

Yet Mr Gageby knew. He knew there was a time to tell you that you were the most stupid woman in the world, and a time to realise you had been so humiliated that any more would be counter productive.

VI

I always called him Mr Gageby. Many times he asked me to call him Douglas but it didn't seem right, so he called me Mrs Snell.

He stood up for me when I annoyed everyone with a report on Princess Anne's first wedding. He praised me for covering a war in Cyprus where my heart was in my mouth and my hands shook so much I could barely type. He let me go to live in London in pursuit of my love without a murmur. He only said 'Try to make the English sound like people when you get there, not like the Enemy'. He was celebratory about any success I had as a writer of stories and bought my books in the French language to increase my sales out there. What's not to like about a man who did all that?

And he was wrong in one thing. I didn't always have confidence. Thanks to my kind, optimistic parents I was happy in myself as a person. But not about work. What I have, and what I believe a lot of us women got from Mr Gageby and his news editor Donal Foley, was something magical: a true and genuine confidence that we were just as good as anyone else.

Douglas Gageby as editor of the Evening Press.

Irish Catholics' favourite Protestant editor

James Downey

One evening in the early 1950s Douglas Gageby, soon to become the founder-editor of the *Evening Press*, strolled into the Pearl Bar in Dublin's Fleet Street. Bertie Smyllie, the editor of *The Irish Times*, was there as usual surrounded by his coterie. He called him over and asked him why he was not working for his paper. Gageby replied, 'I don't want to work for your bloody paper.'

A decade on, Gageby took over the bloody paper himself and achieved greater fame than the man who had asked him the question.

During the many years in which I worked with him in *The Irish Times*, we had countless conversations about newspapers. He told me a lot of things, some of them true. The Smyllie story rings true. Gageby disliked Smyllie, thought his reputation inflated, and resented the implication of the question. For it did not mean, why is a bright young man not working for *The Irish Times*? It meant, why is a bright young Protestant not working for *The Irish Times*? And at the core of Gageby's beliefs, at the core of his being, were a hatred of real though unacknowledged sectarianism and a contempt for the 'old' *Irish Times* as the house organ of the Church of Ireland and Trinity College, tempered (and praised above its merits) with an appeal to a section of the intelligentsia, attracted by its relative sophistication and its stand against the excesses of transmontane Catholicism.

If Gageby had not broken the mould, the paper would not have prospered. It might not have survived. It owes its colossal successes, the standing it has since enjoyed in society, to the labour of many hands, but overwhelmingly it owes them to one man.

Under the two editors of the immediate post-Smyllie period, Alec Newman and Alan Montgomery, it came closer to the mainstream of Irish politics, Irish culture, Irish society and what for want of a better word we may call Irish thought. But it needed a Gageby, and it was fortunate for the paper and the country that it got one. It needed his powerful personality. It needed his ruthlessness, which left a good many victims bleeding in the wake of his chariot wheels. And it needed his prejudices and contradictions, his descents into sentimentality, even his bizarre tastes in literature ranging from Kipling to musty poets nowadays entirely unread, like Ferguson and Rolleston:

'We hold the Ireland in the heart
More than the land our eyes have seen.'

The land described by Gageby and his colleague and admirer John Healy in their numerous romantic moments certainly was a land nobody's eyes had seen or will see. It was a land full of opportunity and aspiration and patriotism and compassion, a land of which Thomas Davis and Wolfe Tone might have approved, in which 'Catholic, Protestant and Dissenter' united to drive out the English oppressors and create a Utopia to fulfil all the dreams of history, and indeed prehistory, and in which Tone and Newgrange were preternaturally linked together in the national psyche.

To be sure, Gageby and the fine journalists who collaborated so enthusiastically with him in the 1960s and later, did not ignore the somewhat less dazzling reality. Michael Viney, Eileen O'Brien and Mary Maher turned over quite a few stones and gave us a look at the loathsome crawling things underneath. But in the success of *The Irish Times* as a cultural phenomenon, the vision, and the manner of its expression, mattered more. The readers, and the much more numerous potential readers, knew in their bones that the editor was 'one of us', and rejoiced in that all the more because he was a Protestant, brought up in Belfast, who had embedded himself in the Irish state and nation and who viewed it, praised it and criticised it from a perspective very similar to their own,

We can't get away from it, can we? The Tiger Cubs of the 21st century don't give a damn if you're a Catholic or a Protestant or recite incantations to some Celtic or oriental deity. In the 1960s and for a long time after, people did feel the difference. It was not a question of morality or doctrine, but of identity and allegiance. Nobody could have any doubt about Gageby's identity and allegiance. He was not so much a token Protestant as a trophy Protestant.

That had been even more the case during his rapid rise in the *Irish Press* group. Not just a Protestant, not just a Protestant nationalist, but a Protestant Fianna Fáiler! And not just any old Fianna Fáiler, but essentially an adherent of the party's green wing, a friend of Major Vivion de Valera and Colonel Matt Feehan, who was editor of the *Sunday Press* at a time when every edition carried gory and overblown accounts of ambushes long ago, prompting Brendan Behan to say that he feared to enter the office for all the bullets flying about.

More oddly, a man with a deep suspicion of everything English amounting almost to anglophobia. He had served during the Emergency (1939–45) under Colonel Dan Bryan, the chief of military intelligence and possibly the most pro-British person in the country, charged with collaborating with Britain (quite rightly, too) in every respect bar permitting an overt breach of our phoney neutrality. Like any educated Irish person, he loved English literature. He must have had some respect, though he never mentioned it to me, for British achievements. Yet he positively disliked visiting the country and clearly felt uncomfortable on his rare trips to London.

If the Freemasons on *The Irish Times* board knew all that, they must have agonised when they made him first, joint managing director and then editor. By his own account, when he was joint managing director they found it hard to get him to acquiesce in their purchase of the moribund (and Protestant) *Evening Mail*. Gageby opposed this act of folly because it was done for sectarian reasons, and because his keen commercial sense warned him against it. In the event, the resultant drain on the company's finances dragged down their Sunday paper, the *Sunday Review*, and went close to destroying *The Irish Times* itself. He told me that they persuaded him to vote for the purchase with the age-old plea, 'Let's make it unanimous.' This is another story that has the ring of truth about it.

Their decision to appoint him editor was soon vindicated. Circulation rose, and so did advertising; there were booms, or at least minibooms, before the Celtic Tiger. When he took over, the stated circulation was about 32,000, but doctored figures were common then and for a long time after, until the Audit Bureau of Circulation clamped down. In one of our conversations, he hinted that the true figure might have been as low as 20,000. Let us take a more kindly 25,000, and that means that between 1963 and 1986 (including his three-year retirement as editor between 1974 and 1977) he more than trebled the circulation.

He had many advantages and plenty of luck. The proportion of educated people in the population rose. Spectacular political events stimulated interest in current affairs and created a demand for more analytical and independent coverage and commentary. Ireland became more open, both internally and in our relations with the outside world, and readers wanted a newspaper which would reflect that. But the achievement was still awesome.

Early in his reign, a magnificent opportunity presented itself. He seized it. The Second Vatican Council seemed to herald an inspirational reform of the Catholic Church, summarised in the Italian word *aggiornamento*, 'bringing up to date'. The hopes of liberal Catholics would be dashed, as hopes are, but John Horgan's coverage of the council in

The Irish Times was superb journalism and required reading for everybody with an intelligent interest in the affairs of the church. Gageby and others claimed that every parish priest in the country felt obliged to read the paper. That was nonsense, but it was splendid nonsense.

One of those liberal Catholics was Gageby's inspired choice for news editor. Donal Foley has gone down in the history of Irish journalism as one of the great news editors. He deserves his reputation, but not in the normal sense of a first-class hunter for news and organiser of coverage with an unbeatable nose for a good story; in that regard there were many better men and, curiously, he shared his editor's lack of attention to detail. Instead, his strength was his instinct for the *Zeitgeist* and how the paper should respond: with passion for church reform, for improvements in education, for the Irish language and culture (traditional music and Gaelic games were becoming fashionable as well as popular) and for what had already been recognised and dubbed 'the liberal agenda' under Smyllie, three editors before.

Foley's political opinions were left-wing, and this was also true, with variations, of many of the paper's most prominent writers. Their views differed sharply from Gageby's, as will be seen in a moment, and were not necessarily reflected in the paper's editorials. But a newspaper's ethos is not expressed only, or even chiefly, in editorial policy. It makes itself felt in a host of ways throughout the publication, in the stories it chooses to cover, in its manner of reporting them, in the prominence it gives them, in the choice of specialist writers, whether staff correspondents or outside experts. Moreover, certain of the leading *Irish Times* writers did not forbear to let opinion—based, for example, on distaste for the Fianna Fáil party and individual Fianna Fáil politicians—mingle with news reporting. The paper had, and kept, a reputation for separating reportage and opinion. It was undeserved, and Gageby often railed against views masquerading as news, but he never succeeded in suppressing the practice.

As a counterweight to the left-liberal ethos, he deployed a device which has been almost universally misunderstood. John Healy is credited with the creation of the 'Backbencher' column in the *Sunday Review*; in point of fact his collaborator Ted Nealon should have equal credit. Backbencher cultivated new ground in Irish political journalism. In place of reports of speeches and turgid, cautious commentary, readers got lively items about shenanigans within constituencies and supposed inside information on the waxing and waning of the influence and standing of ministers and opposition spokesmen—and leaks from the cabinet triumvirate of Charles J. Haughey, Donogh O'Malley and Brian Lenihan, wrongly said to have the approval of Seán Lemass. After the closure of the *Sunday Review*, Healy's column, by then exclusive to himself, moved into *The Irish Times*. It ultimately metamorphosed into the 'Sounding Off' column, no longer a purveyor of information but a parade of prejudices. It became notorious for its adulation of Haughey, portrayed as a heroic figure and the only possible saviour of his country. For Gageby, it served two more significant purposes.

Healy wrote eloquently—most notably in two books which will stand the test of time, *The Death of an Irish Town* and *Nineteen Acres*—about small-farm and small-town life and the decay of the West of Ireland. His descriptions of emigration were both colourful and moving. He mourned the region's loss of its real wealth, its people. But he put forward no alternative; and small wonder, since nobody had then or has now any idea how to stop an inexorable tide, and the time would eventually come for questioning whether the attempt was even desirable. He built up an idealised picture of the remaining peasantry, the salt of the earth, staunch individualists but good neighbours who came together in a voluntary *meitheal* at seasons like harvest when they needed joint effort. Much of this was the fruit of mere imagination, but it gave people a nice warm feeling in an era when they would generally have agreed with Gageby that nobody in Ireland was more than two generations removed from 'the mill or the bog'. It fitted in admirably with the similarly nice and warm feelings experienced by the somewhat more worldly readers who preferred the views of such as Foley, who wanted the country modernised, but humanely modernised.

Nowadays, of course, our Tiger Cubs have never seen a mill, at any rate not a linen mill, and if ever they see a bog their only wish is to get out of it as quickly as possible. But long before there were Tiger Cubs, there were plenty of people who felt no affinity with mills or bogs and who wanted what most of humanity wants regardless of origin, namely, money and possessions.

If the 1960s were a good time for these aspirations, that was emphatically not true of the ensuing two decades. 'Dublin 4' was weary of high taxes and fearful for its children's prospects in life. It might not have thought much of Healy's prescription for a saviour, but it read with satisfaction his denunciations of what he pleased to call the socialist oppression under which we groaned. He devoted much space to the iniquities of 'the permanent socialist government'—meaning that conservative institution, the civil service—and went so far as to maintain that the entire public sector created no wealth whatever.

Perhaps 'he' in those last two sentences should read 'they'. Healy was not alone in thus fulfilling his master's second purpose. Gageby often aired his own preoccupations through Healy, sometimes directly by writing parts of the column himself. Between them, they dwelt in various odd ways on subjects removed from politics. One of the oddest columns was devoted entirely to the quantity of ground water in the country. The point escaped me, and no doubt escaped any other readers who ploughed through it.

At a more important level, he used Healy as a conduit for the paper's enthusiasm for the European project. We had excellent, and equally enthusiastic, people writing on the subject, but Gageby presumably thought that sending Healy to Strasbourg to attend sessions of the European Parliament would add something to our coverage. He may also have had in mind the supposed standing of *The Irish Times* as 'a newspaper of record'. There is no such thing as a newspaper of record, and I have never known why he took to the term rather late in his tenure; it may have been at the urging of some member of the Irish Times Trust. At any rate, it most certainly was not upheld in the immensely long, ill-written pieces in which Healy did not record the proceedings of the parliament but featured generalisations about the long peace and the reconciliation of France and Germany, a theme echoed by Gageby in frequent tedious editorials.

When for some unknown reason he decided to take an interest in Japan, he sent Healy there. Staff members asked me what I thought Healy would make of the country. I said, 'He'll find it's exactly like Mayo.' They thought I was joking, but I was serious, and he did find it exactly like Mayo.

Once the two of them were sitting on the terrace of Gageby's holiday home in the South of France. A farm cart lumbered by, carrying a load of grapes. Healy said: 'That's the same as a cart in Mayo carrying potatoes. It goes to show that all civilisations are based on agriculture.' On hearing this ridiculous anecdote I lost patience and said: 'Wrong, Douglas. All civilisations are based on trade.'

Infinitely more serious was that the paper failed in its duty to the readers by substituting dream for fact in Healy's coverage, and by the editorial treatment of the 1969 Stormont election which put an end to Terence O'Neill's premiership and signalled the coming victory of the extreme unionists. Gageby and Healy convinced themselves that O'Neill would wipe out his opponents, and credited him with wholly imaginary political skills. Most weirdly, Healy wrote about old-time republicans overcoming their prejudices and coming down from the hills to campaign for him in his Antrim constituency. In all my life I have never heard anything resembling confirmation of this. I regard it as fantasy.

Had we (by 'we' I mean the experienced writers and senior editorial executives of *The Irish Times*) had a better gift of foresight, we might have realised that we faced a rough time, during which unwarranted optimism would take over from objective news coverage. The accuracy which the readers were entitled to expect suffered terribly.

There is a marvellous paradox here. The confusions, contradictions and departures from reality mirrored the gut feelings of many readers, perhaps most readers, and buttressed their love of *The Irish Times*. But in 1974 the gap between fact and fantasy reached a point beyond all forgiveness when the paper published the opposite of the objective and easily recognisable truth. On 1 January of that year a power-sharing Northern Ireland Executive was set up with Unionist Brian Faulkner as chief minister and Gerry Fitt, leader of the nationalist Social Democratic and Labour Party (SDLP) as his deputy. From the beginning it suffered a series of disasters which fatally undermined it, the final and mortal blow being a strike organised by the loyalist Ulster Workers Council (UWC) in May. By the end of the month the executive was about to fall under the weight of the UWC strike and the imminent collapse of public services. When the SDLP party, in a doomed last-minute attempt to prop up Faulkner, agreed to dilute and delay the proposal for a Council of Ireland, *The Irish Times* carried the headline 'Council of Ireland to Come in Two Stages'. The day before the calamity, one of Gageby's lieutenants bullied a reporter into changing a story which accurately forecast the event.. On the day itself, *The Irish Times* proclaimed editorially: 'The Executive is Standing Firm.'

I don't know how much these grotesqueries contributed to his retirement shortly afterwards and succession by Fergus Pyle. I know more about the events that led to his return and the removal of Fergus in 1977—the 'Second Coming'—and to his final resignation of the editorship in 1986, but very little of my knowledge came from him. His relations with the members of the Irish Times Trust remain as obscure to me as the Mysteries of Eleusis.

All this notwithstanding that from 1978 to 1986 I was his right-hand man. People thought, or rather assumed, that I was in his confidence. Not so. On matters concerning the governance of the company, he practiced a strict economy of truth. On the details of running the paper—news coverage, design and so on—he grew increasingly eccentric. He had little or no feeling for the importance attached by night editors and chief sub-editors to the choice of the right lead story, the 'splash', and to presenting it in such as way as to denote its significance. He would bring home from France copies of provincial papers and try to persuade us to copy their atrocious front-page design. He made whimsical appointments to key jobs, usually without consulting me and always without explanation. In one instance in which he did consult me, it meant nothing: he overrode my furious protests. Most strangely in a man imbued with printing lore, he had little understanding of the production process itself. He was impatient, not to say angry and ill-tempered, with the accommodations without which it would have been impossible to make the change in very difficult conditions from the old hot-metal system to the new print technology. On one bad night he panicked and said, apparently in all seriousness, that we should abandon the whole enterprise and go back to hot metal. In such circumstances working closely with him could range from the merely tiresome to the utterly exasperating. It put me in mind of the wise man of ancient times who said that he would prefer to be first in a village than second in Rome.

Almost all of this was unknown to the public and indeed to the bulk of the journalists. Legends always grow up about a towering personality, usually the same legends. 'He likes you to stand up to him.' He did not. 'He lets you get on with the job, then backs you.' Wrong again. As a practitioner of second-guessing, sometimes on the pettiest of matters, he had few equals. It would be an understatement to say that he was sparing of praise. He was ungrateful, liverish, erratic, often unjust and dictatorial, sometimes deceitful.

In his later years as editor he was thought to have mellowed. That depends on one's point of view. To water-carriers such as the above-mentioned night editors and chief sub-editors he looked rather different from the benign figure, at once fatherly and heroic, of legend. If anything he grew more tyrannical and capricious. He also grew old, and the older he grew the more he hated to be bothered with trifles; then a time came when he dismissed serious matters as trifles. In the end, he stayed too long. Men of his kind do.

Of course, newspapers are not democracies. Every day, editors and executives have to make literally scores of on-the-spot decisions, approving here, overturning there, which may be right or wrong but must be accepted. Normally their subordinates obey with little question because they trust them. If trust fails disaster follows. Gageby was trusted. He earned it. It was his main strength.

Is that enough? I think not. A newspaper which commands enormous respect and influence should have some 'collegial' element and some consistency. There should be a limit to the extent to which an editor's whims can prevail over consistency, at worst over a rational view of affairs.

I have mentioned the almost comical mistakes of 1969 and the colossal misjudgment of 1974. Had we had so much as a spoonful of collegiality these might have been avoided. In another sense, and in a very strange way, that is true of a bigger crisis which occurred between those two dates.

Gageby's reaction to the arms importation crisis of 1970 was remarkable. Anyone who at a generation's distance looks up editorials he wrote at the time might expect them to have concentrated on constitutional proprieties and the stability of the state. Instead, the tone is one of 'Aha! It's all coming out now.'

The realities of that murky affair supply him with some justification. We still do not know for certain the full truth of the parts played by Jack Lynch as taoiseach and James Gibbons as defence minister. I intend to examine the subject more thoroughly in my memoirs. For the moment, let me just say that the received wisdom that both Lynch and Gibbons behaved impeccably is untenable.

Gageby regarded Lynch with such contempt that he blackballed him from a club of which he was a member. (He was eventually persuaded to relent.) He was infuriated by the scapegoating of the chief of military intelligence, Colonel Michael Hefferon. One might discern here the feelings of one former intelligence officer for another, but Gageby went on to devise a general theory which I believe derived less from disapproval of the treatment of Hefferon, or concern for the proper conduct of affairs, than from political prejudice. He held that a government must stand by its security forces, no matter what. Obviously this is preposterous if members of the security forces engage in gross misconduct or activities likely to undermine the security of the state. Later he took it so far as to deplore the best thing his interim successor, Fergus Pyle, did in his brief and unhappy tenure of the editorship between 1974 and 1977. Gageby told Donal Foley that he would never have published the series of articles which exposed the activities of the Garda Síochána 'heavy gang' and effectively ended the ill-treatment of terrorism suspects. The idea quickly got into circulation that the exact opposite had happened: that Gageby had published articles rejected by Pyle. Such is the unfairness of life.

For all his flaws and all his eccentricities and all his refusal to entertain wise counsel and all his capacity to be grotesquely and flatly wrong, was he Ireland's greatest editor? I say yes. There are probably at most three other contenders for the title, only one a contemporary; and there will be no more. Would he have been a better editor without his caprices and prejudices? Perhaps not; but I do not mean that in any humbug-sense of 'all of a piece' or 'two sides of the coin', or a futile weighing of flaws against virtues. Flaws and virtues can be contradictory, not complementary.

To see Gageby among his family and friends was to see a different man. To talk to him in his unbuttoned moments—which might come from a relaxed mood, or merely a flash of irritation—was to hear a different man. He was a romantic who liked bad poetry, but not all his tastes were absurd or ill-judged. As well as Ferguson and Rolleston, he admired George A. Bermingham, an unjustly neglected writer who showed his own romantic streak in books like *Spanish Gold* and who, like Gageby, thoroughly believed in the unity of Irish classes and religions, but who also had a sharp and very funny knack of revealing a less noble Ireland. Bermingham (Canon James Owen Hannay) was a Church of Ireland clergyman.

And Douglas Gageby, Irish Catholics' favourite Protestant, was a good Protestant. People who might or might not know anything of his beliefs argued about them. I know almost nothing, because he never discussed religion with me. I do know that some of his views about Catholic–Protestant relations in or out of a united Ireland were simply ridiculous. He seemed to have a poor grasp of two points, that Catholics and Protestants relate to their churches in different ways but, contrariwise, Irish Catholics would eventually fight their church on the liberal agenda, and win. But once in a blue moon he would let slip a couple of words about 'private judgment', or Martin Luther, or morality.

It's an arguable though by no means provable proposition that the best editors are atheists and, in politics, either social democrats or High Tories. Gageby was none of these things, but after all he was unique in every other way as well.

The formation of an officer

Colonel Ned Doyle

I want to tell you about a young soldier called Douglas Gageby and his beautiful girl friend Dorothy Lester, and how tens of thousands of men volunteered to join the Irish Defence Forces as the Second World War engulfed Europe, so that the divisions of the Civil War began to give way to the Ireland of today.

The semi-circle of young soldiers around a machine gun had been a common sight all over Europe since the late 1930s. Our course commandant in 1943 said: 'You will be instructing, and assessing instructors throughout your army lives, so we now start with "Methods of instruction". Pay attention.' A sergeant stepped forward. Firmly and confidently he announced:

'What yiz are going on today is how best to teach "Naming the parts of the Bren light machine gun". And note how I've said that—slowly and clearly. Soldiers must be clear about what they are going to learn—so you must be clear also. You are all trained soldiers and know the Bren. The NCOs amongst you will have taught it. Now we'll see how good you are.'

He called two of the class to the gun. A voice behind me said, almost inaudibly,

Today we have naming of parts.

I looked at the speaker—a relatively small soldier with a Northern accent.

Yesterday, (I replied) *we had daily cleaning.*

The soldier answered: *Japonica*

Glistens like coral in all of the neighbouring gardens . . .

So he *was* quoting Henry Reed, although there were neither gardens nor japonica in our training ground.

'Pay attention there in the back,' barked the sergeant, 'We like things done properly here.' Then, very sharply, to the potential instructors: 'Don't stand between the gun and your class; remember to let the recruits see the rabbit.' And he demonstrated how to stand back and use a pointer. Elementary stuff, but these things have been developed in

armies since the old 'hayfoot—strawfoot' way of teaching illiterate recruits to distinguish between their left and right feet. Much has been
discarded as men with better education joined the world's armies, but
the essentials of good instruction remain.

At this early stage of our Potential Officers Course the NCO instructors had not quite worked out all the names. 'Ga-g-eby' (with two
hard Gs), the sergeant said: 'You're an infantryman. Sum up what recruits would have learnt—or not learnt—as you see it. Then we'll have
comments from the class on the good points and bad points. Tomorrow we'll do the safety catch. Think about it. Lives may depend on it.'

And so I got to know Douglas Gageby. A flood of poetry appeared around the beginning of the Second World War. *The Century's
Poetry*, published cheaply by Penguin, was a huge success with British
troops during the phoney war of 1939–40. The *New Statesman* published 'The naming of parts' in 1942. Housman, from an earlier age, still
seemed everywhere—his melancholy fatalism seemed to suit the times,
though he wrote some of the most nonsensical of war poems, as well
as others that are very fine. Criticising Pádraig Pearse for romanticism
and passing over Alfred Housman's 'I did not lose my heart in summer's even' from his 1936 book shows some prejudice:

> *I lost it to a soldier and a foeman* . .
> *That took the sabre straight and took it striking*

I recall a hayfield on a blazing hot day when I was a boy. An old
soldier removed his shirt. He had taken a sabre stroke while a gunner in
some distant Victorian battlefield. It was a frightful-looking wound,
even 45 years later. A cavalry sabre was a heavy weapon and a trooper
was trained to apply all his strength in bringing it down from his seat on
horseback. One could see the over-development of sabre-arms brought
by the hours of practice. Housman's foeman *'kissed his hand to me and
died'*. That hand was hardly attached to a sabre-slashed shoulder.

We talked of these things. Douglas had a well-stocked mind and
had done much reading.

II

Colonel Gallagher, the college commandant, laid out the ground rules
on our first day. He was an impressive man, quietly spoken but firm.
Pubs and other barracks were out of bounds. No walking out of
doors—all movements to be on the run and in combat kit. High standards of physical fitness—anyone unable to keep up would be returned
to his unit.

Our daily life was not encumbered by poetry. We moved in a thunder of running, steel-studded boots. A high standard of drill and personal turn-out was expected. The military college staff were not going to spend too much time inspecting us at this stage, although the Saturday morning inspection of cadets, potentials, college company, etc, was formidable. You conformed to high standards or went back to your unit.

I was a cross-country and 'mile-in-battle-order' runner. My happiest moments on that course came when I heard the order: 'Advance arms—double march'.

This was something I could do very well. Nobody was going to ask me anything I didn't know when I was running. Is the 'mile-in-battle-order' still run? It was a test of stamina and determination. There was a corporal in the Second Brigade I never caught. He was a magnificent runner with great reserves of energy. I think his name was Fanning. How often I looked at his iron heels and knew he could speed up the pace every time I tried to pass him. What a thing it is to be young and fit. Douglas said he was never as fit in his life as he was leaving the military college.

The picked men whom the NCO training schools transform into confident, skilled instructors remain in the memory. Perhaps Reed's 'Naming of parts' and 'Judging distance' can be evocative only for those who have done weapon training under such men, with their patter and practised routines. By being made part of the process we were being shown how good instruction was produced. Douglas was fascinated. He liked Reed's ability to merge mundane weapon training with lyric poetry and he knew more of Reed than I did. He tended to be interested in everything and curious as to how things were done and people were motivated.

In our group of soldiers and NCOs we had pre-Emergency volunteers, E-men (who had joined for the Emergency), some regular soldiers, NCOs and reservists. There was Simon Deignan, a Cavan county footballer, Seamus McCarthy, the Dublin county hurling goalkeeper, Gerry McDermott, a Lansdowne senior rugby player, Herbert McWilliam, a TCD-qualified solicitor who became a High Court judge, Seán Collins (who later set up the Defence Forces School of Cookery, transforming military catering) and a quiet, very competent Engineer Corps NCO with two kit boxes, the second containing a set of carpenter's tools. There was a bank clerk, a pharmacist and a company quartermaster sergeant who had previously been a Post Office telegraphist and then a general civil servant. We also had a few young soldiers, not long from school: one became a doctor in Northern Ireland, another did well in banking in South America; one tends to hear of those who do well. Many of those strong, fit young men are *imithe ar slí na fírinne* now and lie beyond 'brooks too broad for leaping'.

I had trained as a Morse and teleprinter operator in the efficient little telegraph school in the GPO. I also attended night courses at the College of Technology, Kevin Street. One got about three shillings extra a week for passing the exams. On enlisting with a group of Post Office volunteer E-men, we got a short course in the School of Signals in the Curragh. I was then posted to Air Corps Signals at Baldonnel, between Dublin and Naas. I continued to go to night classes, hoping to reach chartered engineer level. Kevin Street, under Hugh de Lacy's influence and drive, was upgrading its courses. Eventually I took almost permanent night duty (midnight to 8 a.m.) to ensure ability to attend the previous evening's 7–10 p.m. classes, cycling from Baldonnel to Kevin Street and back before going on watch at midnight.

When I went on the officers' course with Douglas, almost directly from my NCOs' course, I was a corporal in Air Defence HQ in the Monastery in Clondalkin. Our backgrounds could scarcely have been more different and he had the most unusual background of us all.

He was born in Dublin in 1918. His civil servant father transferred to Belfast in 1922 and Douglas went to school at the Belfast Royal Academy and later studied French and German in Trinity College Dublin. He went to Heidelberg University for two summers and became competent in German. That was the late 1930s: he told of big brown-shirted men collecting donations for *Winterhilfe*, the Nazi party's collection to help poor people in winter. He went to Paris in 1937; he seemed to speak adequate French when I met him. He visited Nuremberg and saw Hitler and Goering. The European sky was darkening although Heidelberg, he said, was beautiful and tranquil. After the war, when he enquired about a Jewish former landlady, no one could tell him anything. He saw and did not forget Europe's march towards its own destruction.

He had wanted to enlist in the Army in 1940 while he was a student in TCD, but was implored by his mother to complete his degree first. With tears, he agreed. He enlisted in July 1942. He said later that it did not make any difference to the Army or the country that he had not joined in 1940; but it made a difference to him. He regretted that he had not spent more years in the Army, which had embraced him; he always thought of it with affection.

His Army record shows that when he enlisted he declared his religion as 'Christian Scientist'. After his officer training he was made a second lieutenant on 9 September 1943.

When we met he still had accommodation in TCD. He brought me in one Saturday morning. It was a foreign land; could the block have been called Botany Bay? The accommodation seemed austere.

III

The first step towards bringing together our heterogeneous group (and many others) had been taken far away and high above us. On Sunday 3 September 1939 Britain and France declared war on Germany. The Wehrmacht had been in Poland for more than 48 hours.

The Irish manpower position was:

	Officers	NCOs	Privates	Total
Permanent defence forces	630	1,412	5,453	7,495
General reserve	202	544	4,328	5,074
Volunteer reserve	254	557	6,429	7,240
Totals	1,086	2,513	16,210	19,809

The general reserve was composed of ex-regular personnel. The volunteer force was set up in 1934 with energy, imagination and a regimental organisation. Historic territorial designations were used, such as the Regiments of Oriel, Uisneach, and Thomond. Its university unit was called the Regiment of Pearse. Shamefully, these resonant titles were killed off after the Emergency.

Training halls (*sluagh*) of simple but functional design had been built. So we had a well-trained body of volunteer reservists to call up in 1939–40. Becoming an officer or NCO in the 1930s volunteers took a considerable amount of a young man's spare time, together with periods of full-time training.

Morale in this country was generally good at the end of the 1930s. We had successfully come through an economic war, though it did damage our agriculture. Support for the government remained adequate. The small farmers, who had suffered most, continued to support the withholding of land annuity payments to England. Payments stopped about 1933–4; the British responded by imposing duties on two-thirds of our exports, including cattle; we taxed British imports. It seemed a struggle we could not win—but neither could Britain, if war came.

The ethos and spirit of a time is made up of the sum of the assumptions, events, certainties and doubts, successes and failures that surround us. They are in our minds and much of them dies with us. How to recapture the ethos of a vanished time? One can read books and documents and apply hindsight. But we may get the balance wrong and the significance of some things may be overlooked. The significance of the land annuities and the importance of the 'economic war' seem unduly diminished. Outside of Dublin they were vital matters, constantly debated and part of the ethos of the time.

The theme most frequently debated in every fair, shop, pub and small farmer's home went like this: 'Nobody compensated our ancestors when the land was confiscated by Britain and given to the landlords. Our people were driven off their lands into a miserable existence. Why should we have to compensate the landlords now? That is a matter for the British government.' The land annuities cost about £4 million a year out of a national purchasing power of about £30 million.

Atavistic?—perhaps. Inaccurate?—no. Practical politics?—just about. Sustainable against the power and resources of Britain?—hardly.

The Fianna Fáil party eventually made the cessation of land annuity payments part of its policy. The opposition was concerned about possible long-term damage to our cattle trade, upon which so much depended. The bigger farmers thought likewise. The opposition also felt that as agreement to continue payment had been part of the 1922 Treaty there was a moral obligation involved. Those were honourable concerns, but the *real politik* of the time was, as usual, little concerned with honour.

In London the civil servants were quietly doing sums arising from the effects of the 'law of unexpected consequences'. War was coming. The population had increased since the First World War. The fall in Irish cattle exports to Britain, and, more seriously, in cattle numbers in Ireland, indicated that the level of Irish beef exports could not be as high as in the First World War. Britain could buy anywhere in peacetime and had a 'cheap food' policy to do so. But a new world war would be a different matter. High Irish cattle exports would be essential. But the Irish were showing no sign of giving up the struggle and the small farmers still supported their government.

An Irish delegation was invited to London in 1938. The land annuities were swept away and we got our Treaty ports back. The complexities, quoted for years, and the reasons why nothing could be done, seemed to vanish. A final payment to Britain of £10 million was imposed. Perhaps it was a sop to the House of Lords and the implacable Tories for whom any concession to Ireland was anathema. It was a mistake. Mr de Valera as taoiseach returned from London and launched a national loan to pay it—'to buy our freedom'. It was over-subscribed in days and the British government had to deal with Mr de Valera right through the war because his party was re-elected.

IV

The winter of 1939–40 was harsh, although it was also described as quiet and a 'phoney war'. Very bloody wars were fought in Poland, Finland and Norway. Nothing effective was done to help Poland, despite guarantees from Britain and France. Poland was even spoken about scornfully for not lasting long in the war. This deliberately ignored the fact that she was invaded from both west and east, by Germany and the Soviet Union. The Poles were the first to break into the German 'Enigma' enciphering system and they brought their results to France and Britain. Polish pilots played a very effective role in the Battle of Britain and their 203 Squadron shot down the highest number of German planes in that battle.

The position is complicated but Adam Zamoyski, in his *The Forgotten Few*, of 1995, sorts out the factors with clarity and impartiality. Polish troops fought in North Africa, Italy and Normandy. They got the blame for the failure of the ground troops to reach Arnhem in time. By the 50th anniversary in 1994 the military historians had cleared their minds: 'A shameful act by British commanders,' was Martin Middlebrook's summary in his excellent *Arnhem 1944*.

A small army is unfortunate to be around when a big one needs a scapegoat. The drumbeat of propaganda will be unbeatable. Perhaps to appease the Soviet Union and the Polish communist government in Warsaw, Poles were not allowed to march in the 1945 London victory parade. The names of their 202 and 203 Squadrons did not appear on the Battle of Britain monument in Dover—erected as late as 1993. The British foreign office was usually represented by a very junior official at the annual Mass to commemorate the Polish war dead. The RAF did its best. A band was sent and a plane flew over, but official disapproval remained throughout the Cold War years and for some time afterwards. Douglas was familiar with much of this.

The essentials of the first 18 months of the war, often lost in the mass of detail, were these:

	Attacked	*Defeated*
Poland	1 Sep 39	27 Sep 39
Denmark	9 Apr 40	9 Apr 40
Norway	9 Apr 40	10 June 40
Holland	10 May 40	15 May 40
Belgium	10 May 40	28 May 40
Britain	10 May 40	26 May 40 [withdrawal started]
France	10 May 40	25 June 40
Yugoslavia	6 Apr 41	17 Apr 41
Greece	6 Apr 41	23 Apr 41

The speed of the German advance through the Low Countries and northern France had been watched by the government here. There had been continuous recruiting during the winter, although the government exempted 2,053 volunteers—mainly students and others in reserved occupations. By early June 1940 the German army was over the Somme. Their moments of truth come quickly and briefly to the small countries and to their armies and governments.

On 6 June 1940 de Valera and Cosgrave, the government and opposition leaders here, issued a united appeal for recruits for the defence forces. No one, least of all the regular Army, expected the response. Recruits flooded in so fast that some had to be sent home to await a call. By 12 July 1940, 12,642 were taken in and another 12,000 had filled in forms. By 31 March 1941 we had 2,138 officers, 6,678 NCOs and 32,626 privates—a total of 41,442 all ranks—more than double the manpower of 18 months before, when war broke out.

In addition a new Local Security Force (LSF) was created. It proved a real surprise. Starting from nothing, it got 44,870 men before the end of June 1940 and 145,306 by the beginning of October 1940. In January 1941 it was subdivided into two bodies, the LSF under the Garda and the LDF (Local Defence Force) under the Army. The LSF had 49,000 men approximately. The LDF's numbers rose gradually, reaching 98,429 in 1942 and 103,350 in 1943, so that the total of the two forces reached approximately 152,000 in 1943.

The LDF consisted of younger men, eventually under Army command. It was a part-time uniformed force armed with Springfield and Lee-Enfield rifles. It was designed as a combat force for protective duties—power stations, dams, communication facilities and so on. It was later incorporated into Army training, exercises and alerts, and had one-week full-time training courses and shooting competitions. The unarmed LSF (under the Garda) had older men and was for local patrolling, aerial and coastal observation and watching for saboteurs and strangers in their own areas. (Exaggerated reports of sabotage and Fifth Column activities on the continent were rife.) Each Garda district had a specially trained Garda officer for the LSF.

Clearly the LDF and LSF had attractions for people engaged in the kind of agriculture we had at that time. Equally clearly the requirement for training officers and NCOs for these forces was large.

There was also a magnificent response from the voluntary organisations such as the Red Cross, the St John's Ambulance Brigade and the Knights of Malta, which trained large numbers of people, especially women. I have been surprised at how many women looked back on this part of their lives with nostalgia. These organisations, and we must include the Civil Defence, regarded women as at least as valuable as men. They brought women out of their homes on a few nights a week and taught them some skills that could clearly be useful in their own families as well as in cases of public emergencies. The meetings provided small social centres for neighbours.

V

Much had been learnt since 1940 about selecting and training temporary officers. The selection process had been broken into two phases. Training was made longer and tougher, with considerable emphasis on physical fitness and weapon skills. Preliminary selection was made by commands and each command ran a course. I would think a little over half of my preliminary course made it to the military college and perhaps pro rata from other commands—memory is fickle. 'Potentials' could still be eliminated at this stage. The emphasis was now on platoon tactics, military law, map reading, etc. We were required to swim a length or two of the Curragh swimming baths in full battle kit and then exercised in river crossing—at Connelford on the Liffey, near Newbridge. We ran almost everywhere but used Army bicycles on some occasions.

There was not enough barrack accommodation in the country for the influx of recruits and some former 'big houses' were taken over. Orderly officers' orders required frequent checks on doors and windows of the houses. I have spoken to some owners or former owners, who had been abroad. They said they were pleasantly surprised to find little damage to their houses. Perhaps the Department of Finance watched over them, shuddering at the potential bills. Bawnjames, Knockdrin, Kilkenny Castle, Shanbally Castle, Dromoland Castle and many others were used.

A junior officer might find himself running a 'local purchase rations account' in one of these houses, so in the Curragh abattoir we were taught to inspect meat. 'Grapes on the pleura' of a cow indicated tuberculosis. We were shown the pleura and the 'grapes'—little nodules, as far as I can remember.

VI

In May 1943, at that longer stage of selection, conditioning and training, the system brought Douglas Gageby and me together in our four-month 'Emergency Officers Course'. Douglas's recruit training in Portobello (Cathal Brugha) Barracks had been interrupted by a short period when he was withdrawn to work on German internees' mail in the Curragh camp. He was glad to get back and complete his recruit training in Portobello and he was a thoroughly trained infantryman when I met him. He was a good rifle and Bren gun shot. His map reading was quick and thorough. Both he and Herbert McWilliam (the two Protestants on the course) were very good at 'judging distance'. He was fit and he was used to slit trench digging and camouflage.

He enjoyed the barrack room experience. The bed-making, with the beds lined up in an exact line, the kit inspections with every item of kit laid out in accordance with a diagram enabling inspection officers to spot deficiencies at a glance. The kit boxes were also packed in accordance with a diagram. It was an ordered life. He fitted in well.

He enjoyed Dublin soldiers with their very different accents, 'straight out of Sean O'Casey' as he said, and mordant sense of humour. He heard one recruit rebuking another who was fussing to get out early on parade: 'Take it aisy. This ain't like a civvy job—you can't lose it.' He had a fund of such stories.

One feature of the 1940 recruiting drive was that politicians' sons enlisted. Some were already in uniform as members of the volunteer reserve. A few of these people went into politics afterwards. They had slept in barrack rooms, queued for their meals, did their equipment and room cleaning and been part of the communal rough and tumble of the soldiers' lives. They broke down the divisions of the Civil War in their common service. They had something knowledgeable to say when defence was discussed in the Dáil. We have few such nowadays.

The boys, who came from Seán MacDermott Street, the Gloucester Diamond, Dominick Street, etc., belonged to families that had been producing soldiers for the British Army for a hundred years or so. They knew and accepted much about army life before they joined. I met two who had been in the same billet with Douglas. Clearly he was a new kind of individual to them 'but he always mucked in' they said. He enjoyed their quick wit, toughness and acceptance of life's vicissitudes. He was fascinated to find that 'spit and polish' actually referred to both the process and the materials used in making boots glitter.

He picked up the training quickly and liked the tricks of the trade. The clear nail varnish on bayonet handles to make them shine, for instance, which was almost a badge of the regular soldier of that time—when, to encourage a high standard of turnout for guard duties, one extra man was always detailed. The best turned-out soldier, in the judgment of the orderly officer who mounted the guard, was given a white stick and excused guard duty. The competition was fierce.

'Where did you get the nail varnish?' Gageby asked someone. 'The sister,' was the reply. I had to explain 'the sister', that institution in north Dublin families, to him. Usually older and working, she was a rock in a big family. 'The sister says . . .' when quoted by a small boy was enough to close an argument, in many cases. She was a source of fourpences for the films or for the Clontarf Baths when the tide was out. She was a boy's shield when he was in trouble with his parents and a benevolent authority figure who was considered very wise, all the more so because she was nearer in age than his parents. It was a bond of unexpressed affection—she might have reared a boy whose mother was busy with a big family. I am speaking as one who never had 'the sister' and I envied the boys who had. I recall a rather inarticulate soldier trying to explain it: 'She's not really just a girl,' he said, 'she's like your mother and the nun in Senior Infants rolled into one. '

Those families are in good housing now, with better health, warmth, dryness and education. We are rebuked for not doing enough for public buildings after Independence. The critics don't mention that our inheritance included the worst slums in Europe. The state's priorities lay, not in neo-colonial dreams of architectural perfection but in the green fields of Marino, Donnycarney, Cabra, Ballyfermot, Raheny, Finglas, etc. One hopes that there is still a function for 'the sister'. The small-sized, street-wise young men were the soldiers I would like to have behind me in a tight corner. They know about fighting—when told to 'get stuck in' and stand fast—and when to wait and fight again if the odds were too high. Douglas had stories about them and seems to have been accepted—Belfast accent and all.

The military college staff officers were young and fit. They set and demanded high standards, but inside those parameters they were helpful and knowledgeable. Douglas always spoke highly of the late Paddy Allen and of Larry Corr, still strong, imposing and indefatigably interested in military matters, the course commandant Charlie McGoohan, gone to his reward—a reward which one likes to think St Michael, the soldier's archangel, reserves for dedicated men, deeply interested in realistic training and incapable of doing things by halves.

The college's NCO instructors had years of experience. They had made good shots of doubtful gun-shy firers and given their own quiet confidence to young men over-awed by their surroundings. They could put their instruction across with the minimum of words and the maximum of effect.

The college had an ethos that seemed to draw the best from people. Douglas watched that happening and admired it. Much depends on the direction and standards set at the top. Colonel Gallagher, in turnout and bearing, was impeccable. He found time to give a few lectures. One was on practical matters in the general conduct of an officer. One was on Clausewitz and the function of his writings. Another was on the importance of chiefs of staff to great generals. The latter two seem esoteric for potential second lieutenants, but why do I remember so much of what he said, to this day?

Douglas later was elected an honorary member of McKee Barracks officers' mess. He liked the atmosphere there and I saw many prominent people there with him. His parties at the annual dinner of the Irish Military History Society were eclectic: as well as his own family, John Hume, Maeve Binchy and many literary and political luminaries appeared with him. He was particularly fond of Sam McAughtry (who wasn't?) and had him to lunch in Dublin on several occasions.

VII

I first saw Dorothy Lester together with Douglas in the Stephen's Green Cinema restaurant in 1943, soon after I had first met him. Her fair hair was held in a kind of loose net. A woman said it was called a 'snood', very new in Dublin then. I was told it was clover coloured, also very new to Dublin. Her smile lit up the room. There was something foreign about her appearance and elegance and she had a slight American accent, picked up in her time in the International School in Geneva.

They met in the Front Square of Trinity College Dublin, in the autumn of 1939. He was 21, she was 17. Both were students of modern languages. He succeeded in the exacting Scholarship examination the next spring (May 1940). He was capped for rowing for the university.

Their attraction seems to have been immediate and mutual. He said that he had never seen a hazel twig snapped down in a dowser's hand when he found a spring of water, but he knew what it must be like, for it happened him when he met Dorothy.

From later acquaintance, I think that she was mature and wise for her age. Her father's international career had taken her to Geneva and Danzig. She had lived and been at school in both places; both she and Douglas had seen and understood more than many of their contemporaries.

I saw Dorothy later, cycling into the Curragh camp. Dublin to the Curragh is about 30 miles: and don't forget the journey back. Douglas sometimes cycled up to Dorothy's relations in Dublin for weekends to meet her. It meant a 5 a.m. or 6 a.m. start back on Monday mornings. What a thing it is to be young! Buses were few and awkwardly timed. It is difficult to explain the importance of bicycles in life, love and work at that time. Petrol was unavailable for private motoring. Everyone took trams or buses or cycled to work. Women cycled to dances, with their dresses in waterproof bags on the carriers. Bicycles were needed for anything that ended after the last public transport, although there were a few horse-drawn cabs in Dublin. The journeys that ended in lovers' meetings could be cold and wet. Dublin, however, was a safe city and one saw young girls walking home.

Douglas and Dorothy married in Dublin on 12 July 1944, when he got a few days' leave from his army duties. Only a small group from their families was present. I dined with them in their first home in Rathgar. In June 1945 he resigned from the Army and started work as a sub-editor on the *Irish Press* newspaper. Their first child, Susan, was born in August 1945 and they decided to take her with them as a toddler, to visit Dorothy's family in Switzerland in the autumn of 1946. Douglas slipped away from that family visit and crossed into devastated Germany. In a solo expedition lasting a couple of months he reported to the *Irish Press* what he saw, and what had become of people he met before the war. It was his first serious journalism.

Dorothy and Douglas were a quietly devoted couple. She supported him thoroughly in his very demanding work. Her mother, the wife of a Belfast alderman and merchant, was an intelligent woman and was considered a very good homemaker and hostess. Dorothy showed similar attributes in her first home in Winton Avenue, and later in their house above the Dodder in Terenure.

Her father, Seán Lester, was a Methodist from Belfast who had been captivated by the Gaelic League and said that he had experienced the splendid hopes of an ancient nation's rebirth. As a young but experienced journalist he had been recruited by the minister for external affairs, initially for dealing with publicity. He later dealt with correspondence to and from our embassies and Britain, then became Irish representative to the League of Nations in Geneva. His hard work and integrity gained him international respect. He became the League's high commissioner of the Free City of Danzig, now Gdansk, (1934–7). The Nazi party was strong in the area and Forstrer, the Gauleiter, was an old friend of Hitler. Lester had a hot three years. Douglas wrote his biography (*The Last Secretary-General*, Dublin 1999). The extracts from Lester's diaries show his clear mind and lucid pen. The loss of such people to our state services and society was a sad result of partition.

Douglas saw the funny side of life and was good company. He was a constructive and undemonstrative patriot, who believed in his country and worked for it. 'Buy Irish and complain' was his answer to those who criticised the quality of Irish goods. Such criticisms are rarely heard now. A good friend whose advice was thoughtful and sound, he was overawed by nobody. Dorothy became a friend of my late wife, Betty. They were similar women—educated, humorous, intelligent and quietly devoted to their homes and families. Dorothy did much work with the Simon Community. Her death was a heavy blow to Douglas.

Three telephones inspire confidence . . . Douglas Gageby at his desk in G2 (Army Intelligence) HQ Dublin 1943.

Mr Gageby's republic

Olivia O'Leary

I'd reach for the phone, groggy, like all newspaper journalists early in the morning. 'Olivia, it's Douglas. Great stuff today. Great stuff. Go back to sleep.'

There was no chance of my going back to sleep. The editor liked it. Much of the time he didn't like it and he was one of the few people in journalism whose opinion I really cared about. He had two modes. When he was happy, he barked. The brown eyes sparkled and he radiated approval. When he wasn't happy, he growled. He'd stand at the editor's door, growling. And sometimes, he'd erupt. 'Where's our Blueshirt correspondent?' he roared across the newsroom at me one day when I'd written a piece he thought was too hard on the SDLP. He didn't want to talk to me. He just wanted me to know what he thought.

He was a confident man and he felt no need to compete with his journalists. He saw us as his most important resource and felt an editor's job was to find, hire and encourage us. He knew that feedback and encouragement were as important as a pay rise. He must have saved the paper thousands.

He didn't tell us what to write. He believed our value was to write it as we saw it and most of us never knew how staunchly he defended us when people complained. John Hume rang to complain about the piece I wrote on the SDLP. Mr Gageby idolised John Hume but he made no concessions.

To me, he was a real republican—a Belfast-reared Protestant who believed not only in Irish unity, but also in liberty and equality. Fraternity he could be a bit irreverent about, particularly when it came to the histrionic attitudes sometimes struck by the newspaper unions. 'Look at so-and-so' he said to me one day, glancing over at our then father of the chapel, normally the mildest of men. 'He's been looking daggers at me all morning. There must be a chapel meeting brewing.'

In a way, the paper was his republic. In a still conservative country, it was a safe haven for liberals. Certainly it was the place where I felt myself liberated and valued as a journalist. He consulted us. He encouraged us. We might see ourselves as dirty-raincoated sleuths with a foot stuck in the door, but he didn't. He tried to smarten us up, to make us think of ourselves as true equals to anyone we met or interviewed and he liked us to behave that way socially.

He was a great man for lunches. 'Take Brian Lenihan out to lunch' he barked at me one day. I didn't need to be told twice. 'Take Bill Craig out to lunch,' he said soon after. Now, this was different. The controversial Northern Ireland home affairs minister who took on the civil rights movement, leader of the loyalist movement Vanguard and of the Ulster Workers Council strike which brought down power-sharing, Craig had always struck me as the dourest of men. To my surprise, he did come to lunch and after the first bottle of a good wine, thawed out and was wonderful company. Whenever we met afterwards, he was always helpful. Mr Gageby's approach paid off.

Douglas Gageby loved Northern Ireland. So did I. I'd worked and lived there and took any chance to go back. For all his republicanism, he had a soft spot for the stout old unionists who continued to hold out behind their stockades—solid citizens like bluff Fermanagh farmer and Unionist leader, Harry West. He asked me to interview Harry. I did. We ran a big picture of Harry in tweeds, gazing out over his lakeland farm. The headlined quotation ran: 'I know these fields will be part of a united Ireland—but not in my lifetime.' There was something about the defiance and the fatalism in that line which appealed to Mr Gageby— something poignant. When he liked a piece, he put it under the sheet of glass on top of his desk. People like David McKittrick, Geraldine Kennedy, Conor O'Clery, Henry Kelly, Maeve Binchy, Mary Maher made it under the glass, not me—except for that piece on Harry West.

He had two sacred cows: Germany and the Irish Army—the Army, I should say. Sometimes I sinned. He would stop in his well-worn track from the newsroom door to his office and growl at me: 'How many armies have we in this state?' 'One, Mr Gageby.' 'What's it called?' 'The Army, Mr Gageby.'

We knew he spoke German and had been in Army Intelligence during the war, interrogating German pilots who crashed here. He believed in a Franco-German-led EU as the bulwark against another war in Europe.

And he liked to look forward, not back. When Carl Carstens, the new president of the German Federal Republic, visited Ireland in May 1980, I got hold of a confidential briefing document given by Iveagh House to the political leaders who would meet him. The briefing document indicated that since Carstens had Nazi connections in the past, there might have been protests against him by Jewish and human rights groups if he had visited Holland or Denmark. He was visiting Ireland first, suggested the document, because we were less likely to protest.

I published all this as part of a not very reverent sketch piece I did on the visit and went on to say that the band had played 'Deutschland über alles' at a ceremony the German president attended.

Mr Gageby was furious. I had got the name of the German national anthem wrong, he announced to me through gritted teeth. It was called 'Das Lied der Deutschen' and, he said, it was the third verse, not the controversial first 'Deutschen über alles' verse, which was sung now. 'Ah, come on,' I argued 'It's still the same tune!' But that only made him crosser. Technically he was right, of course, but his real objection was that my article dug up Germany's past. He felt it was time to move on.

Also, he probably thought I was being smart-assed. He didn't like us being smart-assed. The day before Pope John Paul came to Ireland in 1979, he called us all in to his office, all of us who would be covering the visit. 'Now,' he said 'This is an historic occasion for the people of this country, maybe the most historic occasion any of you will cover in your lifetime. I don't want any of you fashionable liberals sneering at the Pope. You will cover this seriously as the great occasion it is for the people of this country and most of our readers'. It was the only time I ever remember him telling us how we should write, so we knew he meant it. As a result most of us tried very hard to give the Pope a chance. My resolve finally broke down in the rain in Limerick when the Pope effectively told married women to go back into their homes and have children. No woman, I decided, should have to stomach this— not in Mr Gageby's republic.

But I understood what he was trying to do, whether it was with the coverage of the papal visit or with the voice of the country TD in John Healy's 'Backbencher' column. He was determined finally to bury any memory of *The Irish Times* as the voice of Protestant unionism. He wanted us to be liberal but also to be part of the mainstream of Irish life. He was right, but it sometimes led him to be protective about the state, to be cautious about the sort of investigative journalism which could be seen to undermine the credibility of the state or its security apparatus. He was wary about criticism of the Gardaí and of course, of the Army. *The Irish Times* would be seen to be loyal.

When I went to tell him I was leaving, he wouldn't hear of it. I was finding that the time demands of a daily paper kept me too long away from my new baby. That could all be sorted out, he said. He would move me to the features office and I could have a more flexible timetable.

Next day, he came over and sat down beside me. He'd been talking to his wife Dorothy. Dorothy told him that a mother knew what was best for her baby and that if I felt it was best to leave, he shouldn't try to stop me.

After I left, we didn't meet very often. Mr Gageby was no social butterfly—his world was the paper and his family. Thirteen years later, I did a little programme for television about our local railway in Borris, now closed. I'd forgotten he loved railways. Once again I was to lift the phone and hear his voice: 'Olivia. It's Douglas Gageby. Great stuff.'

God help me, I'm still smiling.

The sacking of Alec Newman

Donal O'Donovan

In the lavatory shared by reporters, sub-editors and the editorial staff of *The Irish Times* I had finished throwing up a sizable load of black stout when the editor walked in. He was in need of what he would call 'a pump-ship' but first he noticed my white face.

'Where have you been?' asked Alec Newman in a spirit of genuine enquiry.

'I have been vomiting pints,' I answered.

'Be thankful, Donal,' said the editor, 'that you can still get sick. The time will come when you will no longer be able to throw up.'

The year was 1957. I had joined *The Irish Times* from the *Sunday Independent* three years earlier. I was a sub-editor under Donald Smyllie, chief sub-editor. I had just become engaged and used the £70 I had contributed towards my pension to pay for my honeymoon in Germany. My salary at 29 years of age was 12 guineas a week, the going rate and not enough to purchase pints in the Pearl Bar.

Even then I could see that my conversation with Alec Newman was unusual. My previous employer was Hector Legge, editor of the *Sunday Independent* and proud possessor of his own private lavatory key. Known to me as 'Mr Legge' and to everybody as the terror of our lives, he was tall where I was small, and well-spoken where I was Dublin.

The culture shock I had suffered while I absorbed the free and easy atmosphere of the subs' room under Donald Smyllie was compounded by the fact that I got a single glimpse of God before the editor, Bertie Smyllie, who was Donald's brother, died of diabetes and a heart attack in September 1954. That was just six months after I first set foot in Fleet Street.

I was happy as a sub-editor and very surprised when Donald suggested that I should apply to the editor for a vacancy in his office. Like the reporters' room, the subs' room could discern the high fence that separated us from the editor's room, where they were all Trinity graduates, most having gone straight into the paper from college with no training as journalists. They showed a sense of superiority that reduced contact to a minimum.

The vacancy had been caused by the departure of Martin Sheridan, an editorial assistant who had begun a new life as public relations officer in Córas Tráchtála, the Irish Export Board. Martin was clever, very witty and curiously well suited to the new job, where he carved himself a fine career. I think he was a Catholic by birth. The question of religion was still important then, although in my case (Catholic, Blackrock and UCD). I was not blazing a trail. My cousin, Peter Brennan, son of Uncle Joe, the governor of the Central Bank, had already done a stint in Smyllie's office, and he was Catholic and Cambridge. But Bruce Williamson, Jack White and Dick Gamble were highly polished products of good schools—Shrewsbury, Midleton and St Columba's—and Trinity; and Alec Newman was a classics scholar who had gone on to teach Latin and Greek at High School, Dublin.

Is it any wonder that my reply to Donald Smyllie was: 'Me? I couldn't write a leader to save my life'. 'Have a go,' said Donald. 'It can't do any harm.'

I was full of fear and lacking any confidence when I approached Mr Newman, who asked me to write a piece on the (British) National Health Service. Making use of *Whitaker's Almanack* I produced the article. 'I was going to give you a week's trial,' said Alec, 'but now there is no need.' So I joined the élite.

Sitting at right angles to me was Bruce Williamson, to whom, when I was at school, I had submitted a poem. I was delighted to get a rejection slip that said: 'I am sorry that it couldn't be a cheque. Don't be discouraged, however. I think your poem's rich with promise. Good Luck.'

I had envisaged the literary editor as a fat greybeard of great authority, and was amazed to discover that Bruce was 24 in 1946, a gentle, lovable and deeply unhappy man whose hobby, collecting scale model motor-cars, I shared. He was a distinguished cinema critic and a writer of scintillating leading articles and beautiful poetry. He kept a bottle of gin in his desk and used to disappear from the office occasionally for a matter of weeks. These unexplained absences, I learned later, were spent in a nursing home. Bruce's wife Millie had been one of the grain merchant Odlum family and regarded Bruce's occupation as beneath him. They had a son, Howard, whom I also met. He too was unhappy.

The third man in the room was Dick Gamble, who doubled as motoring correspondent. Dick was low-sized and had a gammy leg. He felt the insecurity that went with his appearance and he drank as heroically as the rest of us. He was married to the beautiful Jean Dunne who later married Hugh Crawford of the motor distribution business. Dick went to England, where he died years later. His place was taken by Fergus Pyle—later to be editor between Douglas Gageby's two sessions. Alec gave him a month's trial but before Fergus's month was up Alec had left, in circumstances as dramatic as any staged in the other Fleet Street in London.

Our room had been partitioned so that the editor had a small and accessible glazed area beyond ours. There Alec held court, wrote his leading articles and gave work to Marion Fitzgerald, the editorial secretary who began her journalistic career writing 'pup' leaders. The pup was a third leader, usually a comic comment on a strange news story. Marion had a gift for pups, which sometimes were also contributed by Alec Reid or R. B. D. French, both lecturers at Trinity College. Marion went on to have a career in more substantial journalism and to marry Brian Fallon, who made a European name for himself as *The Irish Times*'s art critic.

On the far side of the editor's room sat Jack White in his own room, a handsome man as tall as Bruce. Features editor and a novelist, he also wrote an award-winning play, *The Last Eleven* (Abbey Theatre). Jack had written a memorable leader on the dropping of the bomb at Hiroshima on 6 August 1945. One of Alec's unpleasant traits was to call White 'Jacksie' from time to time, a deliberate insult to indicate contempt.

Jack did not retaliate, but the nickname was part of an obscure game of office politics being played at the time. Jack was looked on by a number of people as the natural heir to Alec, but there were obviously some, including Alec, who were determined that another editor could be found. Jack, the Cork-born son of English Congregationalist parents, was aware of the moves being made (he advised me that anybody with ambitions would be wise to change jobs by the time he was 40). He made the move himself, departing for the new pastures being sown in Telefís Éireann.

Thus he left Chairman Frank Lowe and the board (including Douglas Gageby) free to apply a sharp hatchet to Alec's neck without the risk of White's succeeding him. Alan Montgomery, chief reporter, would not have wanted White as editor for he disliked him. Alan, who was not a graduate, was the son of the essayist 'Lynn Doyle', a drinking friend of the old editor R. M. Smyllie. In 1940 Smyllie had made Alan the paper's chief reporter, as a wedding present.

Various other journalists did not want White because they considered him arrogant or 'English' or both.

I don't remember his words myself, but when Alec came back from his fateful meeting with the board he told Marion and Bruce, and then others: 'The bastards have got me.' (Hugh Oram *The Newspaper Book*, Dublin, 1983, page 282.)

What nobody had counted on was that Bruce and Marion would decide to depart with the sacked Alec, leaving Dick Gamble and me to cope with the immediate and surprise appointment of Montgomery as editor. The board's appointment of Alan was a surprise because he wasn't really editor material. Bruce had been the deputy editor and, as I recall it, had been offered the succession but turned it down.

Alec had joined *The Irish Times* in 1930 when he was 25. A Waterford man, he went to the Royal Belfast Academical Institution and became a distinguished classics scholar at Trinity. He taught classics at the High School in Dublin but was a poor disciplinarian and used his writing ability to get a leader writer's position in *The Irish Times*. When Bertie Smyllie became editor in 1934, Alec was appointed assistant editor and spent the next 20 years using his encyclopaedic memory as a panel member on Radio Éireann's 'Information Please' and the BBC's 'Round Britain Quiz'.

Alec was married twice; first to Maureen Rossiter, an old school friend of my mother's and a Catholic. In those days, there was a lot of nonsense about mixed marriages and Alec had to spend time in London to fulfil some regulation that would allow him to marry. When she died he next married Mary Frances Keating, who for many years was a cookery writer for the *Sunday Independent*. She was a sister of Seán Keating the painter.

Alec and Mary Frances (another Catholic) had no children but Mary Frances bravely undertook the care of Francis, his severely handicapped son by Maureen, who had also given him a rather beautiful daughter called Sorcha. With Francis, Alec helped, mainly by pushing the wheelchair around Ranelagh, but there was a pub that held more attraction later in the day and there was the Palace and then the Pearl Bar and there was the Irish Times Club in Fleet Street, where I was at times despatched to get whiskey from Charlie Long, the manager. I am tempted—I will tell—of the night Alec himself made the long journey upstairs to demand: 'Charlie, give me a scrotum of malt—two balls to take away in a bag.'

Who knows the pressures on the board to get rid of Alec Newman? He and Bruce executed a campaign against the autocratic and conservative Catholic archbishop of Dublin, Dr John Charles McQuaid. When the archbishop refused to celebrate a solemn votive Mass for the first Dublin Theatre Festival, the paper used its liberal reputation to castigate McQuaid for his narrow-mindedness. A more balanced view might have been conveyed to readers by acknowledging the archbishop's right to disapprove of some of the plays to be staged.

McQuaid's relationship with Smyllie had been more civilised. They had dinner at the archiepiscopal palace once a year and ritually bantered about the Union Jack that formed the badge on McQuaid's Standard motor car. McQuaid's brother Matt was the salesman for that make.

One of the causes that *The Irish Times* fought in a way that enhanced its developing liberal character was the Fethard-on-Sea boycott of the local Protestant community in 1957. It was ugly and it was conducted by the parish priest. It deeply involved the *ne temere* papal decree of 1908 which compelled the non-Catholic partner in a marriage to bring up children as Catholics. It brought in the Belfast lawyer Desmond Boal and it caused the mother, Sheila Cloney, to take their two daughters from the family home to live in Scotland. It ruined her father, a prosperous farmer. Some local IRA veterans of the War of Independence fought the boycott and Taoiseach Éamon de Valera called the boycott 'ill conceived, ill considered and futile, unjust and cruel'. It famously ended with the parish priest buying a packet of cigarettes in the shop worst affected by the boycott. The film, *A Love Divided* (1999), was based on the Cloney family's story.

The Fethard-on-Sea saga was the kind of story *The Irish Times* needed to boost its pathetically low circulation (at that time perhaps 35,000 and sinking). I can recall the agonising that sometimes went into a necessary rise in price of ½d. How long, we speculated, until the immediate drop in sales would be balanced by the increase in revenue?

Another consideration in favour of getting rid of Alec Newman that must have weighed with the board was his *modus operandi*. When the first copy of the country edition was delivered in to the editor's room, a long period of dissection, analysis and change would begin. How long it lasted, with us on our knees and the pages spread over the floor, would depend on how drunk Alec was. Sports pages were ignored, but everything else was scrutinised; alterations were made, pictures could be substituted and an hour could be spent on the redrafting of a headline. The trains waiting at Kingsbridge or Amiens Street were forgotten and the printing and circulation staff were fuming. There was, as I recall, a fine to be paid for every delay on the railway.

The fallout from the night of the long knives was widespread. Alec had neither money nor a job. He was 56 and addicted to alcohol. Mary Frances had a bleak future, though her sister Claudia and her brother Claude helped where they could. It was a while before the *Irish Press* offered Alec some work as a leader writer and commentator on current affairs. He worked until he had a stroke, and he spent his last years in the Royal Hospital in Donnybrook, where George Leitch, the chief photographer of *The Irish Times* and my best friend, used to visit him with me. He died in 1972.

Because his family owned large tracts of Belfast, it was wrongly assumed that Bruce Williamson did not need a job. Douglas Gageby showed his real heart at this time, trying to entice Bruce back into the fold. But Bruce had his pride and it was some years before he made his return. Marion married Brian Fallon and, apart from going on with her journalism, fulfilled her ambition to have seven children. She and I are the only survivors of that time in that strange place in Fleet Street known as the editor's room.

The invention of financial journalism

Nicholas Leonard

In January 1963, a small classified advertisement appeared in the *Financial Times*. It read roughly as follows: 'IRISH TIMES seeks financial editor. Some journalistic experience desirable'.

At the time I was working on the city pages of the *Evening Standard* in London and William Davis, the highly energetic financial editor of that paper, drew the ad to my attention the day it appeared because, he said, I was always going on about wanting to go back to Dublin and work there.

I liked *The Irish Times*. It was the first newspaper that had ever printed anything I wrote: a letter I sent it as a teenager in about 1955 to tell its readers that I had had the unusual experience of seeing a fox prowling down the main street of Killiney where I was living.

My late father, Ralph Leonard, who was the publicity manager of Aer Lingus at the time, was also an enthusiastic reader of the paper. Like many in the media world in Dublin in those days, he was worried about whether it could survive financially and he was fond of saying that it could maintain its circulation of around 33,000 even if it had to quadruple its cover price which at the time was just 6d in old coinage.

By a happy coincidence, Norah Raitt, the Irish girl who operated the telex machine in the city office of the *Evening Standard*, was a friend of John Arnott, the London editor of *The Irish Times*. She rang him, introduced me to him over the telephone and we arranged to meet for a drink in a Fleet Street pub.

Sir John Arnott, it turned out, was a good deal more than just a London editor of the paper. He was also a significant minority shareholder who was extremely frustrated and anxious about its trading and prospects. Behind a façade of affable bonhomie and effusive hospitality, John concealed an extremely incisive and prescient mind which not only enabled him to write brilliantly readable columns for the paper but also gave him insights into what needed to be done with it.

One of those insights was the opportunity to enhance its financial news coverage. It is hard to imagine now but in 1963 there were no full-time financial journalists in Dublin. Clerks in stockbroking offices contributed some weekly notes on a freelance basis while the majority of the daily editorial consisted of UK material supplied from London on a syndicated basis.

John had seen the impact of charismatic financial editors like Frederick Ellis on the *Daily Express* and he believed, rightly, that not only was there an opening for *The Irish Times* to follow suit and improve its readership and coverage but also that such an enhancement would prove extremely attractive to advertisers because of the above-average income of those readers.

When I met John for the first time, the only financial information I had on *The Irish Times* was disconcerting. The company, whose preference shares were quoted, had shown an annual loss of over £30,000. In other words, it was losing about £1 a year for each of the 33,000 or so copies it sold each day.

At the time I was 23 years old and had 'some journalistic experience', having worked for 10 months on the *Investor's Chronicle*, my first job after university, and a further five months on the *Evening Standard*. Despite some obvious qualms about whether this experience was sufficient, and possibly because of the lack of any plausible alternative candidates, John decided to introduce me to Alan Montgomery, who was then the editor of *The Irish Times*, and to Douglas Gageby who was its joint managing director.

Like John, they told me they were worried about my being so young. My concerns were somewhat different: would *The Irish Times* survive to continue employing me and could I afford to live in Dublin on the salary of £1,300 a year which was about 30 per cent less than I was getting as a novice city reporter on the *Evening Standard*?

William Davis, who had been appointed two years earlier as city editor of that paper by Lord Beaverbrook at the age of 26, gave me two invaluable pieces of advice: get your by-line on the financial pages every day and do interviews with major business people as often as you can.

I think I was the first person to be given a by-line on a daily page in *The Irish Times*. The new business and finance section, consisting of a page and a half, appeared on 20 May 1963 and when I went into work that morning I found a neat, hand-written note from Douglas Gageby congratulating me on how it looked and read. I think in retrospect he must have been relieved that there was a financial section there to read since the only reporter was myself and I was also responsible for organising the layout and proof-reading with the help of a sub called Ned Barry, the only man whom I ever met during my career in journalism who wore a green eyeshade, Hollywood-style, at work every day.

I had virtually no further contact with Douglas until November 1963, a traumatic month in the history of the company when, a few years after being forced to close the *Evening Mail*, it reluctantly decided to abandon its loss-making tabloid, the *Sunday Review*, as well.

Douglas, who had had an outstanding editorial career at the *Evening Press* and the Irish News Agency, replaced Alan Montgomery as editor. The contrast in style between the austere, intensely focused and self-disciplined Gageby and the gregarious, companionable charm and warmth of Montgomery, could not have been greater. I can still recall the sense of shock we all experienced at the afternoon editor's conference when Alan produced a bottle of whiskey, poured us all drinks and told us that Douglas was replacing him.

When Andrew Whittaker asked me to write about Douglas, I was initially reluctant because I did not feel that I ever knew him well enough to make a meaningful contribution. But on reflection I very much doubt whether anyone ever knew him that well. He was a very private person in the workplace but an extraordinarily able, hard-working and insightful editor, who had the crucial ability to lift the game of those working for him. Being an effective editor is a very different skill to being an effective journalist but Douglas was equally talented on both fronts.

He and John Arnott turned out to be absolutely right about the opportunities for expanding financial journalism in Ireland. It is strange to reflect now that in 1963 it was quite commonplace for substantial companies, like John Power, the distillers, and Thomas Dockrell, the builders providers, to ban reporters from their annual meetings. Maurice Dockrell, the chairman of the latter, used to personally bring me out a glass of sherry after the meeting and graciously inform me that all resolutions had been carried without dissent.

The Irish Times turned out to be extraordinarily well placed to take advantage of the cultural and social changes that had been triggered by the success of the government's programmes for economic expansion. I remember that soon after I joined it, I had to write a story about British Drug Houses and the outlook for its new drug called Volidan. I went to the editor and asked whether it was permissible for me to mention that Volidan was an oral birth control pill. (It was duly allowed but it is hard to believe now that I thought it necessary to ask, the reason being that I knew it was against the law to promote contraception).

Ironically, it was the closure of the *Sunday Review*, for which I had written a weekly column, that indirectly led to my departure from *The Irish Times* the following year. The *Review*'s centre spread was a lively gossip column by Patsy Dyke, whose husband, Cathal Óg O'Shannon, was one of the outstanding reporters on *The Irish Times*. When her column came to an abrupt end, Patsy went into public relations and a few months later invited me to join a press trip to Dromoland Castle Hotel, which she had obtained as a client. Also on the trip was Nuala McLaughlin, the editor of *Creation*, who suggested to me that I should interview her husband, Hugh, who had launched numerous publications during his career. When I met him for lunch in April 1964, he told me that he had always wanted to start a financial weekly magazine and he invited me to be the editor. I gave *The Irish Times* my three months notice and left it in August 1964. The first edition of *Business and Finance* appeared on 18 September. I will always be grateful to John Arnott, Alan Montgomery and Douglas Gageby for the opportunities they gave me. I know they were disappointed that I did not stay longer with them but, as I pointed out to Douglas on the only occasion that our paths crossed many years later, they had the consolation that the circulation of *The Irish Times* rose steadily after I left. The initiation and the subsequent development of its financial coverage played a key part in that.

Aggiornamento

John Horgan

When I first attempted to join the staff of *The Irish Times*, I hadn't even heard of Douglas Gageby. I had an introduction to Séamus Kelly [1] and worked that line for a time until, after dozens of phone calls to the 'Irishman's Diary' office which—to my innocent surprise and eventual disillusionment—were never answered and never returned, I knocked on the door of Conor O'Brien at the *Evening Press* and got a job.

Not much later, now working for Des Fisher at the *Catholic Herald* in London, I ingratiated myself with Donal Foley and John Arnott [2] by re-writing press releases as paragraphs for their 'London Letter' in *The Irish Times* on an unpaid basis during my lunch break. A job prospect materialised in some curiously unspecified fashion and, after an interview by Alan Montgomery at a Formica-covered table in the Kardomah Café in Charing Cross, I was hired. With the arrogance of youth (and probably at Donal's instigation) I responded to the job offer with an audacious request to Monty for an assurance that *The Irish Times* was not about to go bust. Even more amazingly, I got it. I still hadn't heard of Gageby.

I worked for a couple of months in *The Irish Times* office in Printing House Square, the headquarters of *The Times*, before coming back to Dublin in September 1963. The man who had hired me was gone—to a sinecure in Guinness's from which he dispensed countless buckshee barrels of stout to any journalist (myself included) who rang him up on the eve of a party. Douglas had by now taken his place. I must have met him shortly after my arrival, but have no memory of our first meeting: it was probably brief, courteous, and just the right side of peremptory. The firm handshake and the straight gaze didn't encourage small talk: with Douglas, there was always a job to be done, and the niceties could wait.

---

1 Sole proprietor, for many years of the 'Irishman's Diary' column, as well as theatre critic.

2 Deputy London editor and London editor respectively. Arnott was the last surviving link with the newspaper's once-owning family. Foley came back to Dublin to become news editor in late 1963, just after my return.

There was a whiff of change in the air, almost undetectable, but unmistakable when identified. My arrival in the newsroom was the occasion for subterranean growls, partly occasioned by an extraordinary decision (again, I suspect Donal) to run, as a main page news lead, a feature article I had written from London about Irish emigrants returning to the homeland in search of the prosperity that was then emerging. It had been based on a survey of one—myself. The growls turned to barely concealed mirth when, a year later, my first by-line appeared, as 'By our educational correspondent'. This sort of nonsense, I was assured, would never catch on. Catch on? The photo by-lines are now crowding out even the headlines.

In retrospect, it can be seen that two things were happening. One was that the relationship between Douglas and Donal was beginning to bear fruit. Certainly Douglas never interfered with Donal's running of the newsroom, and their intermittent disagreements enriched that relationship rather than imperilled it. It was important to both men, and doubly important to the paper, which was sloughing off its past and fashioning a new identity.

The second thing, which was probably more Douglas than Donal, was the sense that the new kid on the block—television—stood, in relation to newspapers, in a totally different relationship than had its predecessor, steam radio. It was a voracious rival, gobbling up advertisements, poaching journalists and cannibalising audiences with equal appetite. Its current affairs programmes were staffed by a new generation of (usually graduate) interviewers and reporters who had not had to serve the long apprenticeship of local and provincial newspapers, and who took on their new role as masters of the media universe with rare glee and a profound disrespect for their elders. Newspapers had to up their game if they were to challenge the glitzy new medium and, under Douglas, this is exactly what *The Irish Times* did.

The 'educational correspondent' was only one of a number of innovations which, taken together, broke radically with the idea of the newspaper as a dreary, pre-programmed mixture of news, finance and sport, and started to address the varied interests of a new generation of young Irish men and women, no longer growing to maturity in London or Manchester or New York, but in Dublin and Cork and (probably even) Roscommon, and justifiably impatient with the shibboleths and the tired old nostrums of the past. By the mid-1960s the three political party leaders of the older generation, Seán Lemass, James Dillon and William Norton had all gone and there was a palpable sense of excitement. It is important to remember, though, that although the economy was improving on an almost hourly basis, much of the excitement was not about money, but about ideas. And, in Douglas's *Irish Times*, the ideas fizzed like champagne.

His other huge contribution, at this initial stage, was subtly to change the paper's centre of gravity, so that writers now became of prime importance. The prominence allocated to people like Michael Viney, Desmond Fennell, Michael Foy, Mary Maher and many more underlined this commitment to style. This did nothing to dilute the potent mixture of truth-seeking and exhibitionism that fuelled the new breed of reporters: I still cringe with embarrassment at the memory of the arrogance with which I walked the length of the newsroom to ventilate my displeasure at a hapless sub-editor who had changed one of my semi-colons into a full stop.

If there was hubris, there was also comeuppance—and I had my first taste of the latter at Douglas's hands. I was on Sunday evening town,[3] the grave-yard shift, and one of my few responsibilities was to report that night's 'Thomas Davis Lecture', broadcast on RTE. The topic was the change of government in 1932. The speaker was some Fine Gael academic. The task was to make some sense of his remarks from the tiny squawk-box high up on the wall behind the news desk through which the RTÉ broadcast came into the clattery newsroom.

As the speaker trumpeted his praise of W. T. Cosgrave for handing over the reins of power to Éamon de Valera in 1932 'like the democrat he was', my already fragile grasp of Irish history (the Leaving Certificate syllabus in 1957 had probably ended with Poyning's Law) weakened even further, and my report, as printed, informed the startled readers of *The Irish Times* that the democrat being praised was, in fact, Mr de Valera.

When I turned up for duty the following morning I was informed that the editor wanted to see me. There was a smell of sulphur in the air. Apparently a large proportion of *The Irish Times*'s then modest readership had been on the phone to tell Douglas that they needed no further proof of the dark suspicions they had harboured since he had assumed the editorial chair—that *The Irish Times* had finally, and definitively, sold out to Fianna Fáil. I entered the sanctum hesitantly, expecting to be given my cards.

Douglas looked up from his desk. 'You made a right fuck-up of that, didn't you?' he remarked mildly. 'Don't do it again.'

This was light touch regulation several decades before the concept had even been invented, and I came to recognise it as one of the distin-

---

3 The shift traditionally devoted to the mind-numbing practice of phoning Garda stations and fire stations to find out if there had been any unnoticed disasters in the city.

guishing characteristics of Douglas's editorship. It was not that Douglas didn't have opinions, or was remiss in expressing them, sometimes accompanied by military-style rhetoric. But he expressed his most considered opinions in the taut, idiomatic, carefully worked and deeply personal prose of his editorials, which still bear re-reading almost half a century after he penned them. Generally, his leader (or leaders—there were many evenings when he did two) had been dictated by about 5.30 p.m. He would then repair unobtrusively to the College Mooney pub— comfortably adjacent to the office, but at a safe distance from the Pearl Bar, which was the principal watering-hole of the other members of the editorial staff—for about an hour, before returning to carry on the night's work.

The rest of the paper was a play-pen for the writers he trusted, and he found the space for them, on occasion, by throwing out advertisements or increasing pagination, to the consternation of the commercial side of the house. There was an occasional editorial cuff on the ear. An article which I had written for Fergus Pyle, then features editor (and later Douglas's successor) suggesting mildly that we had no need for a standing army was excised from the features section at page proof stage, and only reappeared a week later cheek by jowl with a salvo from one of Douglas's military buddies arguing the exact opposite.

There was a printers' strike in 1965. I still have my copy of the protective notice, signed by Douglas, which every reporter got. I was one of the lucky ones—kept on the payroll, contributing my RTÉ appearance fees for news programmes to the National Union of Journalists' hardship fund. Then the strike ended and, within a few days, Douglas approached me in the newsroom: at little more than a week's notice, he wanted me to go to Rome to cover the fourth (and final) session of the Second Vatican Council.

It was an extraordinary time for Catholicism generally, and more particularly for the Catholic Church in Ireland. In fact, relatively little of what was happening had, until then, percolated to the Celtic fringe of Europe. With the exception of RTÉ, which had sent Seán Mac Réamoinn and also Kevin O'Kelly out to Rome for part of each of the first three sessions of the Council, no Irish news medium had done more than publish the hackneyed and stereotyped dispatches from the international news agencies.

Irish Catholicism, despite the first three sessions (and years) of the Council, was still in a state of torpor. John Charles McQuaid, a stern-visaged autocrat, had been archbishop of Dublin for almost a quarter of a century, during which the power of the institutional Catholic Church had been extended and consolidated. Catholic attendance at Trinity

College Dublin was still technically sinful. In more rural areas, Catholic attendance at the weddings and funerals of Protestant neighbours could still be problematic. Irish Protestants—the most quiescent minority in any country in Europe, as Gageby's friend the Presbyterian minister Terence McCaughey provocatively described them—complained intermittently and ineffectually about the effects of the Vatican's *ne temere* decree, which forced the Protestant partners in religiously mixed marriages to bring up their children as Catholics. It was a society, and a culture, in stasis.

To be taken out of this milieu and thrown into the cultural and theological maelstrom that was Rome in the autumn of 1965 was challenging, liberating, fascinating, and (occasionally in more senses than one) intoxicating. You were pulling yourself up by your own intellectual boot-straps, scraping together enough knowledge to make sense of what was happening around you, and at the same time trying to find the words to make sense of it all to those at home, and to convey the excitement and intensity of it all.

Back in Westmoreland Street, Douglas sat back, watched, read, and let it happen. For three crowded months I wrote an average of about 1,000 words a day, six days a week. Sometimes it was even more. To the best of my knowledge, not a word was cut. On one occasion, imbued with Douglas's ideology of giving all sides a fair crack of the whip, I interviewed a Spanish cardinal only a short theological step removed from Torquemada. It was a lengthy interview and, from memory, it was given the best part of an entire page when it was published. On the other side of the ecclesiastical fault line, my fairly orthodox, middle-class, vaguely liberal Irish Catholicism had to come to terms with continental theologians who combined the sort of personal piety that would not have been out of place in a small Irish village with what initially seemed to my untutored ears to be rank heresy. There was the novelty—shock, almost—of the Mass in English, and the curiously mixed feelings engendered by the sight of a row of bishops, gift-wrapped in their scarlet belly-bands, kneeling in a queue for confession in a side-aisle of St Peter's basilica like so many altar boys.

Personal experiences apart, what strikes me about this in retrospect is that we were all, without consciously being aware of it, engaged on that most precious of journalistic missions—not the mission to convert, but the mission to explain. It was Douglas's editorship which nurtured that mission—the light but sure touch that sensed a popular mood and knew how to key into it. By the end of the Council—and after the Synods which succeeded the Council in 1967, 1969 and 1971—*The Irish Times* had escaped the protected habitat of the rectory and the manse and was to be seen, if not exactly flaunted, in an increasing number of presbyteries and, for all I know, even in the odd convent. Ireland itself was changing. More significantly—and certainly I was only a small part of that journalistic revolution—the landscape of Irish journalism was beginning to change. Before Douglas took over, the battle royal was the one being waged between the Irish Independent group and the Irish Press group: well before the end of his first term as editor, *The Irish Times* had become, unmistakeably and irreversibly, a player.

The even-handedness that Douglas inculcated now moved up a gear. Fresh from the Vatican, I was now posted by him every year to the Presbyterian General Assembly in Belfast, to the Methodist Conference in Belfast, Dublin or elsewhere, and to the General Synod of the Church of Ireland in Christ Church, Dublin. In turn I was fascinated by the rhetorical richness of the Presbyterians as they argued about 17th-century theology, astonished to find the Methodists more socially radical than any political party in Dáil Éireann, and baffled by the barrack-room lawyers of Irish Anglicanism as they argued their way through their parliamentary procedures.

Douglas's light touch was evident also in another potentially critical area. We were contractually obliged to seek his permission before writing for any other publication, but one permission seemed to act as a sort of general absolution. Particularly on Saturday mornings when, in the absence of a Sunday paper after the *Sunday Review* folded in 1964 there was nobody on duty, the newsroom echoed to the hammered keys of the old stand-up typewriters as reporters plied the export trade.[4]

Curiously for a man who inspired such loyalty, he never stood in the way of anyone on the staff who felt he could better himself. I once asked him for advice after Jim McGuinness had offered me the editorship of the *RTÉ Guide* (the fact that I felt no diffidence in asking for his advice is itself emblematic of the relationship he had with us). 'Think of the amount of money that would make it worth your while to move,' he advised me, 'and, if they agree, take it.' By the time I had worked out that £1,500 a year (I was then on about £950 at the *Times*) represented the height of my financial ambitions, I had also worked out that no amount of money could compensate for leaving Westmoreland Street, and I turned the offer down without a qualm. Much later, Douglas was to wave goodbye to John Healy, a.k.a. 'Back-bencher', as he departed for Tony O'Reilly's empire in Abbey Street, and welcomed him back equally cheerfully at the expiry of a contract which had cost O'Reilly a great deal of money, and in the course of

---

4 Writing articles and news reports for other (usually UK or American) publications was a handy additional source of income.

which not a single word Healy wrote had been published because the National Union of Journalists at the *Independent* had blacked his copy.[5]

I can recall only one occasion on which he asked my advice. It was late at night in the newsroom, and he showed me a letter from a reader complaining about an article that had been written by one of my colleagues. 'What would you do about that?' he asked. 'I'd publish it,' I answered, with the insouciance of youth, and a total absence of professional solidarity. 'It's not as simple as that,' he commented. 'X [the journalist involved] says that if I publish it, he'll sue *me*.' The letter never appeared, and I had learned, to my surprise, that not even Douglas was omnipotent.

The benign neglect of one's outside activities already mentioned was probably responsible for the fact that when, in 1969, I stood for and was elected to the Seanad in the National University of Ireland constituency, the thought of asking Douglas's (or anyone's) permission never even crossed my mind. It became an issue only four years later, when the onset of the 1973 election coincided with the agreement by Douglas, Major T. B. McDowell, the chairman, and the board to launch *The Education Times* with me as editor. They would have preferred me to stand down from the Seanad, but agreed to a compromise: I could be editor while a senator, as long as I maintained my status as an Independent. The final move in that chess game was towards the end of these negotiations, when McDowell summoned me to the boardroom to say that they were very happy to launch the new title, but also to ask me whether I was aware that, by taking this route, I was effectively removing myself from consideration as a future editor of *The Irish Times*? The words 'bird', 'hand' and 'bush' sprang to mind. I never regretted my decision. I was 32.[6]

The years before the launch of *The Education Times*, however, had been already full of many other things besides religion and education,

---

5 Healy had always refused to join the NUJ. He bought a Rolls Royce with the money from his *Independent* contract, and later gave O'Reilly a present of one of his paintings of the West of Ireland. O'Reilly was to say that it was the most expensive painting he had ever bought—which at that time it probably was.

6 When a combination of factors, not least the horrendous economic situation in 1973–5, later made it obvious that *The Education Times* would not survive (which would have meant the end of my contract in any case), I joined the Labour Party, and was again summoned to the boardroom. I was reminded by Major McDowell that I had now broken my contract and would have to leave the employment of the company (i.e. be fired) with my contractual three months' notice. Pat Nolan, father of *The Irish Times* NUJ chapel, took up the cudgels on my behalf and won me a year's salary (£6,400) on which I fought and won a Dáil seat in 1977.

the two areas in which I specialised. In the late 1960s the paper, not least because of the dramatic increase in circulation under Douglas, had begun to make money. Douglas loved spending it on his reporters. In 1968, as the ethnic conflict in Nigeria boiled over into civil war, he asked me to go out and cover the conflict. With the foolhardiness of youth, I agreed, and almost immediately found myself as one of half a dozen passengers on an ancient Super Constellation, loaded mostly with ammunition, flying at night into the secessionist province of Biafra, which at that time seemed to be run partly by General Ojukwu's rag, tag and bobtail army, and partly by the Irish Holy Ghost missionary order.

It was an extraordinary assignment for a number of reasons, not all of them apparent to me at the time. For one thing, communications between Biafra and Dublin were literally non-existent, and after flying into Biafra I effectively went off the radar for three weeks. (After I returned to Dublin, I heard that Douglas would inquire at editorial conferences, quizzically, whether I had perhaps been eaten.) It was a war of attrition. Hostilities were sporadic, and sometimes, for weeks on end, not a shot would be fired by either side. The sole occasion I felt in any personal danger was when I was interviewing Ojukwu and heard an aeroplane overhead (the only planes in the air during daylight hours were Federal Nigerian MiG fighters piloted by Egyptian mercenaries).

A problematic aspect of the assignment was the requirement—again a Gageby trademark—that I should also file reports from the Federal side of the conflict. Accordingly, when I left Biafra, I posted (yes, gentle reader, posted) my typewritten Biafran articles from Rome before flying back to Lagos, and enclosed with them a plea to Douglas not to publish any of them before I had safely exited the Nigerian capital. Unbelievably by today's news-hungry standards, he acceded—but only just. The first of my Biafran articles was published in *The Irish Times* (and duly publicised by the Biafran radio) on the morning of the day I was due to fly out, creating all sorts of apoplexy at the Nigerian ministry of information and ensuring that my taxi journey to the airport was more nerve-wracking than anything I had experienced in Biafra itself, as I anticipated being prevented from leaving the country.

The oddest thing of all about this saga was that I missed one of the most important parts of the story entirely. At least I was in good company. The Irish missionaries wanted the story to be about the persecution and starvation of their loyal Ibo flock and, by and large, that is what they got. There was certainly enough truth in it to make it stick. But the story behind the story, which most reporters (innocent of the realities of geopolitics) were slow to see, was that behind the secessionist struggle, and intrinsically related to it, France and Britain were fighting each other in a proxy war over the control of the oil-rich Niger delta. Not for the last time, an innocent and impoverished people were being caught up in a deadly conflict between international capitalists. And, for neither the first nor the last time, most of us failed to dig deep enough to uncover the roots of the story.

Later, there were more trips to Africa. One of them was to Rhodesia during the period when it had unilaterally declared independence from Britain and was defying, not only Whitehall, but the tide of change that was sweeping Africa. Here, the Antrim-born Bishop Donal Lamont of Umtali offered unexpected insights into the racism of some expatriate Irishmen. The Mashonoland Irish Association, he once abruptly informed its astonished officers (who had invited him to address their all-white St Patrick's Day function), should be re-named as the Orange Order of Rhodesia. Another was to Zambia, where another contact from the conciliar days in Rome, Bishop James Corboy, helped to provide the short cuts to knowledge and experience that reporters, pressed for time, so often need. A third, paid for by the Benguela Railway Company (I have a feeling that all media were much more relaxed about this kind of financial support in those days), brought me to pre-independence Angola, where the Portuguese were trying to persuade the rest of the world that their form of colonialism was colour blind and therefore deserved a fair hearing. I managed to offend my hosts in a series of articles which pointed out that although, unlike South Africa (which I had also visited briefly), none of the housing, or public or private amenities, was racially segregated, the same could not be said about the money.

As if all this wasn't enough, there was Cuba, 10 years after the revolution. In sending me, Douglas wisely hid from me the fact that Jack White had gone there for *The Irish Times* almost a decade earlier: he simply wanted me to see things for myself without the complication of feeling I had to match my impressions to those of the journalist who had gone before me. It was as astonishing an experience, in its own way, as Rome. There was a different kind of culture shock, and the sense that—despite the depressing militarism of that society, and the lack of some freedoms that might seem commonplace, indeed essential, at home—its value system had more to recommend it (and very much less in common with Soviet-style collectivism) than traditional European anti-communism might suspect.

Another aspect of this journey, however, was emblematic, not only of Douglas's style, but of the sort of ethos which lay behind his editorial management. In a sense, it was almost 19th century in the relaxed way in which those of us who were sent abroad were allowed to work. He didn't just send me to Cuba. He allowed—no, encouraged—me to spend three weeks travelling slowly south through the United States, taking time out to do a story about members of the Ku Klux Klan in Mississippi, who were sitting around the same table with black workers as part of a strike committee at the huge Masonite pulp mills. Another detour, arranged at short notice with encouragement from the home base, was to report a young Senator Ted Kennedy speaking from a platform in the centre of Memphis, where I was the only pink object in a sea of black, expectant faces. At the end of this, there were three weeks to be spent, at the expense of *The Irish Times*, attending Ivan Illich's language centre in Cuernavaca in Mexico for an immersion course in Spanish so that I could make the most of my impending visit to Cuba. It was not only the year, but the month, that Mexican soldiers had massacred students protesting in Mexico City's main square. There always seemed to be another story around the corner, each one more fascinating than the last.

The magic ingredient in all of this was time—time to think, time to learn, time to take the soundings and develop impressions, time to write the story. Although we were working for a daily newspaper, and there were inevitably pressures associated with this, there was never a rush to judgement. Perhaps this work ethic—speed moderated by sensibility as much as by the need for accuracy—was Douglas's greatest contribution to the journalism of his era, and it is something that modern journalism is in danger of losing. Along with this was the passion, which he shared with Donal Foley, for what is now called 'fresh air journalism'. This meant getting up off your behind, forgetting about the telephone, leaving the office and the comfort station of the Pearl Bar, and actually finding out what real people were thinking, saying and doing. Today, when so much journalism has been reduced to mouse-minding, and when every story seems only to be a click away, perhaps we need to re-learn that lesson too.

In the early 1970s Douglas asked me if I would be the paper's first full-time correspondent in Brussels. He was, as ever, ahead of his time. I was the younger man, but the more conservative, and I turned it down. I should have known better.

Behind his cultivated stance

Bruce Arnold

I joined *The Irish Times* as a sub-editor in November 1961 after I had finished my degree in Trinity. It was unusual to do so at the time. Experience on a provincial paper was the usual requirement, but through the good offices of Jack White, who was about to leave the paper and go to RTÉ, I got the job. Just over a year later I also took over Jack's position as Dublin correspondent for the *Guardian*, a job he could no longer perform. It came about accidentally. There had been a bomb planted in Cork, under a stage on which Éamon de Valera was to speak. It went off prematurely and a man was killed. The *Guardian* rang the news desk where I was looking for copy for early subbing. Matt Chambers, the news editor, took the call and gave me an odd look. 'You're a *Guardian* kind of chap,' he said. 'They want a piece on that Cork story,' and he handed me the phone.

Douglas Gageby was joint managing director of *The Irish Times* when I approached Jack White and it was Gageby who employed me, not the editor, Alec Newman. I don't believe I even met Alec until I walked into my first day's work. But Alec was my first editor, and his deputy was Bruce Williamson. They stood for the old, R. M. Smyllie *Irish Times*, but not for long. Alec was put under editorial pressure by Douglas Gageby. Gageby sought a significant change in one of the paper's leaders. At first Alec Newman agreed, but during the course of the evening felt that this threatened his editorial independence and changed his mind, reinstating his original copy. He was removed as editor and Bruce Williamson left with him, in sympathy. This happened not long after I joined the paper.

Alec Newman was replaced by Alan Montgomery who had been news editor and was from Malahide. He stayed in the job for about a year. He was pleasant to work for and remained a casual friend for many years afterwards. But he did not suit the paper's direction at the time, and though he accepted Gageby's editorial involvement, they did not suit each other. Journalists would have favoured him. On balance I think he was probably better than Newman, who was a *Spectator* kind of writer, as his later columns in *Hibernia* demonstrated. When presented with the financially attractive opportunity of moving to Guinness's to head up the press office there, Montgomery departed in 1963.

There had been an adverse NUJ reaction to my appointment, and for a time I was moved into the leader-writers' office where I worked beside Fergus Pyle, also a Trinity graduate, and we wrote leaders together.

The Irish Times was going through a low period in its fortunes and two editors leaving in such a short space of time was a worry. There was also the closure of the *Evening Mail,* which had been acquired by *The Irish Times.* Then there was the *Sunday Review,* edited by Ted Nealon and John Healy and for which I did extra work sub-editing on Saturdays. I was paid £11 a week and the extra was necessary since I was married and needing to do some daytime tuition to earn extra money.

Douglas Gageby became editor of *The Irish Times* after Montgomery. The difficulties with the NUJ had been ironed out before this and I became a card-carrying union member and returned to the sub-editors' desk, sitting opposite George Burrows. He was correspondent for the *Daily Telegraph.* We collaborated over the stories we sent to our respective English newspapers, phoning them usually in the early evening and running telephone accounts with the paper which we paid monthly. On our respective nights off we covered for each other.

Douglas Gageby was a competent but uninspiring editor. He had as his deputy Donal O'Donovan, and a close editorial associate in general terms was the literary editor and novelist, Terence de Vere White. They were slightly detached from other senior figures. Séamus Kelly, who was Quidnunc, otherwise author of 'An Irishman's Diary', was a law unto himself—and rather a poor law, in my opinion, from the writing point of view. The kindest men in the paper were Donald Smyllie, chief sub-editor, who was the much younger brother of the former editor, R. M. Smyllie, Noel Fee and Matt Chambers. Younger journalists included Cathal O'Shannon and Tony Kelly.

I had poor relations with Douglas Gageby more or less from the start, and also, it must be said, with Donal O'Donovan and Terence de Vere White. I think each, in different ways, disliked my Englishness and my supposed arrogance; I was self-assured, confident in my views and not without experience of life. Years later Donal O'Donovan had the good grace to ameliorate retrospectively what he described as his mistaken views about me. Terence de Vere White never did, nor did Douglas Gageby.

What I wanted was to escape the rather dreary work as a sub-editor and write for the paper. Even under Alan Montgomery I tried to change my position in the paper, wanting to write rather than to sub-edit. The best he could do was invite feature articles, which I delivered, but still working on the sub-editors' desk.

I made several attempts to persuade Gageby to extend my range as a writer for the paper, but to no avail. After all, I was writing pieces for the *Guardian* on Irish politics, social and religious affairs, and reviewing occasional theatre and art exhibitions for them. But the best I could get in *The Irish Times* was limited feature writing and book reviewing. This might have been fair to begin with, but after two years I wanted the more fundamental change that would give me a regular voice as a journalist. I felt, not unnaturally, that I was wasting my talent and making no real progress.

A good deal later Fergus Pyle as features editor allowed me to start a weekly column on the Fine Arts. I wrote under a pseudonym, 'Jonathan Fisher', and the column became quite widely read. These were early days for such specialisation. Only a couple of English journalists, Geraldine Norman being one of them, were writing about saleroom news and prices, and there was growing interest in the subject which coincided with my own activities and the work I began to do for my first book, *A Concise History of Irish Art*.

In addition to my work for the *Guardian* I was editing the *Dubliner*, a literary magazine, and working for other publications and outlets, including RTÉ.

There was a pleasant camaraderie about the sub-editors' desk in those days. Gageby sometimes attempted to be part of this, but with no great success. Unlike Smyllie and Fee, he was not a 'stone man'; he did not revel in the oil and ink of the case-room nor venture, at print union peril, to touch the metal. He came from 'upstairs' and that remained a defining aspect of him.

Noel Fee was a particularly witty deputy chief sub. I remember being on duty on the momentous night of John F. Kennedy's assassination on 22 November 1963 and subbing the main story. Fee, to lighten the intense atmosphere that prevailed, quietly said at one point, 'He must have been eating meat.' It was a Friday, and the reference to Kennedy's Catholicism made us all laugh.

By the middle of the 1960s I felt that I was blocked. I was at the time very critical of *The Irish Times* and of Douglas Gageby. I thought him a rather complacent editor, often, though not quite always, missing the point, as well as adopting predictable views and responses. The issues that dominated debate at the time included Irish-American relations, the threat of Communism, the challenge of EEC entry, the fairly lamentable state of the two opposition parties—Fine Gael and Labour—the growing impact of television, launched at that time, and the issues surrounding Catholic Church authority.

As 'a *Guardian* kind of chap' I had pretty radical views on these and other matters, and believed that the newspaper I worked for, which had tenuous parallels with the one I was correspondent for, did not come up to scratch. I knew enough of the older *Irish Times* traditions from Donald Smyllie and Noel Fee to feel that the new direction, following two rapid changes of editor, was not hard hitting enough.

I regularly subbed copy from Michael McInerney, a diligent political correspondent and doyen of the Dáil, but neither aggressive nor confrontational. As a subscriber to the English *Spectator* and to the 'Taper' column in it written by Bernard Levin, I believed in a different character and direction for political comment in *The Irish Times*.

Douglas Gageby's office door gave directly onto the sub-editors' desk, a corner of which was given over to the financial pages, presided over by Nicholas Leonard, who more than anyone else at the time was doing the kind of journalism that I favoured. This approach on financial matters was not evident in coverage of politics, world affairs, religious issues or the moral and social stories that were related to the way we were ruled over by a government and church working in what seemed too close a harmony.

I got on with my other tasks. Sitting at a subs' table can be intermittently busy and then idle. I was good at the job, often getting the main lead to deal with, and this in part militated against any move into other work in the paper. My continued requests to Gageby to be considered for writing articles for the paper met with negative responses whether in the political, features or literary areas.

Rightly or wrongly, I also felt at the time that Gageby lacked both judgment and courage. His views on Northern Ireland—unexceptionally, since we all suffered the same blinkered judgement, though he had the advantage of coming from the North—were naïve. He read Charles Haughey entirely wrongly and came too much under the influence of John Healy, who had worked for him in the Irish News Agency, the *Evening Press* and the *Sunday Review* before *The Irish Times*. Healy was a country boy, a 'scoop' news journalist, aggressive, with enormous chips on his shoulders, and his commitment to Haughey's political interests was brazenly partisan.

Like so many people, Gageby was respectful of Seán Lemass without seeing his shortcomings. Indeed he seemed to share in the complacency that was at least part of Lemass's last years in power. For a Northerner he was far less perceptive about the North than Ernest Blythe.

I thought at the time his concern was with financial recovery, possibly at the expense of editorial strength and the courage of a firm set of principles. From the paper's point of view this was an understandable objective. *The Irish Times* was in poor standing in the years when I was there, 1961 to 1966, and Gageby did achieve change, bringing financial stability.

I think it was George Burrows who warned me of Gageby's dislike for English people. One colleague, with me on *The Irish Times* in the early 1960s, made the same point. He also had some interesting observations about Gageby, saying that his views and some of his prejudices derived from his Northern Ireland origins. Like so many Northerners, he was quite covert: 'It was only very rarely that you got a firm statement from him of his thoughts.' Yet he was not consistently so, espousing more openly the oddly simplistic idea, shared with Northern nationalists and of course with many in the South who never visited Northern Ireland, that unionists could be invited into a united Ireland and would come.

My judgement of Douglas Gageby is a much wider matter than the personal coolness between us and the feeling that he deliberately ignored my potential at a time when *The Irish Times* had few good writers.

He became editor of a paper that had definite, if old-fashioned, objectives and clear political, social and other views. It was the closest Ireland had to an international paper. It bridged the divide between Britain and Ireland, between Protestant and Catholic within Ireland and between North and South. The whiff of unionism, in the best sense, that pervaded its history at the time I joined it, was a potential benefit. I mean loyalty to the British connection and to Protestantism, things loathed by Gageby but which had been significant during the Second World War and its aftermath and which were still significant factors in the 1950s. I feel now, had that dimension remained a central part of *Irish Times* thinking, both readers and the country would have benefited.

Douglas Gageby should have built on this. He did the opposite. He seemed to neglect what I thought of as much of the quality and character of the paper. At times I thought he sought to efface it, even that his ill-formed political ideas led to poor political judgment. The whole 'Backbencher' promotion by the paper was evidence of this. He seemed at times to be under the spell of John Healy, who wrote that column, and this was an inappropriate stance for him to have. It is no place for editors to join with their columnists in the way Gageby did.

At the same time, and in contrast to this espousal of Healy's quite dogmatic and rather crude writing, he had no real sense of campaigning, of necessary causes within Irish society. He failed to confront the indifferent and often lazy and complacent political attitudes during the 1960s when Ireland could have made far better progress than it did.

In a rather smug way he wanted to be all things to all men and therefore avoided aggression and confrontation. He was a coterie man;

he had his favourites, to others he was distinctly chilly. Newspapers need to be deliberately challenging, even obnoxious, to some of the people all of the time, to all of the people some of the time. He did not think that way. I have always held that view and have followed it in my own writing on politics, the arts and the social and religious life of Ireland.

Far from that being the hallmark of Douglas Gageby's approach, his priority was to increase sales and raise the profile of the paper. At the same time he made a personal fortune out of transferring his shares in the paper to the new Irish Times Trust. The sale of his financial interests was worth tens of millions of euros in today's terms. One former colleague of mine in *The Irish Times* described it bluntly in the following terms:

> 'The owners of the ordinary shares in the paper asset-stripped *The Irish Times*, got the Bank of Ireland to bank-roll it and set up the Irish Times Trust, and left the former owners [themselves] in charge of running the whole operation. And they were sainted by the Irish establishment for it because they prevented the dross, like Tony O'Reilly, Hughie McLaughlin *et al.*, from getting their filthy paws on it. I have been in awe of their skill for years.'

It is, to me, inconceivable that earlier *Irish Times* directors like the Arnotts would have done the same. Their course would have been to put everything to the survival and growth of the paper, like the Chances and William Martin Murphy, who probably saw the *Irish Independent* as a family public relations company.

It was for other reasons connected with Douglas Gageby's early editorship of *The Irish Times* that I decided, early in 1966, to resign from the paper and become a freelance journalist. I did so with much relief. I wrote to a friend, Bill Webb, who was literary editor of the *Guardian*, and told him 'I despise the people I work for and I detest the work. Risks and all, I think I shall be much happier'. And I was.

To say I never looked back is not quite true, but it does come close to how things developed afterwards, with a successful writing career within the Independent group of newspapers, beginning with Hector Legge and the *Sunday Independent*. Legge took me seriously as a writer and gave me *carte blanche* within the paper he edited. Nicholas Leonard took me on as political correspondent for *Business and Finance*, and, as a result of this, Bartle Pitcher asked me to join the *Irish Independent* and write a weekly column on politics.

I continued to work as a freelance journalist for *The Irish Times*, writing the weekly column on the fine arts under the pseudonym Jonathan Fisher. Through this I maintained contact with Fergus Pyle, who by then was features editor. I liked and admired him and we remained friends until his death. But any attempt at the time to get articles accepted was, as before, difficult. My last exchange with Douglas Gageby was about Jonathan Swift and the tercentenary coming up in 1967. I had done a good deal of research and offered articles. He passed me on to Terence de Vere White, who was in charge, and I sent him some Swift quotations for the supplement, not quite what I had meant. Gageby turned down the main offering I made at the time, and Terence was otherwise lukewarm about any work.

It is difficult to identify what Douglas Gageby believed in or what he felt strongly about. And I do not believe there were any issues he pursued with true integrity or any notable courage. He did achieve growth and stabilised the paper, but at some cost to its identity, a cost that successive editors have largely failed to rectify.

Behind the cultivated stance, the patrician accent accompanied by the deprecating, faintly mocking laugh, the sense of 'civilised man' adjudicating upon the society to which he never seemed really to belong, I never thought there was much there. I still feel the same about him. And the lightness of weight became, both under him and afterwards, something of a hallmark of the paper he no doubt influenced and changed, to its commercial value, its bank-rolled security, but not necessarily any more than that.

Douglas Gageby's Northern roots, and especially the ideals of the United Irishmen, were important to him. As the obituarist in The Irish Times *put it 'he called himself something of a "romantic nationalist" and when unveiling a plaque in Belfast commemorating the founding of the United Irishmen in the city in 1791, he said they were "not failed revolutionaries—they were realists. They had in common the spirit of Wolfe Tone's dictum of the name of Irishman replacing that of Protestant, Catholic or Dissenter."'*

The mantle of Wolfe Tone

Wesley Boyd

On the surface Douglas Gageby and I had much in common, which is probably why we agreed on so little. He was born in Dublin but reared from an early age and received his early education in Belfast. I was born in Fermanagh and reared from an early age and had all my education in Belfast. We were both from Ulster Protestant stock but had strayed from the orthodox flock by believing in a united Ireland. He went to the posh fee-paying Belfast Royal Academy, the oldest school in the city, and then to Trinity College in Dublin. I went to non-fee paying schools and joined the *Tyrone Courier* in Dungannon at the age of 18.

The Royal Academy was a school for the middle and upper classes and was also favoured by the Jewish community; to us in the mean streets of North Belfast it was known as 'little Jerusalem'. Its pupils were sheltered from the sectarian savagery that afflicted the lower orders and enjoyed a liberal and progressive regime. The school and its headmaster, Alec Foster, had a profound influence on the young Douglas. In his introduction to John Hume's book, *Personal Views* (1996) Douglas recalled that Foster was a Derryman. 'He was a classical scholar, but Derry was somehow brought into study and conversation with a relevance that was not always apparent to his pupils,' he wrote. 'He pronounced it "Durry", which is close to the Irish *Doire*. Derry—there was no place like it. (And there was no such place as Londonderry in his canon.) Derry was one of the great cities to him, and to everyone— apparently—who was ever born there.'

Douglas had fond memories of the Academy. It, however, seems to have forgotten the man who was described, on his death in 2004, in the *Irish Examiner* as a 'colossus of journalism' and by a former assistant editor of *The Irish Times*, Donal O'Donovan, as 'the greatest journalist that this country has produced'. Among the former distinguished pupils listed on the school's official website are the late Sir Francis Evans, the British ambassador to Argentina, Jack Kyle, the Irish rugby international, Kate Hoey, a Labour minister at Westminster, and John Cole, the former BBC political correspondent. No mention of Douglas. Distinction south of the border is not highly rated in the northern groves of Academe.

[77]

Another of his Ulster heroes was Armour of Ballymoney—the Rev. J. B. Armour, a veteran Presbyterian minister andoutspoken champion of Home Rule in the early years of the 20th century. There were occasional allusions to Armour in his editorials on the North. Douglas regarded him as a true disciple in line and in spirit of the Ulster Presbyterians who led the rebellion of the United Irishmen in '98 and of Wolfe Tone and Henry Joy McCracken. This romantic view of the Protestant activists may have been shaped not only by the teaching of Foster but the daily view he would have had from the Royal Academy grounds of the mighty Cave Hill looming over Belfast; it was on its summit, at McArt's Fort, that Tone and his comrades had gathered to take their oath of fidelity. It was a place that Douglas came to know well. 'He wears the mantle of Wolfe Tone,' Donal O'Donovan says of Douglas in his autobiography, *Little Old Man Cut Short*. (Dublin 1998).

It was this mantle which influenced Douglas's editorial judgment on Northern Ireland affairs. He viewed the evolving events there, certainly up to the start of the Troubles in 1969, with benign optimism. When Captain Terence O'Neill succeeded Lord Brookeborough as prime minister in 1963 he saw it as the dawning of a new era of harmony amongst Protestant, Catholic and Dissenter. He was much encouraged by O'Neill's reformist programme which manifested itself with visits to Catholic schools, shaking hands with nuns and promoting stronger cross-border economic links. In January 1965 O'Neill sprang a surprise—even on his own cabinet colleagues—by receiving Seán Lemass, the taoiseach, on an official visit to Stormont. The meeting angered many unionists and gave a rising far-right politician, the Rev. Ian Paisley, a new and potent platform. He declared the threat of a united Ireland had been opened up by the prime minister's 'treachery' and launched his 'O'Neill Must Go' campaign.

Douglas stood by O'Neill. He did not realise that Ulster unionism had changed little since the setting up of the first Northern Ireland parliament in 1921. It had only one political objective—the maintenance of the union with Britain. There was no wind of change to stir the mantle of Wolfe Tone. His remoteness from the mass of unionists, and particularly from the sectarian working classes, was understandable. He had returned to Dublin in 1937, after his sheltered days in the Royal Academy, gone to Trinity, joined the Army and lived and worked in the Republic for the rest of his life.

O'Neill decided to challenge his unionist critics by calling and winning a general election in February 1969 and Douglas was delighted when the parliamentary party endorsed his leadership, albeit without the support of two of his strongest ministers, Brian Faulkner and William

Craig. He was inclined to dismiss the views expressed by myself and Dennis Kennedy, who, like myself, had worked on the ground in Northern Ireland for unionist newspapers. We maintained that the election had left a legacy of bitterness in the party which O'Neill could not overcome. The Captain felt obliged to resign two months later and was succeeded by Major James Chichester-Clark. (Paisley remarked he had brought down a captain and could bring down a major as well.) While holding different views Douglas would not attempt to dictate what one should write and tolerated a diversity of output.

It was not until the IRA campaign of violence got under way in 1969 that the media in the Republic began to take a serious interest in Northern Ireland affairs by opening substantial editorial offices in Belfast. Before that the *Irish Independent* and the *Irish Press* had small editorial staffs in Belfast but their work was largely to service their northern editions. *The Irish Times* maintained a commercial office but relied on freelances for its coverage. RTÉ's resident correspondent worked from home and rarely used the services of a camera crew. The northern media also demonstrated a woeful lack of interest in the affairs of the Republic. With the exception of the *Belfast Telegraph*, which had a sizeable circulation in the border counties, none of the daily papers had a resident correspondent in Dublin. They depended on freelance contributions, as did the BBC and UTV. This tradition of lack of interest and neglect went back even before the days of partition.

When I worked on the *Northern Whig* in Belfast in the 1950s staff reporters were despatched to Dublin for only two events, the Horse Show at the RDS and the Church of Ireland Synod. My editor at the time, Bruce Proudfoot, a long-time employee, recalled being sent to Dublin twice, once to cover a debate in the Dáil and again to report on the entry of de Valera and Fianna Fáil into the same establishment in 1927.

The southern media reciprocated and ventured on only a few journalistic forays into the North. No wonder editors and their readers were so ill-informed about what was happening on the other side of the fence which ran across their island.

Things were beginning to change when I joined *The Irish Times*. I had been London editor of the *Northern Whig* for nine years or so and when it closed for economic reasons in 1963 (after 139 years of publishing) I joined the London newsroom of the BBC. Alan Montgomery, then editor of *The Irish Times*, offered me a job as a specialised correspondent in Dublin. Monty, as he was known to all, wanted new blood to move the paper away from its old staid Protestant reputation; in the same month he recruited Nicholas Leonard from the London *Evening*

Standard and John Horgan from the *Catholic Herald*. Nicholas set about revolutionising Irish financial journalism and John brought a sharp edge to the reporting of religious and social issues. When I arrived Monty was about to leave to be succeeded by Douglas Gageby.

Monty's departure could have sat neatly in one of his father's Ballygullion stories. (Montgomery senior, an Ulster bank manager, wrote comic fiction under the pseudonym 'Lynn C. Doyle'.) Monty was asked to sit on the interview board to appoint a public relations officer for Guinness. It quickly dawned on him that the pay and conditions for the post were much superior to those he had as editor. He offered his services, was accepted and departed for the brewery after a lifetime in the newsroom of *The Irish Times*.

As editor Douglas accelerated the pace of change. One of his early moves was to promote Donal Foley from reporter in the London office to the post of news editor in Dublin. Donal had injected a much-needed touch of Irish realism into the London office which was staffed by the Hon. John Arnott, a scion of the family which had owned *The Irish Times* since 1873, and the Hon. Michael Campbell, son of Lord Glenavy. John, an old boy of Harrow, concentrated on British politics, and Michael, a budding novelist, on arts and culture. I got to know Donal well during our days in London and he rang me at home in Dublin, to tell me of Douglas's offer (conveyed to him in person by Major T. B. McDowell, the new managing director. He was nervous about accepting a job he knew nothing about but I assured him he could do it without difficulty. At the time the news desk was manned by people who showed little initiative or imagination, assigning senior journalists to cover social events such as a lecture at the Publicity Club or the annual dinner of the Institution of Engineers which yielded only a few lines of copy.

As a specialist correspondent I had a fairly loose rein, although I did not entirely escape from trivial work. On my own initiative I sought and got an interview with Terence O'Neill with whom I had become well acquainted during his regular visits to London as Brookeborough's minister of finance. From then on I was regarded as the expert on Northern affairs and travelled there on many assignments encouraged by Douglas and Donal.

Douglas and Donal made a powerful team and they continued the policy of recruiting new talent, including several bright young women. Their enthusiasm led to clashes with the National Union of Journalists. Entry into Dublin daily journalism was confined almost exclusively to those who had following the traditional path of serving three or four years on weekly newspapers. Only a few recruits came directly from the universities or other professions. The traditional path was zealously guarded by the union, which at the time was striving to enforce one hundred per cent membership (or, in the parlance of the employers, the closed shop) in the hope of improving pay and conditions. As the father of the NUJ chapel in *The Irish Times,* and honorary secretary of the Dublin newspaper branch, it was my unwelcome task to round up the strays and oppose the recruitment of non-union journalists. Of the two strays in the newsroom one, Terence de Vere White, the literary editor, moaned that he had left the legal profession to avoid joining things. The other was a member of the Plymouth Brethren who said in conscience he could not associate with non-believers. Terence agreed to join 'if it helps' and the Plymouth Brother salved his unease by paying his union dues directly to head office. The crusade led to several rows with Douglas and Donal, who insisted they had the right to employ the person best suited for the job. Once Douglas described me as 'a dirty little Belfast Communist'. Thereafter he opted to leave negotiations with the union to the soft-spoken and patient assistant editor, Ken Gray, and compromise was reached by introducing a probationary period of employment for new recruits.

Another great influence (and I suspect his real love) was the Army. He joined it as a private in 1942 and was commissiioned in 1943.. There was no worse sin in his editorial lexicon than to describe it as the Irish Army. 'There is only one Army and one Army only,' he would declare. Once an English-born sub-editor let the term appear in the paper (presumably to differentiate it from the British or American force). For evermore he was known to Douglas as 'that f——— stupid little Cockney sub'.

During my term as director of news in RTÉ he and I served as judges for an annual journalistic competition in *An Cosantoir* for members of the defence forces in memory of Captain Séamus Kelly, who for countless years was drama critic and diarist of *The Irish Times.* The awards were always announced at a lunch given by the chief of staff in McKee Barracks. Sitting among the senior staff discussing topics such as who was the best general in the Second World War—the vote always went to Marshal Georgi Zhukov of the Soviet Union—Douglas would radiate happiness and enthusiasm. He was at home.

At a Civil Rights march in Derry in 1969—Douglas Gageby, on the extreme right of the photo in a duffel coat, notoriously refused to appear in photographs in his own paper, but this one slipped through.

Gageby's Northern crusade

Fionnuala O Connor

Douglas Gageby was editor of *The Irish Times* for the first five years of the Troubles in Northern Ireland (1969–74) and again during the bleak, remorselessly violent late 1970s and 1980s. Until the negotiation of the Anglo-Irish Agreement in 1985, those were years of near-despair, when British and Irish policy often seemed to amount to no more than containment and no exit route from the Troubles was evident. When it would have satisfied many to settle for crude caricature, Gageby's championing of John Hume and his SDLP party reminded the South that Northern nationalists were not all gunmen and bombers.

By 1973, when I was taken on in the Dublin office and then sent north in advance of the elections to set up the first Assembly, it was widely recognised that Gageby's ten years as editor had largely created a new identity for *The Irish Times*: as the liberal voice of a modern Ireland. Gageby had also established it as the paper of record. As the Troubles broke out, he insisted that it record the news across the border as conscientiously as in the Republic.

Michael Viney's fortnight-long 'Journey North' series in 1964 made a huge impact, though very much as news from another country by a foreign correspondent of considerable adroitness. Viney emphasised that the series was a personal view from 'an Englishman domiciled in Dublin, reared in a mildly Anglican environment but now a Christian of no denomination.'

Gageby's appointment of Fergus Pyle to Belfast in the late 1960s stepped up the commitment and changed the approach permanently. Pyle was styled 'Northern Editor' and encouraged to put the paper on the local political map. The years immediately before the Troubles erupted were full enough of incident and omen but even arid debates in the unionist-dominated parliament at Stormont got *The Irish Times* treatment. A fond in-house obituary of the legendarily verbose Pyle noted as 'newsroom lore', no doubt tongue in cheek, that the sub-editors of the day found his Stormont reports were sometimes longer than those of the official Hansard.

We were the next team into Stormont, when the dust-sheets came off and Parliament Buildings re-opened for what was conceived as a new kind of legislature in the summer of 1973. Four of us alternated shifts on every day the Assembly met. This was decades before e-mail and laptops. Labouring to spell out unfamiliar names to weary telephone copy-takers, struggling to speak neutrally so that our northern accents caused no further befuddlement, was no harder than explaining to family and friends how you had spent the day, or explaining your presence to the *Belfast Telegraph*, *Irish News* and *News Letter* reporters in the press gallery.

Few in the North, beyond the Assembly members and their immediate families, were as interested. The other Dublin papers turned up for occasional debates and at times of crisis but lacked the staffing or interest to do more, and had none of the motivation lent to us by our editor's sense of mission.

We puzzled many—when we paused to think about it we were ourselves puzzled—but some envied us. The poor *Sun* reporter with the public-school accent and the desperately serious desire to write analytical accounts of the Loyalist Workers Strike—John Ware of 'Panorama'—wrote long reports but was lucky to get 400 words into his paper.

We went away to churn out lengthy news stories, comprehensive sketches on the Stormont mood, and vast swathes of verbatim debate which sometimes occupied two full pages of the paper. Gageby's insistence on reporting 'what the man said' meant a full day of telephone dictation: sometimes the phone line to Dublin would be open for up to eight hours. No other paper, based in Belfast, Dublin or London, gave their staff anything like the same space. We owed our latitude to Gageby.

He was good to us. Substantial expenses drew few complaints from Dublin, where the long hours we put in were recognised if not always warmly appreciated. (A rare exception to this was the Dublin-based reporter who, sent up to write a profile of North Antrim, carried out a day-long tour of the constituency in a taxi, running up a mind-boggling bill.) When a bomb damaged the *Irish Times* office Gageby immediately had it re-located to a suite in the Europa Hotel. While suitable new premises were located staff worked in the Europa for almost a year at a cost which can only be imagined. It put everyone involved in daily contact with journalists from abroad, some of them serious and well-known; heady stuff for people in their first big job.

The paper's investment in time and effort and attention failed to add any considerable number to the sales figures: in fact it was said that sales would drop when a Northern story was used as the lead. But what readers we had seemed to take us as seriously as *The Irish Times* took the North.

Looking back, I'm sure that some of this was snobbery. Unionists and nationalists both recognised that the old *Irish Times* of the Ascendancy was in the midst of transforming itself but I think for some its upper-class past—or an idea of what that might have been—still had a pull. For a few of the best informed, the enigma of Gageby was magnetic: the Northern Protestant gone native, as far as Northerners knew a unique creature in public life in the South.

Politicians and individuals, who might perhaps be lumped together as a political class trying to stay afloat in a tide of violence, treated us with becoming seriousness. I doubt that any of us were deluded into thinking that we impressed contacts by our own innate ability: we were too young and raw for that. The paper's Anglo-Irish origins probably maintained some unionist sympathy. Some others on first approach heard only the 'Irish', assumed you were phoning from the Catholic *Irish News*, and ended the conversation.

By and large, though, if you phoned an academic or lawyer for advice on some complex measure, or asked a senior unionist late at night, as I once did, to describe the house of Sir Norman and James Stronge, who had just been shot in their library by IRA men who then set fire to the building, you got patience and helpfulness over and above ordinary civility.

From our perspective as lowly operatives on the ground, the editor's philosophy about Northern coverage was simple. Indeed, he never made much attempt to indoctrinate us beyond a few superficial sermons, delivered over the dinner table. When he arrived up to treat us at a hotel he liked just south of Hillsborough, the White Horse, conversation was heavy going and one-sided. He asked us questions in turn about our work, what enthused us; he made awkward jokes like an old-fashioned father with adult children. Perhaps it was a management thing, or the officer in him: Gageby almost always met us three underlings from the Belfast newsroom, David McKittrick, Walter Ellis and myself, without the Northern editor, Conor O'Clery.

Looking back, I think we were ill at ease and, for journalists, pretty inarticulate. He bought us expensive brandy, and smoked a cigar or two. He said the same things each time, or so I remember.

Why didn't we write more cheerful pieces? Would one of us not go and climb Cave Hill, for God's sake, and write about Jemmy Hope and Tone and the meetings under Napoleon's Nose? We could have done more in that direction, but such ideas seemed jarringly out of place at a time of political deadlock and hundreds of killings taking place every year.

Gageby had charisma, made people want to impress him. To us young reporters in *The Irish Times* Northern office in the early Troubles, he was a figure far above us, but in one sense he was contradictorily closer to us than most of his newsroom officer class. His fervour for the North was something we scarcely understood, but from daily contact with the news desk and occasional visits back and forth, we knew that the editor's passion was unusual in Dublin. To judge from what went unsaid as well as the tone of most communication down the line, the politics and violence which both fascinated and exhausted us in Belfast left most in head office not just cold but chilled.

The witty partnership of Jim Downey and Dick Walsh—who as political correspondents recognised the baleful influence of the Troubles on the Republic, and the need to keep abreast of developments— was very much the exception. To a great extent, it was the willpower and determination of one man that decided the newspaper's commitment to supplying an extraordinary amount of Northern coverage.

Gageby's Northern crusade—for that was how it came across— became a distinguishing feature of *The Irish Times* and had a unique effect. The status of the revamped paper and Gageby's own standing lent clout to its 'line' on Northern Ireland. At a time when the decline of the civil rights movement and the explosion of violence led many to turn their faces away from the subject, *The Irish Times* checked the mood.

In the teeth of indifference and dislike, without and within the paper, the volume and style of our coverage made an impact. It mattered that Southern readers saw stories from Belfast on the front page of the most influential newspaper day after day, no matter how awful the content of stories. It is not too much to say that Gageby's personal convictions became a check on the national consciousness, perhaps even a moral precept for a generation of politicians. The platform the paper gave to Hume, the SDLP, and less often to unionists such as Roy Bradford, was a stimulus to the efforts of Department of Foreign Affairs officials in Dublin tasked to work on a practical policy for successive governments to adopt in the face of the Troubles. Though it was scarcely surprising that it should have been so, it was Hume's articulation of a moderate nationalist position, coherent and above all else non-violent, that became the guiding principle of Southern policy.

In the early 1990s, when Hume came under huge criticism for attempting to keep the then controversial peace process alive, Gageby wrote a crisp, concise letter to *The Irish Times*. It read:

'Many years ago my wife Dorothy and I were observing the progress of a large civil rights crowd across Craigavon bridge in Derry. On the west side we were stopped by the RUC. A young man in a check jacket turned round and motioned us all to sit down. He went forward to speak to the police. I was told his name was John Hume. He was unperturbed, cool and steady. I will never get that picture out of my mind: the demonstrators on the bridge, the wall of police and the young man crossing the open space on his own.'

The esteem in which he held John Hume endured for decades. The irony is that while Gageby's Northern hero was Hume his Southern hero was Charlie Haughey, who famously trailed those clouds of arms trial sulphur around with him and despite them became Fianna Fáil leader and taoiseach. The further irony is that Haughey resented Hume's qualities rather than admiring them, at various points working to undermine him.

But to the chagrin of unionists and considerable if covert distaste in Dublin, the SDLP became the Irish government's representative in the North, as one of its members once put it effectively—regardless of who led that government.

The Gageby–Hume relationship may have benefited the Northern politician more than the newspaper editor. Gageby's mantra of the equality of Protestant, Catholic and Dissenter became one of Hume's guiding principles, and helped define an image of him in the Republic as that rare thing, a Northern political figure superior to the bitterness and inward-looking tribal allegiance that so repelled the South.

For years before Gerry Fitt gave up the post of SDLP leader, Hume had become the favoured contact of Dublin diplomats, the man whose thinking on the way ahead must be heeded. Gageby liked Fitt for his hard-drinking humour, his rumbustious style, and he was amused by the SDLP's other avowed socialist, Paddy Devlin. For a naturally conservative man, Hume's conservatism was bound to be even more congenial, in addition to his cerebral approach, didactic style, and willingness to begin building a European dimension into his thinking—surefire attraction to the German-speaking, Francophile Gageby.

And there was a side of Gageby that enjoyed bringing on younger talent, encouraging younger men to more ambitious projects. Hume's regular appearance in *Irish Times* columns, either reported or writing his own essays, gave him an early launch-pad and then essential continued visibility. Hume has said his first commendation to Gageby came from John Healy, Gageby's guru on Southern politics. The boost Hume got from Healy and *The Irish Times* generated much envy in the Dáil, but helped to armour the SDLP man against back-biting.

The admiration we young staffers had for our imposing boss depended not at all on liking, and lacked even a glimmer of warmth. Nell McCafferty's radical reports from the courts and a women's page had been introduced into a stuffy newspaper on Gageby's watch. But he was in his mid 50s—old to us—and a man of his era, a man's man who reportedly loved army company. He was courtly and formal, eyes twinkling as though on auto-pilot, but still managed to give the impression that what you said to him went in one ear and out the other. I don't think he found the male reporters easy conversation either but he seemed particularly stumped by me, and it cut both ways.

Though the first sizeable intake of women came in his time, I always imagined that he thought the job unfeminine and its effects on women lamentable. But he was what we thought editors should be. I don't think any of us imagined that should include familiarity, or a personal relationship.

What we knew of Gageby was mainly second-hand, perhaps stylised and rewritten by gossip and the need for myth. The newsroom had it that he defended his reporters, that when complainers came calling he gave them short shrift before coming out to chase up the story in question—after that he might well lace into the writer, but it would be on the back of the story, not the complaint. Legend said he swore people out of his office. This was thought to be a good thing.

David McKittrick recalls that several politicians, such as Paddy Devlin, complained to Gageby about his coverage. The key point is that McKittrick only discovered this years later, and completely by accident: Gageby simply never mentioned this to him. He sent to Belfast fine journalists—Viney, Pyle, Henry Kelly, O'Clery *et al.*—and he printed what they reported, even when it conflicted with his views and aspirations. There was very occasional pressure on them but this was exceedingly rare: almost invariably his method was to make his own views clear but not to penalise or censor anyone who disagreed with them. We knew he sent no messages through his news desk to cut or censor our copy. We appreciated that.

We thought it especially fine because it was clear from our awkward chats with him that he had an idealised picture of Northern society, and Northerners, which our daily stories rubbished. He once had lunch with Andy Tyrie, then leader of the Ulster Defence Association: Gageby urged the paramilitary boss to join with the Republic, saying it would be 'a 32-county Ulster.' He said we must read for ourselves about 19th-century Presbyterian and Home Ruler 'Armour of Ballymoney' but I don't believe any of us read a word. His other guiding light was Hume, and while nobody ever told us directly that we should pay Hume special attention, that was unnecessary. In the way of newspapers, the editor's guru compelled attention. In time we became admirers ourselves.

Hume's approach chimed with Armour's speeches and writings, which sustained Gageby in the hope—we thought it a delusion—that unionists might yet discover their Irishness and make common cause with nationalists to create a new Northern Ireland. Hume's pragmatism struck a similar chord. IRA bombs had finished off the initial wave of Southern sympathy, and much of the interest in what had become horror without apparent end. It was Hume's insistently optimistic voice that became Gageby's lifeline, and the touchstone of Northern coverage.

The tragedy was that he was so alive and engrossed in the North, but that his editorship coincided with an awful, dismal, lethal time when violence was remorseless, when his own solution of Irish unity stood no chance. He must have wanted to hear that violence was receding, political reconciliation possible, community relations improving, but he was fated to be an editor in times when all of that seemed cruelly remote. He never gave up on it though: he stuck with it, his commitment to the North unshakeable. The IRA and the loyalists could set off as many bombs as they liked, but they never succeeded in removing his belief that there would one day be an agreed united Ireland, delivered by diplomacy and not violence. Wishful thinking on a heroic scale, we thought, and perhaps the essence of what made him a great editor.

6 January 1969: group photograph recording a presentation to Mary Maher on her marriage—(from left) Donal Foley, Norine Linnane, Wesley Boyd, Mary Maher, Dan Duffy, Douglas Gageby, Henry Kelly, Michael McInerney (behind), Gerry Mulvey (in front). Four years before the ban on married women working was abolished in the Civil Service, Mary was the first woman journalist to marry and not leave her job on The Irish Times.

The Gager and the workers

Mary Maher

In the office we called him The Editor. In the pub we called him Gageby or The Gager and discussed him endlessly, the best and the worst of him.

The worst. There was the conference, for instance, at which some-one suggested we should expose the inadequacies of the Garda train-ing system. According to my highly reliable source, the proposer strength-ened his case with the comment that all they learned in their training school in Templemore was how to shine their buttons.

In this context 'the conference' refers to the thrice-daily event that is central to the life of a daily newspaper, an assembly of senior staff responsible for deciding the contents of the paper. The evening con-ference is short and sharp and focused on the front page. At the earlier gatherings, dialogue is expected as heads of departments, flanked by assorted other seniors, list their choices for communal pondering.

Conventional wisdom holds that this is sound teamwork, a bond-ing exercise that draws on collective intelligence. Ordinary members of staff who don't attend the conference tend to see it more as a point-scoring exercise among people jockeying for position. One way or another, it's difficult to think of a better mechanism for exchanging information and opinions and getting the paper out on time.

That said, the pressure to participate does yield some strange contri-butions. On this particular day, someone piped up to remark that when he was in the RAF, the squaddies had special buttons that didn't need to be shined. Douglas Gageby peered up over his glasses and said in his drawling ironic tone, the one that chilled bone marrow, 'Is that so . . . when you were in the RAF you didn't have to shine your buttons. Wasn't it well for you—you fucking traitor.'

Tolerating fools, even momentary fools, was not his strong point, quite apart from the fact that any whiff of West Britism brought on thundering wrath. But idleness, carelessness or—most unforgivable of all—compla-cency: those were his breaking points. From time to time whole depart-ments were under suspicion of the last, sports or features or arts.

Business and commerce he had a brooding distaste for, and their importance in news terms only served as a further irritant. Thus the incident of the dollar, worse than that of the buttons (highly reliable source again), which occurred at a late afternoon conference. This was sometimes a skittish affair, as one or more of the gathering may have taken a jar or five on board at lunchtime.

The finance representative had just begun his familiar and mysterious recital on the rise and fall of the American currency when the man at the helm fixed him with a glare and roared, 'Fuck you and your fucking dollar! It'll soon be five o'clock and you can go home like the little fucking bank clerk you are!'

Oh, he could be a hard one, fol dol the di do, he could be a hard one, I tell you.

There were no doubt other outbursts of personal abuse that I've forgotten or never knew about. But the same can be said of many editors of his generation, and indeed many bosses in general. It was, as the banks said when offshore accounts were uncovered, the culture of the time.

In his case, such lapses from grace were heavily outweighed by several factors. For one, he was reassuringly transparent. If someone was for it, you'd know by the way he strode scowling into the newsroom. He didn't work behind the scenes. As a colleague has observed, 'The thing about The Gager was that at least he did his own bullying.'

For another, we took into account his army background. He did see journalism as a battleground, us against those who wished to hide what the public had a right to know. If he marshalled us like troops, he also kept close to the action, often arriving at two or three in the morning in the case-room, sleeves rolled up to work.

His style was military: the quick decisions, sometimes genial and sometimes brusque; the gruff bark of anger, the ease at exercising authority. He would engage with insubordination—journalists are infected with it—but never impudence. There was once a jaunty department head who made a fundamental change without consulting him, and when summoned to explain replied with a cheeky note quoting the newspaper's ad of the time, 'Keep up with the changing times.' The man's tenure ended swiftly and silently and without sympathy from the rest of us.

There was too that breathtaking command of barrack-room idiom. The Editor's blue language was at master class level. I have heard several versions of his famous response to the photographer who produced pictures of pretty girls to illustrate—depending on the version— fine weather or sunny beaches: 'That's not what I wanted,' he is said to have said. 'That's cunt. If I wanted cunt, I'd have asked for cunt.'

It is also in keeping with his code of behaviour that I've heard the stories but not the language. No matter how angry he was, The Editor deleted expletives in the presence of women, and if a vulgarity did slip out he apologised immediately.

He could apologise—always the mark of a superior boss—and the finest apology in my memory followed his famous rage during the papal visit of 1979. The Editor took to this event with stunning enthusiasm. Not everyone shared his buoyant view that this was a marvellous historic moment; a number of us were jittery about the net impact the occasion might have on a country already bedevilled by religiosity of one kind of another. Our running joke was that he had overnight become the paper's first Catholic editor.

But he was having none of our apprehension. The Pope had come to call on us, he wanted to see all of us, and *The Irish Times* would not be bested in its welcome. Squadrons of staff were assigned to cover the visit, and The Editor announced he himself would write a feature on the Phoenix Park appearance.

On the night in question reports descended in a landslide on the sub-editors struggling to patch together page after page of the papal experience. In those days copy was printed in long galley proofs, which were then cut to fit into columns on the stone, where the metal lines of type were assembled into pages. The dread fear of all subs was a transposition of a few lines, or sometimes an entire section of copy that made nonsense of the story, a fool of the reporter, and a villain of the sub.

The worst happened. Among other disasters, The Editor's transposed story attributed to the Pope a cheery recollection of fish being served on Friday in the army barracks.

The features sub who hadn't spotted the calamity knew what he had to face the next morning, and knew that it was no excuse to point out that the deputy editor who proofread the pages hadn't spotted it either. On cue, The Editor flung open the door of the features department, charged across the room and fired a furious tirade in his face. We froze at our desks and gave thanks that fate hadn't fingered us.

That was Friday. On Monday The Editor threw the door open again, once more bringing us to a halt. He strode over to the sub and said 'I read your letter. You're right. I'm sorry,' and departed. Mystified but relieved, we went back to work, under the impression that there had, after all, been exonerating circumstances.

Some time later I learned that his battery of insults had included a reference to a personal loan the sub had been given by the company. I don't think anyone had taken that in. The sub had written him a penitential note but registered his offence that this private matter had been mentioned in public. It says something about Gageby that he repaired the damage where he inflicted it.

So much for the worst. There was much more of the best. In his book about his father-in-law, *The Last Secretary-General: Seán Lester and the League of Nations,* Gageby commented 'Lester took people as he met them; he had no airs,' and the same could be said of himself. Most of the time, his management approach was that of a good father, benevolent but watchful, and he directed not by giving orders but by hinting, encouraging or chiding.

We knew what he believed in and we knew his political vision. We knew, because he often told us, that his grandfather was the only man on the Shankill Road who wasn't a member of the Orange Order. For pub diversion we invented imaginary front pages covering his pet subjects—trees, Wolfe Tone, the Rev. Armour of Ballymoney, Henry Joy McCracken, Jem Hope, the Moynalty Steam Threshing Festival and of course, the Army. (Anyone unenlightened enough to describe it as the 'Irish Army' was squelched with a violent blast of 'It is THE Army here!')

But in daily practice we had to refine the art of second-guessing. Department heads had to be alert to the fleeting remark indicating that he had a preference they hadn't chosen or even noticed. The production staff had to listen for the same sidelong comment when it came to arranging order of prominence for stories on the pages.

One night, on an inebriated bet, a reporter with a gift for mimicry phoned the chief sub's desk from the pub. 'Ahhhh, Gageby here . . . ,' he murmured. 'I just saw something on the telly . . .' He mentioned a minor sporting event and then added '. . . just wondered if we might have a picture . . . ah, no matter, not important at all . . .'

The next day's paper had the picture. The reporter and his cohorts kept their heads down and were never caught for what was definitely a hanging offence. But oh, what a let-down for the poor dupe who'd rung around frantically to get a copy of the photo, and should have been in line for the prized reward, a few words of praise from The Editor as he ambled by.

It only took a few words—'good story' or 'grand picture that' or 'you did well'—to set you up for the day. The opposite might be an equally brief phrase. 'Placard waving again,' he remarked to me more than once, and I hung my head mentally if not physically.

He had other paternal tricks, such as flinging people into inventive mode with a casual request that they drop down to see him with a list of stories planned for the next few weeks or months. His method of dealing with tantrums was nothing if not fatherly. One night an exasperated sub burst into his office waving several page proofs, ranting that he was overloaded with work and couldn't possibly get all this read in time. Gageby studied his face for a moment and said 'You can't do it? Here, give them to me. I'll read them. You go on home now and have a rest.'

The sub backed out, mumbling sorry, didn't really mean it, just wanted to point out . . . sorry, Mr Gageby . . .

He also knew how to bolster the sagging spirit. The feature writer felled by alcohol and carted off to hospital told me she woke to find none other than himself sitting quietly at her bedside with flowers and a basket of strawberries. As for falling down on the job, I'm not the only journalist who made a major mistake on a major story and, wishing for a fast flight to exile or early death, got the calm early morning phone call from The Editor: 'All right. You got it wrong. Now come on in to work and get on with it.'

His high regard for his own family, and especially for his wife's opinion, only underlined the paternal image. Séamus Martin, who joined the staff in 1983 and shortly after became the editor of the daily features page, remembers being called down after the first week of a summer series called 'Places Apart' and told 'This series is no good. Come back to me with another set of ideas over the weekend.'

'I sweated bricks and came back to him on Monday with a dossier of ideas. He asked "What's this about?" I said I was responding to his instructions. "Oh, the 'Places Apart' stuff. No need to replace it. Dorothy thinks it's very good".'

Séamus was one of a handful who had a drink-and-debate relationship with him. On Fridays after the late afternoon conference Gageby would frequently arrive at his door with a beckoning finger, knowing there was no feature page on Saturday. That meant a long session in Bowes pub, always brandy, and Séamus was not allowed to buy.

They had one flare-up during the period when Séamus was editing the 'Saturday Column', a collection of miscellaneous items that included contributions from staff. The Editor wanted to publish a letter attacking Séamus over an item someone else had written. Séamus told him if the letter appeared he'd sue, and then rang me, more or less as a National Union of Journalists representative.

We met in Bowes and weren't there five minutes before Gageby arrived. 'Is this your lawyer?' he asked, pointing at me. Then he turned to Séamus and said 'You're right. You would be defamed and you could sue. So what are you having?' I escaped as fast as I could.

The Editor regarded the NUJ as the organisation of the lower ranks, not his affair unless it threatened to interfere with his prerogative. I'd learned that lesson in the early 1980s when I was mother of the chapel (shop steward).

With all the vigour of the naive, the chapel committee had written a note to the personnel manager protesting at the employment of a foreign correspondent who had joined a rival journalists' organisation— now, as far as I know, defunct. Not satisfied with protest, we added for flourish that we couldn't be expected to work with such a turncoat.

Having rattled our sabre we forgot about the letter. A day or two later The Editor suddenly commanded the staff to assemble in the newsroom to discuss the chapel's ultimatum. I stood up front, with the then deputy father of the chapel (FoC), the late Howard Kinlay, next to me. Howard asked in a whisper if my knees were shaking the way his were. Yes, I replied, and he hissed that women had an advantage because no one could see mine under my long Laura Ashley dress.

The Editor's address was to the point. He was the only person who made decisions about who worked for the paper. If the NUJ didn't withdraw this letter there would be no paper in the morning.

In my fairly lame reply, I attacked the personnel manager, insisting that he was out of order in showing our letter to The Editor, since it was only a volley in an ongoing battle about the NUJ's role and rights and wasn't intended to be taken literally.

'Ah, I see,' he said mildly. 'You didn't mean it. That's all right then, you can all go back to work.' He turned and strolled back into his office, leaving us to the outrage of the chapel members. We humbly admitted a blunder, resigned en bloc, and were all duly re-elected. The foreign correspondent's position was permanently secured.

When Paddy Smyth was FoC an unspoken accord was achieved. When the freelance members of the NUJ went on strike in 1984, Paddy managed to see that the paper got out every day without using any material that was normally done by freelances. The Editor was aware of what was happening and ignored it.

When Wapping broke on the newspaper industry in 1986, Michael Foley was FoC and dealt with matters adroitly. NUJ members had been instructed not to handle copy from The Times service. The instruction was largely a counsel of perfection, since full compliance would have brought on more disputes than the union could have handled. But Michael saw to it that the instruction was obeyed in The Irish Times.

Weeks went by before anyone noticed. When The Editor finally realised he'd been bypassed, he called Michael in angrily, saying among other things that 'The Irish Times doesn't take instructions from the Unionists or the union.'

There was another round of chapel committee resignations, and another re-election of the same team. Michael seized his new mandate by persuading Gageby to meet the chapel committee. It was the one and only direct negotiation between the union and The Editor, and Michael put a number of points Gageby couldn't but agree with: for one, the fact that no one had noticed meant the service was hardly worth keeping; for another, the fall in standards under Rupert Murdoch.

A compromise was reached. One item only, something not controversial, would be allowed into the paper to assert the rights of The Editor, and the service would then be terminated. It was a triumph and cut our links with Wapping.

To be fair to the senior management of the time, most of them would have deplored Murdoch as much as The Editor clearly did, both for his brutal tactics and for his deleterious influence on journalistic standards. I can't say we were deeply appreciative of this. Foolish as it may sound today, we took it for granted. We continued to regard the management as the sinister enemy, at least formally, and chapel meetings were occasions to vent anger and suspicion.

Only Mary Holland would occasionally be driven to interrupt a tirade demanding 'Do you know how lucky you are? Do you know how bad things are in Britain?' Only Mary Holland, whose commitment to trade unions was beyond question, would get away with this.

The Editor kept his distance from the NUJ during his tenure. But Séamus Dooley, now Irish secretary of the NUJ, remembers that at the 1995 case against Liz Allen and Independent Newspapers for breach of the Official Secrets Act, Gageby, by then retired, crossed the courtroom and sat next to him, saying 'I'd rather sit with the NUJ than with the opposition.'

He was called as an expert witness by Independent Newspapers on two counts, as a retired editor of unrivalled renown, and as a former specialist in Army Intelligence. His evidence was tart and amusing, the gist of it being, that 'gardaí think everything is an official secret because they don't want anyone to know anything.'

When the proceedings concluded, Gageby shook hands with the then editor of the *Irish Independent*, Vinnie Doyle, and told him 'I'm not here for Tony O'Reilly, or for Independent Newspapers. I'm here because the issue is important.' He had helped carry the day for press freedom, not for the Middle Abbey Street opposition.

In the last years before his retirement, Gageby used to ramble through the paper suggesting in a jocular but pressing way to this or that staff journalist that they should go for the job when he left. Whether he was preparing us for his departure or rehearsing it for himself, it was a way of saying farewell to the family.

It was probably the last years in which the staff was a family. The small and eccentric community created in the 1960s by Douglas Gageby and Donal Foley—Michael's father—was larger by 1986, but not so large that we didn't still share a sense of loyalty and a common identity and purpose. That's almost impossible to sustain as an enterprise expands and grows prosperous.

Working for Gageby was a straightforward proposition. We thought he was a heroic leader and a great editor. We wanted to win his approval, not so much for promotion—there weren't that many openings in those lean times—as for pride. We were proud of him, we wanted him to be proud of us.

He was, too. One of the most prominent journalists of the Gageby-Foley era, John Horgan, had won seats in the Senate, Dáil and European Parliament between 1969 and 1981. In 1983 he applied for a senior lectureship in Dublin City University and sought a reference from his former editor. Gageby was presented with a form requesting all manner of detailed information. He didn't fill it out. He scrawled across it 'You'll be lucky to have him'.

What better accolade could anyone have, coming from The Editor?

The task master

Conor O'Clery

I know from experience how, as editor of *The Irish Times*, Douglas Gageby went about recruiting the team that took the paper through the turbulent 1970s and 1980s. When I was in my final year studying English at Queen's University Belfast I wrote to him looking for a job. He replied saying: 'Come to Dublin on the train. We'll give you a fiver to cover the fare.' That was January 1972. I prepared hard for the encounter, but I needn't have bothered. Whatever he saw in me at the interview—in which he showed more interest in the trees of my Co. Down home than in my general knowledge—he was satisfied that he had found what I later heard he had wanted: a Catholic from the North who had some experience in student journalism and who might help redress the balance in the traditionally Protestant paper. In those days *The Irish Times* didn't hire by committee. It was the personal choice of the editor, or more often than not his legendary news editor, Donal Foley. 'There'll be something here for you when you graduate,' Gageby promised me. I was delighted. My aunt on the Falls Road wasn't so pleased. 'Could you not get a job on a Catholic paper?' she asked.

Three days before my finals ended, I rang *The Irish Times* from Belfast to ask when I should start. Gageby apparently had forgotten all about me. Only that his secretary Helen Gygax recalled my visit, and got him to take the call, my journalistic career might have ended there and then.

Gageby took me on and tested me right away. He put me onto the 'graveyard shift', 9 p.m. to 4 a.m., to learn sub-editing and headline writing, telling me cheerily that I might not see daylight again for some years.

I revelled in my new job. I loved everything about *The Irish Times*, the clanking of the hot metal machines, the smell of ink, the warren of corridors, the characters who inhabited the newsroom, including our jazz correspondent Hoddy who slept there, the end-of-night poker games with Eugene McEldowney and Stephen Herron, the thrill of seeing my headlines in print (my first effort: 'Library Seeks to Balance Books' over a story about a library seeking extra funds), and the guilty joy, as a former civil servant, of not working nine-to-five.

Most of all I loved working for Douglas Gageby. He was the sort of editor whom one wanted to please because of his air of infallibility and his sureness of touch. He inspired confidence and kept everyone on their toes. Someone once observed that Gageby was like your father: you were terrified of his wrath but you always knew he was right. To be singled out for his censure was doubly distressing because he was much loved and respected, and you felt he would never get angry without good reason. He went around the newsroom with a slight, amused smile on his lips. If that disappeared you knew it was trouble.

It wasn't always easy to please him. When I became news editor he was still testing me. There is nothing that keeps a news editor alert like an editor-in-chief with the habit of asking first thing in the morning, 'So what have you got for me today?' He would address me in a friendly manner as if inquiring about the weather, but if I didn't already have a handle on the day's likely stories, with one or two ideas to catch his imagination, I would get a pretty abrupt response.

Gageby never threw tantrums but we all feared his cryptic put-downs at the editorial conferences held in his room overlooking Fleet Street, where the windows were kept shut tight to keep out the diesel fumes from the buses below. He liked blunt talk but not excuses. If I had missed a story that was in the *Irish Press* or—worse still—in the *Irish Independent*, he would set a verbal booby trap by asking me, as we filed in for the conference, 'What do you think of the paper today?' I learned to say something along the lines of, 'Not much, I screwed up badly.' That might be the end of it but I would definitely have been cut down to size if I had attempted an excuse or put the blame on someone else.

All of us sitting around that room on an assortment of chairs, clutching our news schedules, feared most of all the unanswerable question. Once, after fulminating about a sloppily written story on the financial pages, Gageby asked the financial editor: 'Did you read this rubbish before it went into the paper?' He himself had read most of *The Irish Times* before retiring the previous night. Gageby liked his staff to be on top of everything, and above all to have read all the morning papers, and especially *The Irish Times*, from cover to cover. Not one for dropping compliments, the highest praise I ever knew him to give his dedicated chief sub-editor Noel Fee was to tell him he was the only person in the paper who knew where every story was and what was in it.

I recall one occasion when Gageby asked David McKittrick, then our London editor, who was on a visit to Dublin and was sitting in on the editorial conference at my invitation, what he thought of our coverage of some story or other. McKittrick said: 'I don't know.' 'What do you mean you don't know?' asked Gageby. 'I haven't been reading the paper,' McKittrick replied. Jaws dropped around the room. 'Why not?' asked the editor. 'I'm on my holidays,' protested David. 'You'll be on your fucking pension,' snapped Gageby and ignored McKittrick for the rest of the conference.

But while Gageby's tongue was feared, the tongue-lashings were strictly in-house. He never put up the white flag when a journalist came under attack from outside. Once when I was Northern editor, the Social and Democratic Labour Party MP John Hume rang Gageby to lodge a furious complaint about something I had written. He defended me, even though Hume had a point. I never even heard about this until weeks later when Hume himself told me.

Gageby could disarm outraged readers who wrote to complain about something in the paper by ringing them up himself and saying, 'Gageby here. You are absolutely right, I'm just as annoyed by that article as you are.' This sometimes ended up with the letter-writer apologising to him for taking up his time.

The only person really on equal terms with Gageby inside the office was Bruce Williamson, the sedentary poet and much-loved wordsmith who acted as letters editor, leader writer and general wise man, and who occupied a huge desk in the centre of Gageby's office from where he would magisterially conduct the editorial conference in the editor's absence.

Bruce would pen erudite foreign leaders in longhand while Gageby would take himself off to a little cubby-hole beside the men's lavatory to write political leaders on a portable typewriter. Gageby wrote deft and opinionated editorials. His advice on writing them was to figure out one or two things to say and stick to that. In his editorials he would sometimes let fly, especially if his feelings were well-fuelled during the day. Once, over a couple of stiff brandies in the RAC club where we had repaired for lunch, he said of Taoiseach Jack Lynch's new cabinet: 'What a bloody awful government.' 'Why don't you say that in a leader?' I retorted, similarly fortified. He did, and got quite a lot of criticism for it.

But Gageby didn't worry too much about the reaction of people in power. He rarely met them. Unlike other editors in town, he hardly ever attended social functions. He did not want to be compromised by close relationships with politicians making the news. He told me once that he thought it unwise to socialise with those whom he might want to criticise in an editorial, or about whom his reporters could be writing unfavourable stories. Above all he didn't want to know things that might make him hesitate to say what he should be saying in the leader columns—a purist approach which would be disputed by other newspaper editors who believe they should equip themselves with as much information as possible before passing editorial judgment. Also I suspect Gageby couldn't be bothered with Dublin's social round as he had a very low boredom threshold, and he was also quite a shy man. During my brief spell as assistant editor, he delegated me to attend a few functions and I quickly realised that representing the paper at lengthy self-congratulatory dinners could indeed be a tiresome business. He kept a low profile, rarely going on radio and instructing staff that his name should never appear in the paper, unless in exceptional circumstances. He discouraged the rest of us from getting above ourselves, on the grounds that newspaper people should not be part of the élite.

Gageby didn't talk to politicians much on the telephone either but there were exceptions, like John Hume. He had a soft spot for Charles Haughey but he had little direct contact with the Fianna Fáil leader, leaving *Irish Times* 'Backbencher' columnist, John Healy—who had a line into Haughey's Kinsealy, Co. Dublin home—to act as an intermediary. This enabled him to avoid writing off Haughey's career on the famous night when the *Irish Press*, generally sympathetic to Fianna Fáil, published his political obituary, for which it was never forgiven. Haughey had told Healy that rumours of his imminent resignation were premature.

Furious with the bad press he was getting in those days, Haughey started calling on the major news outlets in Dublin to make his displeasure known. News quickly spread of heated encounters over lunches with the editors in RTÉ and the daily newspapers. *The Irish Times* was last on Haughey's list. Gageby asked me to go along with him when Haughey summoned him to lunch in the Burlington Hotel. The night before, I spent hours in the *Irish Times* library briefing myself thoroughly on our coverage of Fianna Fáil, checking the space we had given Haughey, and assessing his treatment at the hands of our political correspondent Dick Walsh, in anticipation of a frontal assault from the great man. *The Irish Times* editorials had in fact been fairly easy on Haughey, and Dick Walsh, despite his personal distaste for him, had been fair and accurate in his reporting.

The lunch was in an alcove of the hotel's dining room. Haughey arrived accompanied by his *consigliere*, P. J. Mara. Trees again dominated the discussion. Over the soup, Haughey and Gageby talked about the trees they had planted and tended. Arboreal talk continued over the lamb chops and through to the dessert. As the crème caramel arrived P. J. turned to me and said, 'What in the name of Jesus are we doing here?' Haughey, I realised, had no intention of confronting Gageby directly. The lunch itself was the message. Gageby's only advice to his host, uttered quite seriously, was to stop reading the papers and to get on with running the country.

This reflected Gageby's scepticism about the influence of newspapers on the events of the day. He liked to portray himself as a newsman rather than as an advocate of change or reform. He didn't plot grand strategies to influence the policies of the government or to expose corruption. He didn't particularly urge us to seek out wrongdoing in high places. In those days the media climate was not conducive to investigations of such things as the source of Haughey's wealth. Gageby was courageous and supportive of his editors when they did try to go out on a limb, though I suspect he would have been uneasy about running the famous investigative stories into the 'heavy gang' in the Garda that were published when Fergus Pyle was editor, such was his regard for the people in the security institutions of the Republic.

But he was very much a crusading editor when it came to the North. Gageby was a Northern republican and in his editorials frequently invoked the late 18th-century Wolf Tone, who espoused the unity of Protestant, Catholic and Dissenter, and the 19th- and early 20th-century liberal Presbyterian home ruler, the Rev. John Brown Armour, known as 'Armour of Ballymoney'. The voice of unionism was not stilled under his editorship—Northerner Dennis Kennedy on the editorial staff saw to that—but Gageby let everyone know where he stood. When one editor mentioned at a conference that he had served in the RAF, Gageby muttered, 'Bloody Blueshirt.'

He became the first editor to open up the pages of *The Irish Times* to coverage of political events in Northern Ireland, sending Fergus Pyle to write stories from the Stormont parliament that rivalled the Hansard reports in length. When the Troubles heated up, he poured resources into the Belfast office of *The Irish Times*. Whatever about his own reluctance to engage with politicians, his advice to me when appointing me Northern editor in 1973 was to be prepared to stay up late drinking with the likes of Paddy Devlin and Bill Craig. He told me always to have money in my pocket as one of the most embarrassing experiences of his own earlier days in newspapers was not being able to buy a round of drink with some important contacts.

He broke new ground for a 'Protestant' paper with a unionist tradition by championing the SDLP and encouraging the idea of power-sharing and a Council of Ireland. He didn't give us editorial direction however. He interfered only once with what I wrote from Belfast. That was when the Sunningdale power-sharing government was crumbling in the face of loyalist resistance. The day before the Northern Ireland Executive fell, its Unionist chairman, Brian Faulkner, issued a statement saying that the Unionist-SDLP-Alliance executive remained united, despite the growing anarchy in the streets. It was clear however, at least in

The Irish Times Belfast office, that Sunningdale was finished, and I wrote a story for the front page saying the executive was hours away from disintegrating. Shortly afterwards I got a call from Jack Fagan on the news desk asking me to write a more upbeat lead. I refused. Then Henry Kelly, at that time working from the editor's office, came on the line with the same request. It was Gageby himself, I realised then, who was insisting that *The Irish Times* should not go down in history as 'abandoning' the power-sharing politicians in their darkest hour. Perhaps John Hume had been on the phone to him. I succumbed. The paper's splash headline the next day, above my name, read, as far as I recall: 'EXECU-TIVE SHOWS UNITED FRONT'. As I walked into the Europa Hotel that morning I was greeted by Derek Brown of the *Guardian* who commented, 'How embarrassing for you! The executive has just resigned.'

This incident apart, the fact that Gageby did not in general interfere with reporters' copy underlined his strong belief that the correspondent in the field should be fully trusted. The rule was that news copy could only be cut from the bottom for length. Gageby presided over what was one of the great writers' papers in the world. He might grumble but he did not interfere with reportage.

We divined, of course, what his wishes were. When I was news editor I knew there were some events he favoured that I should never overlook. In July the Orange parades had to be covered by a team of reporters. In August we had to send a colour writer to the Oul' Lammas Fair in Ballycastle, Co. Antrim. Most important of all was to arrange extensive coverage of the ploughing championships every September in Moynalty, Co. Meath, where Gageby had a fishing lodge. You could miss a big political scoop but neglecting his beloved Moynalty was out of the question. It was very definitely an 'editor's must'.

We also instinctively knew what his limits were. He would not tolerate malice, especially of the type that flourished then in the British tabloids and has now spread into Irish journalism. Under the glass top of his desk there were a few typed quotations that had caught his fancy. One was the famous epigram of Humbert Wolfe:

> *You cannot hope to bribe or twist,*
> *thank God! the British journalist.*
> *But, seeing what the man will do*
> *unbribed, there's no occasion to.*

This wasn't to say that he did not have an eye for mischief, as evidenced in the case of the Berrington letter. The American embassy's cultural attaché Robin Berrington had sent an end-of-year letter to dozens of his colleagues in the US state department with scathing comments about Ireland of the time—the early 1980s. It was leaked to *Irish Times* reporter John Armstrong who brought it to me late one evening when I was on the news desk. I conveyed to Gageby the import of the epistle—that Ireland was damp, strike-torn and uncultured, and that it was 'small potatoes' for diplomats like him with no great issues 'burning up the wires between Dublin and Washington'. Gageby agreed to publish a story about the letter, with the stipulation that we run it as a humorous, bottom-of-page-one, story, that we carry a 'soft' headline, and that I promise that Berrington would not be fired the next day. I promised. Berrington was fired the next morning by American ambassador, William Shannon, and sent straight back to Washington, an act of great stupidity as Berrington became an instant celebrity in Dublin, praised by Gay Byrne on RTÉ and other commentators as the one honest diplomat who at last had told the truth about Ireland. (I met Berrington years later. He told me he had always wanted to be posted to Japan, and as 'punishment' for the letter was exiled to Tokyo.)

As editor, Gageby appreciated the power of fine colour writing to attract readers. He championed the idea of the off-beat page one article and of the parliamentary sketch, penned in those days by talented writers like Olivia O'Leary and Maev Kennedy. He laid the groundwork for the establishment of permanent foreign outposts by his successor Conor Brady. He relished sending reporters abroad to write about important foreign events. He sent me to the Soviet Union for a month to write about the USSR in the run-up to the Moscow Olympics.

He could be impulsive. When I nagged him to let me go to Teheran to write about post-revolutionary Iran he said, over his shoulder as he left the office, 'Why don't you go to Afghanistan?' The Russians had just invaded Afghanistan. I did go, on the first possible flight, and as a result *The Irish Times* was one of the first western papers to get a reporter into Soviet-occupied Kabul.

Gageby always insisted on attention to detail in foreign reporting. When Conor Brady was dispatched to what was then Rhodesia he told him to describe what the country smelled like. If someone came back from an assignment abroad and was heard telling 'what it was really like' Gageby was likely to snap, 'Why did I not read that in the paper?'

Gageby still had some way to go regarding equality for female journalists. He felt that military stories were not for women to cover, and sent a male—me—to report on the deployment of Irish soldiers in the UN force in southern Lebanon. I only learned afterwards that the news editor at the time wanted to send his best hard-news reporter, Renagh Holohan, instead. It was a tough assignment indeed for a woman: it involved dining on pepper steaks by the Mediterranean most evenings with congenial company like Brendan Keenan of RTÉ, and Michael Keane of the *Irish Press*.

Also visible under the glass top of Gageby's desk was a cutting with the words of the great Chicago editor, Finley Peter Dunne, that a newspaper 'Comforts th' afflicted, afflicts th' comfortable'. Gageby identified with this sentiment, especially the first part. While not a campaigning editor, he was committed to the creation of a liberal society. This was evident in the kind of reporter he took on during his two spells as editor, such as Nell McCafferty, who combined colour and advocacy in writing on social issues and is celebrated for her damning reports from Dublin's juvenile courts. Donal Foley is given credit for hiring Nell and other talented women journalists such as Maeve Binchy, Mary Maher, Mary Cummins and Fionnuala O Connor; but it was Douglas Gageby who gave Donal his freedom, and in my case and that of several colleagues, he took a hand himself in the hiring.

Which brings me back to the time I was taken on. When I phoned him that day from Queen's University he asked me, 'When are your finals over?' 'Friday,' I replied. 'Start on Monday,' he said. And that was it. I had hoped for some post-exam holidays but this was clearly my first test. If I had told him that I was exhausted and needed a break he might well have retorted, 'Don't call me, I'll call you.' To the day I retired, nobody in *The Irish Times* ever asked me if I got my university degree.

My Kaufman Starter

Sam McAughtry

By 1981 I had been contributing to BBC and RTÉ programmes including 'Sunday Miscellany' for three years, following publication of a successful first work *The Sinking of the Kenbane Head* four years earlier. I was
happily writing another book plus the articles for the Belfast newspapers, which I'd been doing for 30 years, when Douglas Gageby first
phoned me as I was leaving RTÉ's Belfast studio.

I was coming up to retirement age in the Northern Ireland civil
service and I was delighted with life. I couldn't imagine myself going a
yard further with my ambitions. When most men would have been in
the garden, or on the golf course, or looking forward to the monthly
meeting of Rotary, I was tearing around the 32 counties giving keynote
speeches, doing radio shows and television appearances and shoving
an oar into Ulster's politics. I was a long time member of the Labour
Party, which is allowed under civil service rules, but when I was a working
civil servant I stretched things a bit in election canvassing, coaxing house-
holders to support my local heroes, Paddy Devlin, Gerry Fitt and David
Bleakley. I was also an active trade unionist.

A couple of well-known media figures claim to have recommended
me to Gageby but when I first took his call I don't think it was on
anyone's recommendation, I believe that he had been looking me over
for some time. That was his style. I certainly knew little about him
except that his grandfather, Robert Gageby, had been a splendid advocate for Labour in the early years of the 20th century, and his father had
been a civil servant.

He asked me on the phone to write six pieces for *The Irish Times*, in
a series bearing the unlikely title 'I Love Belfast'. They were splendidly
illustrated by the late Rowell Friers, the popular Holywood, Co. Down
cartoonist and painter. After the first couple of articles had appeared
Gageby rang, mentioning that the setting for one of my tales had been
North Belfast's Cliftonville Road, the location of his old school, Belfast
Royal Academy. We talked at length about the way in which this one-
time quiet, lower-middle-class area had suffered due to the Troubles:
gradually the conversation began to tease out the early strands of my

own political and social background. Although my parents and brothers and sister were unionist, I had come out of the Second World War with socialist preferences. Also, due to my mother's scrambled egg background, I had Catholic uncles and cousins. We talked about this and about the convulsions that had driven thousands of working class Catholics out of estates where, from the 1960s, they had been living and mixing with unionists.

This meant that unionists, in their turn, were driven out of areas like the New Lodge, to the cold Shore Road, to make room for the dispossessed Catholics. Both sides had my sympathy, the more so since my own brother Jack, a harmless bachelor, and an even-handed transport chief inspector, had been driven out, his windows smashed with hurley sticks, from our old family home in Hillman Street near Duncairn Gardens. He ended up at the top of the Shankill Road and until he was rescued by another brother and moved to Lurgan, was pressed by the UDA into sentry service, watching out for republican raids each evening.

Gageby was interested to learn that I considered myself to be Irish by nature and nationality and British by wallet, and I still remember his laughter over the phone. He himself had an understanding of Protestant fears but he had a distaste for the Orange Order, despite the fact that he was the first editor of *The Irish Times* to give broad coverage of the Twelfth Day demonstrations across the North, and he was later to send me right inside the prestigious Orange Hall on Carlisle Circus in North Belfast, to interview the likes of the Rev. Martin Smyth MP, and other provincial office holders prior to the start of the march.

When the 'I Love Belfast' series had run its course I forgot about *The Irish Times* and got down to some radio drama, but in a matter of a few weeks I had another call from him. He wanted to meet me for lunch in Dublin, I think in Bloom's Hotel. It was then that I realised that I had never seen him, and hadn't a clue as to what he looked like. Luckily, the day before the appointment, an Irish historical series appeared on BBC television, the presenter being one Douglas Gageby. I thought, watching him, that, for a newspaper editor, he looked extremely relaxed as he stood on hillocks and beaches and talked about invaders, ancient and modern. Presenting outdoors on TV is no easy job, and editors, by their nature, don't go public a lot, especially outdoors, talking to the camera. His gaze looked to be very sharp, and for someone brought up in Belfast, his accent had a pronounced Southern rhythm though not the South County Dublin variety

Before he'd ever made that first phone call to me he'd sent Belfast-born Eugene McEldowney, the paper's then industrial correspondent, to interview me ('On meeting McAughtry one is surprised: he is a tall man, with a mop of white hair . . .') and Eugene had mentioned to me that Douglas had been in the Irish Army during what was known in the South as the Emergency, 1939–45. This was pleasing news: ex-servicemen bond easily never mind their armies.

In the event he had Colonel Ned Doyle, the retired head of the Irish Army's Signal Corps, with him. In a recent RTÉ programme I had described the joys and trials of signalling from the air, using the old-fashioned radio transmitter/receiver, trailing aerial and Morse code. The colonel had come up the communications ladder to the top and my little memoir had carried him back to his Morse and semaphore days. We had a very pleasant time yarning about military and general matters, and as a consequence, I was later to spend time with, and write features, about, the Irish Army, Navy and Air Force.

I also yarned to both men about pre-war working-class Belfast, describing for example the blank astonishment on the loyalist side at the amount of attention Catholics were showing in 1937 about the Spanish civil war. ('As if they hadn't troubles enough,' they used to say.) On my way to work I passed newsagents on both sides of the divide: the Catholic one had a placard screaming: 'Nuns Beheaded in Guernica' and the Protestant shop placard shouted: 'Linfield Reach Irish Cup Final'. I noted how Gageby's eyes narrowed when I recalled some such item regarding Belfast, or Protestantism, or aired my view of loyalism or nationalism. I was soon to get to know that little signal, in the six years ahead.

Soon after the luncheon Douglas Gageby invited my wife and myself for dinner at his Dublin home. It turned out to be a bit of an anticlimax: I arrived suffering from a cold that had almost taken my voice away. At frequent intervals through the meal my wife Phyllis would say: 'It's a pity about Sam: he would give you a quare answer to that one,' but it was nevertheless a very enjoyable evening and I managed strangled replies and nods to the more relevant passages.

As we were leaving to go back to our hotel Douglas said to me: 'It would be interesting to hear the views of someone like yourself who knows so little about Dublin.' He already knew that, up until then, I had only been to Dublin five times, four day trips, two of which were Gaelic football finals, one with the Belfast Corporation transport department social club's disbursement of extra funds trip, and one as chairman of a body that arranged discounts for civil servants. The fifth was for the annual Irish Congress of Trades Unions conference: 'Could you go out and about tomorrow? Give me six hundred words, leave them into the office on Saturday evening, if it appears on Monday morning's issue I'll give you a ring.'

During the visit I had arranged to meet in my hotel three Dubliners who had been in touch with me through the publication of my Belfast stories. The first was an unfortunate homeless alcoholic who wanted to know more about the main thrust of my last book. The second was the late Éamonn MacThomáis, the amateur historian, who could bring back the Dublin of the twenties and thirties in the most entertaining style. Apart from his accent it was as if we had grown up next-door neighbours.

The third one was Lar Redmond from Bray, by way of the Dublin Liberties, a very popular 'Sunday Miscellanist'. This RTÉ programme at that time was setting a standard that would be hard to match today. Regulars in the studio were Benedict Kiely, Tom McIntyre, Michael Mulvihill, Bryan MacMahon, John Ryan, Caroline Swift, Val Mulkerns, and Maureen Charlton, to name but a third of the cast. Douglas Gageby listened in on a Sunday morning and if one of my pieces touched ever so lightly on the Northern problem he would ring me up at home and discuss it with me.

I confessed to Éamonn MacThomáis that the editor had commissioned me to write about Dublin and I hadn't the faintest idea where to begin: 'You come from a dockside neighbourhood,' he said, 'why don't you go out to Ringsend and do your thing. There are dock labourers and seafarers, it's a tough neighbourhood, like your own, and they'll take to you if you're straight with them.'

The next day, as it happened, was Grand National day: a good omen: it meant that I could walk into the Ringsend pubs, verbalise on the big race, and make contacts. I arrived with my notebook at the ready, and began to ratchet up the racing talk with the locals a couple of hours before the off. I mentioned that I was doing a story about Ringsend. At first this brought frowns: I then talked to them on dockside matters, and compared contemporary conditions then with those in Belfast in the fifties and earlier: this approach brought a flood of reminiscences and then a result:

'If you want to learn about Ringsend,' I was advised, 'go and talk to Lyrics Murphy. He's been writing down Ringsend stories for years.'

I went out and about, the big race was run, Hello Dandy won it, I didn't back it, my fund of racing talk was exhausted, I had quartered Ringsend and Irishtown but no Lyrics Murphy. I was sitting in the Sally O'Brien pub with a sore throat, looking at my notes and not fancying them a yard, when somebody touched my shoulder from behind and a voice said: 'I hear you're looking for me.' It was The Man.

He filled me in with lovely tales about Ringsend past and present. In particular he wanted me to know that the place was famous for the nicknames hung over the years on certain of its residents: 'I've written them all down and I'm wondering how to get them published,' he said. I promised to mention it in my piece. In the event I chose my favourite among them: it was applied to a 1940s particularly officious policeman: the name was Lousy Shoulders O'Shea.

I typed the piece up in the newsroom of *The Irish Times* and left it on the news editor's desk. On the Monday morning I went to my newsagent in Comber, Co. Down and bought *The Irish Times*. There, along the bottom of page one, was the heading: 'If You're in Ringsend, Ask for Lyrics'. I have a yellowing copy of it among my souvenirs. I received the editor's call later that day. He wanted me to write a weekly column and colour stories and features. 'Give me a nano-second to think about it,' I said.

Some days later, at Douglas's invitation, I arrived at the D'Olier Street headquarters and he gave me a tour of the building. It was comprehensive: I even met the editor of the financial pages. 'I got the cheque all right for the stories about Belfast,' I told him. After a moment's puzzlement both men explained to me that the financial editor dealt with items more global than payments to contributors. At a later stage of the tour somebody mentioned that *The Irish Times* had its own drinking club across the street: 'Don't give Sam any drink,' Douglas warned sternly. 'He's off it: his pub stories are myths.'

Since it was Douglas who had brought me on to the paper I assumed that he would direct me: all my dealings with newspapers had been by post, or visits to the literary or news editors' desks, so I wasn't familiar with the working routine. I set off on the train to Dublin shortly afterwards but a severe storm had almost paralysed the city, and I was turned out of the train at Drogheda because of the packed ice on the line. I rang Douglas on the stationmaster's phone to report failure of the mission: he gently asked me to contact the features editor or the news editor at such times and so I came to know Paul Tansey in features and Conor O'Clery in news and a working relationship began with these two that made me feel that I was in heaven with all my sins forgiven. They not only listened to my ideas but they tossed out new ones as to the manner born. Both got on well with Douglas, and Conor, since he was from the North himself, as well as being a very pleasant and disciplined editor, knew exactly how I felt as a working-class Protestant trying to get to know Southern people and their Southern ways. Another Northerner was Eugene McEldowney, whom I'd seen at annual AGMs of the Irish Congress of Trade Unions, although we'd never actually met before his profile of me in 1983.

On the subject of profiles, Douglas saw me once in the newsroom and asked me what I was doing. I told him that I had just returned from visiting Seán MacBride at his home: 'He talked about things that everybody knows,' I said, 'his history is familiar to all: I couldn't get him to talk about things personal to him, he was so . . .'

I was searching for the word: Douglas supplied it: 'Olympian,' he said, and walked away.

I had been happily doing my thing for a month or so for the paper knowing nothing about the fact that Douglas had been brought back from early retirement for the fight-back. He had brought Dr Conor Cruise O'Brien on as a weekly columnist as well as John Healy, an old time, well-read columnist with a good knowledge of the North. Healy was also Douglas's regular fishing partner. ('Fish or cut bait,' he would write when he meant 'Get your finger out.') The news team was leading the recovery, figures were rising and morale in the paper couldn't have been higher.

For part of the day Douglas shared an office off the newsroom with Bruce Williamson, a man with a divine writing touch. He had once worked for a paper that collapsed: 'What shakes you most about the experience,' Bruce said to me, 'is the suddenness of the thing. I reported in for work and was told to go home, right out of the blue.'

The general standard of writing in *The Irish Times* was so high that I hoped to find acceptance from my colleagues on the paper first and the public after that. Sharing space with Donal Foley and Maeve Binchy seemed to me to be like a pub singer joining two operatic stars on stage. Bruce Williamson's writing was beautiful: in his last contributions he even managed to make gorgeous prose of three-line film crits. However, when I got in front of the typewriter I just let rip anyway. Maeve and Donal and everyone else were nice to me. Donal Foley once said to me: 'You know, Sam, you are our remembrancer, don't lose that,' and Maeve gave me the title of a memoir I published later, when she said to me at Donal's funeral: 'You're always on the outside, looking in.'

Douglas Gageby wasn't the sort to say things like that. He would listen, and select, and suggest. I remember once talking to him about my strong Church of Ireland upbringing. My mother brought our whole family up in the church. Our Sunday programme started with Holy Communion at 8.30 a.m., morning Sunday school at 10 o'clock, morning service at 11 o'clock, afternoon Sunday school at 3 p.m., choir practice at 4 p.m. and evening prayer at 7 p.m. The rest of the Sabbath was our own.

I sang in the choir and when my voice broke I pumped the organ. On the way to church I used to see young Catholic lads in muddy soccer togs and I recalled feeling resentment, not because of their faith—

a matter of one measly chapel call before lunch—but because they were playing soccer while I was pumping the bloody organ. I used to read paperbacks as I pumped the organ. In order for sufficient pressure to go into the instrument it was necessary to keep a lead weight on a string above a mark scratched on the wall. After many warnings finally I was sacked for missing too many notes while reading Apuleius's *The Golden Ass* translated by Robert Graves.

Still on church matters I told Douglas Gageby about the Orange banner affair at the top of Cosgrave Street one year. The men of our district had hoisted the banner and were standing under it when our rector, the Rev. R. Dixon Patterson, came upon it. He stopped, put on his glasses, read the messages on it, and froze with rage. Across its width were the usual place names, Derry, Aughrim, Enniskillen and the Boyne, but there was a new message: 'The Road to Hell is Paved with Popery'.

Our rector was furious. He walked to the men who had hoisted it: 'That is nothing short of disgraceful,' he said, 'I am going to a Vestry meeting and I demand that you remove those offensive words by the time I come back.' The men nodded hastily, and ran to fetch their ladder. On the way back the rector paused, put on his glasses, and immediately turned purple. The words that had been removed were 'Derry, Aughrim, Enniskillen and the Boyne'.

'Put that in,' Douglas said. I did work it into a piece, and after that I told it on 'Sunday Miscellany'. Around that time I was invited to a party to celebrate Paddy Devlin's 70th birthday. Everybody there was telling stories so I told the banner tale, whereupon a founder member of the SDLP shouted: 'I'm sick listening to that story. I'm hearing it everywhere. Is that the only story that you know?' I told Douglas about that and he said: 'I hope you told him that he read it first in *The Irish Times*.'

The first time I saw Douglas administer discipline I was really impressed. I was sitting in features working alongside two young staffers both of whom were later to develop into fine reporters, when Douglas charged into the room. It was the first time I had seen him in this office: he was more inclined to go out into the newsroom with copy in his hand, but he'd climbed the stairs with a mission and the young cub he singled out wasn't long in knowing about it. His competence was challenged, his intellect was questioned: the Editor stood over the desk looking down on the hapless youth and by the time he had finished the young fellow was almost in tears

Watching him, I remembered that Douglas had been an officer in the Irish Army, after enlisting as a private, and served in Intelligence. As an ex-serviceman myself, I could, for those few moments, appreciate the economy of words, the clarity of the rebuke, the gap in rank, all being emphasised. He was giving a shellacking to a cadet lieutenant, and the rest of the staff in the orderly room, including the features editor, were holding their breath, in case anybody else there had been an accessory after the fact.

Although he had handled the television broadcast on Irish history referred to earlier capably, I noticed that he was too direct to be a politician. I happened to hear him on a radio broadcast in the mid 1980s in the wake of one of the North's many outrages, this time by loyalists. When someone in the studio happened lightly to touch on the fact that the event was a purely Northern matter, not to be handed to the Republic for debate, Douglas snapped quite angrily: 'For heaven's sake, we're only a hundred miles down the road: of course we're involved.' In those few seconds the strength of his republican beliefs became crystal clear. Later I heard him address the Irish Association in Belfast and in a short and pithy talk he made it clear that he was a separatist, whilst holding firmly to his affection for the place where he had grown up.

Going back to D'Olier Street matters I still remember how Douglas held Kevin Myers back during his editorship. It seemed a pity to turn the volume low on that amount of energy, and to plug that deep well of knowledge. I knew little about the origins of Douglas's umbrage: the charitable explanation could be that *The Irish Times* had been through a trying time, Douglas was nursing it back to health, his remedy was take it easy, turn out good, steady work, don't make waves.

When Eugene McEldowney was the National Union of Journalists' man in *The Irish Times* chapel he invited me to dinner at his Dublin home, where I met his lovely wife and family. In the course of the evening Eugene reminded me that the paper had been through hard times and that my contributions had helped on the road back: 'You are making a serious contribution,' he said, 'you should ask Douglas for a rise to senior journalist rate.'

'Do you think he'd give it to me?' I asked, anxiously. To tell the truth I'd have worked for the current unemployment benefit rate, but being a gold-medal-carrying trade unionist myself I was carried away by the notion of the rate for the job, so the next time Douglas sent for me I mentioned the matter:

'Who's been talking to you?' he asked, sternly. I was so scared that I ratted at once: 'Eugene McEldowney,' I confessed.

'And he thinks that you should be on senior journalist's rate?'

'Well, yes,' I said, 'it wasn't me.' I was ready to take a severe cut in my existing money, if it would get me out of there still in work.

'Well, just pay attention to this,' the editor said, 'to be a senior journalist on this paper means that you would have to be on immediate call, that could be in the middle of the night or it could be half an hour after you thought you had completed a day's work and you're on your way home. It would be a hell of a lot different to writing colour stories, and it would certainly interfere with your life as a fiction writer. You can go away and think about that,' he said, turning back to his work.

I got up, went to the door, opened it, looked back: his head was down and he was looking over the top of his glasses at a sheet of paper. A madcap thought came to me: how about if I were to say at the door: 'I take it that's a No?' God, he would brain me with a paperweight. I left, without bothering.

Later, though, he helped me with the rent of a house off the Malahide Road. I kept it for a year when I was putting in a great deal of my time on the paper. It was Douglas's own suggestion, for by the hokey, there was no way that I was going to ask for a rise ever again.

On the same subject, around 1986 I was asked by Val Lamb, its editor, to write a racing column for the *Irish Field* (then owned by *The Irish Times*) and the fee I was paid for this weekly column was fixed by Valentine after talking it over with Douglas. I was to write for the *Field* for another 18 years and in all that time I neither asked nor received a rise, even though the tools of the trade went from the typewriter by way of the fax to the computer and the cost of travelling tripled. At the same time I have to say that *The Irish Times* itself paid very fair expenses incurred in the line of reporting duty.

One of the areas of the paper that seemed to have escaped the tidying and mental vacuuming that had been necessary to pull *The Irish Times* back to where it belonged was the arts and studies office. It was like some scene from a Dickens novel. It reminded me of my days in the civil service when I was sent to take over a section that had been suffering from sick leave-itis. There were books and papers on the desk, on the floor, on shelves and behind the door. In the six years that I was with the paper I only went there once and the jaundiced looks that I got there beat me back to the clear and positive climate of the features office.

My reason for the one visit stemmed from an interview I'd had with an award winning children's author, a young man who had had his first novel adapted for the cinema and who, when he took up children's stories, went straight on to the bestsellers list. His own story was something else: he had nearly lost his life when a no-warning bomb exploded nearby, in a seaside town. For many months afterwards he had been unable to concentrate on writing and the process of recovery had been a most difficult one. I had left his latest book into arts and studies for possible review but up to and beyond publication my phone queries brought only vague replies.

I mentioned the matter to Ben Kiely and he just nodded resignedly: 'They don't want to review the book: that's how they let you know,' he explained. Fair enough, I thought, that's their privilege, children's books probably have to wait until Christmas, but they might have told me in time before the publication date. Still, for all I knew, maybe that's how the books department of every newspaper worked.

To mark the anniversary of the ending of the Second World War Douglas asked me to go and revisit some of the places where I had been stationed. I went first to Padgate, near Warrington in Lancs. In 1940, just off the boat and 18 years old, I had fallen asleep here, sitting on the floor, waiting for the mass enlistment process: a voice woke me up, I thought it was my mother calling up the stairs and when I looked around at uniformed drill corporals, the bleak furnishings and the dozens of glum, conscripted Englishmen, I felt like deserting the flag. But it passed and from Padgate I visited, after 40 years, St Athan in South Wales where I trained as a flight mechanic. From there I went to the officer cadet training centre and RAF College at Cranwell in Lincs., and lunched with the officer instructors. My final visit was to the Greek island of Samos, the scene of my Beaufighter Wing's attack on a German minelayer. I learned from the islanders that we had killed a good many German and Italians in the attack, but unfortunately a local baker's boy had been on board, and he lost his life in the attack. This was news I didn't want to hear.

My reports on these visits and photographs covered two or three days in the paper. Douglas earlier had sent me to Cuba. My father is buried there, having died while still at sea, at the age of 69. That story was carried on the front page of one of the paper's first colour supplements. At around the same time I recorded a radio commercial for *The Irish Times* that ran on RTÉ for some weeks. The BBC made a film about me: Douglas was asked to contribute: he said, *inter alia*, that although I was not for an All-Ireland, at least I didn't believe in leaning on Catholics who were.

At the time of writing this, I met McEldowney again. He was news editor of the paper before his retirement, and we talked about Douglas Gageby. 'He was a wonderful editor,' Eugene said, 'we would have done anything for him. He loved the North, he was brought up there and he never forgot it, for all his opposition to Unionism's Stormont rule.'

In the months when I knew that he was leaving, my work went

downhill. In my wartime days the engines of our planes were started from cold by a contraption involving an explosive cartridge. It was called a Kaufman Starter. Douglas Gageby was my Kaufman Starter. Whatever he asked me to do I went out and did it, at maximum revs. At the end of every year we would shake hands on the next year's contract. When he began to prepare for retirement my work went flat. It hadn't the same fizz. I took up radio presenting with the BBC and RTÉ, and I worked for six years in the peace movement. A couple of years after leaving *The Irish Times* a new novel of mine was launched in the Writers' Centre in Dublin. He was there with his wife Dorothy to wish me luck. He hadn't long before had an operation: he looked very ill, but he shook my hand and at the door, leaving, he turned and smiled at me. I never saw him again.

He supped with statesmen: his papers, including his editorials, are with Dublin City University. (In one editorial he even mentioned me.) I left *The Irish Times* to do other interesting things; I was six years with the paper, but I was only a moment in his distinguished career. Still: what a moment.

Douglas Gageby's estimation of Charles Haughey was driven by his reliance on the judgement of his columnist John Healy, whose close connections with Fianna Fáil were undisguised.

By that sin fell the angels

Kevin Myers

There were many differences between Douglas Gageby and me: age, politics, accent, to start with. But the greatest difference was that whereas I disliked but respected him, he disliked me and felt no respect for me whatsoever. He did not tell me why he felt like this. It was just thus. What follows will, alas, not please his family, and I regret this, because I am in particular a great admirer of his daughter Susan, who I hope one day to see as chief justice. However, my job is to tell the truth, not to make myself popular with powerful people.

After seven years working in Belfast, I drifted into *The Irish Times* in 1979, doing casual shifts as a reporter. The regimen was easy in those days. We would sit at the desks, waiting to be given a press statement to reduce to usable proportions. The work was so undemanding that I used to bring novels to pass the time while waiting for work to be given to me. I was reading a novel in the newsroom, when Gageby came over to me and asked what I was doing. 'Reading a book,' I said. 'Why aren't you working?' 'I have no work to do.' 'But . . .' he began, stopped, thought for a moment, then walked away. Thus the beginning of a relationship in which you could say the love-interest was minimal.

The position of diary-writer, which had been held for some 30 years by Séamus Kelly, had been vacant since his death in 1978. I had occasionally read his columns: they were excruciating stuff, often enough composed of the opinions about Dublin of Americans he had drunkenly lunched with the day before. Post Kelly, the job of filling the column circulated around the newsroom: no-one actually wanted to write a daily diary. In the summer of 1980, as a casually-employed journalist, I wrote my first 'Irishman's Diary', and it seemed to go down well. More often than not over the coming months, I was marked to do the diary by the news desk, and accordingly obliged. But the news editor, Conor O'Clery, needed to have a full-time diary-writer, and he told Gageby that he wanted to give the job to me.

Gageby vehemently opposed the appointment. O'Clery said that for budgetary and administrative reasons, he had to appoint someone, that it was an appointment within his gift, and that I was the one and only candidate. Moreover, he wanted me. Gageby gritted his teeth, and finally assented to my appointment, but only on the grounds that though the appointment of a diarist would normally merit an announcement by *The Irish Times*, in my case it wouldn't. If any announcement was to be made about my appointment, it was to be by me, in my column. And so, shamefully, it was.

What did Gageby dislike about me? My accent, no doubt. My English birth, very probably. My anti-national opinions, unquestionably. At an editorial conference one day discussing the morning's paper he said: 'A good "Irishman's Diary" today. Pity it's not by an Irishman.' That was an unusual compliment, though admittedly a not entirely fulsome one. Growled asides were the more common response to whatever I had written.

He came over to me one day, his eyes glinting with suppressed ire, waving my column at me, like a furious Red Guard brandishing a heretically Mao-less little red book. 'There's not a single name here. Not one. People read "An Irishman's Diary" for names, not your opinions.'

I assembled some vertebrae in a vaguely upright condition. 'Well, I hardly ever printed names in the columns I wrote before I got the job,' I managed to respond. 'So I'm only doing what I've been doing all along. If you didn't want me writing that kind of column, you should have stopped me getting the job. You didn't.' He glared at me, boring two long straight holes through my brain, then walked away. I sat still for a moment, before slithering to the floor, unconscious.

Some time in 1984 (I think) I wrote what I felt and still feel was a seminal piece about the Irish in the Great War. I had hitherto adverted to this subject in many columns, and in a couple of features, but this was a full-blooded thrust at the nationalist narrative which then held total sway in the popular imagination. 'There it is,' I wrote. 'One narrative. One band of heroes. One single tale, binding Irish history in a single glorious, seamless whole.' I then spoke of the (at that time) forgotten story of the other Irish, the hundreds of thousands who had served in the two world wars.

Gageby came over to me. 'That was a good strong piece today. But it was in the wrong part of the newspaper. "An Irishman's Diary" is not for your opinions about Irish politics or the Great War. Just leave it alone, okay?' I didn't argue with him, because one really didn't, not unless you wanted to be turned into a mournful spot of grease on the carpet—but nor did I obey him either. I continued to write about the neglect of the Irish who had served in the forces of the crown. When I mentioned in one column that my grandfather had been an RIC man, and I felt no shame at that, Gageby came out to me and said wryly but

I think approvingly: 'What are you up to? Are you trying to get us burnt out, or what?'

He was not always so positive. One day he sent out his deputy, Ken Gray to me. Ken was a genial man, but with a certain quiet authority. 'The editor has been wondering whether there's any chance of you not writing about the First World War any more?' he asked. 'You're at it again tomorrow.'

'Of course I'll stop writing about the Great War, Ken,' I said.

'Excellent, excellent,' he replied, turning to go.

'But only when this state officially formally recognises the tens of thousands of Irish who died and have been forgotten.'

'That means no, I take it.'

I think I just shrugged my shoulders.

'Good man,' he said, which was an accurate description of himself.

To be fair to him, Gageby could at any time have spiked my columns on the Great War. He didn't. But he did spike two columns in which I asked where Charlie Haughey got his vast amounts of money. The first time he came over to me and said very coldly, 'This is not your bailiwick. We have political correspondents to cover this area.' The second time, he put his hand on my desk, lowered his face so that it was next to mine, and said to me in tones that brooked neither dissent nor debate: 'I am editor of this newspaper. You will not write a party-political piece like this again. I do not employ you to do the job of our political correspondent. If you think you can do a better job than him, then apply for his job. But never, ever write anything like this again.'

When he was in that mood, I would have more enthusiastically tweaked Bismarck's nose than contradicted him. Moreover, this episode revealed what was central to his sense of self. He really did identify with Fianna Fáil, with its ethos, with its fundamental anglophobia (which is quite common amongst southern Protestants who have seen the republican 'light'). He did not always agree with Haughey—but his was disagreement within the camp, as was that of John Healy whose repeated encomia to Haughey in his 'Backbencher' column in the 1980s were masterpieces of sycophantic drivel, and a disgrace to the traditions of *Irish Times* journalism. But Gageby clearly loved them. The abysmal phenomenon of Charles Haughey—and all the horrors he embodied—were in part made possible by the abject acquiescence of a few figures in moral authority in Ireland—and none was more important than Douglas Gageby.

In the roseate hue of retrospection, it is easy to see the past in a kindlier light than it deserves. *The Irish Times* of the 1980s was a better written newspaper than it was 20 years later: its staff usually knew where apostrophes went, and were totally conversant with the differences between 'rob' and 'steal'—something as baffling for the creatures emerging from DCU today, with their usually worthless journalism degrees in their mitts, as the differences between Aramaic and Hebrew pluperfects. But the idea of a newsroom of impartial reporters had, under Gageby's supervision, long since vanished.

Most journalists were left-liberal—and this included myself. We were instinctively opposed to the Catholic Church, to big business, to the US and to the Irish Management Institute. Indeed, in some circles (especially sub-editors) to dismiss a suggestion, you merely had to sneer: 'Oh Jesus, that's real IMI stuff.' Idea, dead.

This was a world of stereotypes, in which white, middle-class Catholic males were fair game. Gonzaga was a regular target for the gratuitous mocking aside in a news story. We had imported the wholly British concept, baseless in Ireland, that inherited wealth was the cause of Ireland's failure. Gonzaga in this witless parable was the equivalent to Eton. Gageby, of course, was not responsible for inculcating this adolescent and classically post-colonial misconception: but he certainly tolerated and even indulged it.

At the worst and lowest level, long before my time, he even had a reputed member of the IRA writing a regular column in *The Irish Times* from Long Kesh prison, presenting himself as a purely innocent individual caught in a fiendish British scheme to quash peaceful dissent. But right across the board, there was a steady dripfeed of socialist republican commentary into the news pages: this was strictly of the Official Republican variety, when Official Sinn Féin (the Stickies) was a formal ally of the Soviet Union, still had weapons, and was still engaging in occasional terrorism. One Official IRA member of staff even brought a revolver into work, for safe-keeping: and why not? What police force in their right mind would raid a newspaper looking for guns? Would *The Irish Times*—and other newspapers—not denounce them from a hysterical height for doing so, regardless of the justification?

The Stickies were especially powerful amongst sub-editors, a species which has long been vulnerable to subversion. Subs are rarely happy, and even more rarely feel appreciated. They are accordingly ripe for the activities of the revolutionary. Moreover, journalists regularly found their copy had been tampered with between typewriter and publication. The late Christina Murphy—a model of an impartial educational journalist—found a story which she had written about a career in banking had had the following line added: 'Better still, banking allows you to enjoy a career of financial crime, for which you will never go to jail.'

Incandescent at this, she went to Gageby demanding action. He went to the chief sub, who refused to identify the person responsible. Since the time of Gutenberg, subs have retreated behind the arcane wizardry of the guilds, and only the chief sub knew who had done what. And according to these medieval freemasonry rules, the chief sub alone could identify and punish miscreants. Quite clearly, even the powerful Gageby was able to impose his will only so far. Till the day she died, Christina never found out who was responsible for doctoring her copy.

She was unusual as a woman journalist of the time: she was a straight-forward deliverer of news and analysis, with no political or social agenda. Most of the other women journalists were not. Brought in largely by Donal Foley, the news editor, they were almost all colour writers: Maeve Binchy, Maev Kennedy, Elgy Gillespie, Nell McCafferty, Mary Cummins—they got the soft-focus markings, where the chances to emote and to use adjectives were more plentiful.

These were tendencies which—in those days anyway—I rather shared, which is probably why Conor O'Clery, still news editor, asked me to go to Israel in 1982, after the latest invasion of Lebanon. Perhaps it was also because he knew I had been under fire in Belfast on more than one occasion. Well, I spent much of the summer that year in Israel and Beirut, nearly got killed a couple of times, filed a few good stories, and then went home to Dublin, reporting for duty the day after my return. Some people were kind about my work: walking by, Gageby merely paused, looked at me over his spectacles with those unwavering, glinting eyes, and walked on. That same summer Olivia O'Leary— an outstanding journalist—was reporting from Argentina during the Falklands War.

The following January, he came over to me and said: 'Have the Benson and Hedges people been in touch with you?' (They sponsored the 'Journalists of the Year' awards of that era.)

'No,' I said.

'Ah,' he said, his face falling. 'Well. So I have to tell you.' He stopped, unbearable grief momentarily overwhelming him, before he recovered. 'You've just been made Journalist of the Year for your stuff from Beirut.' Another pause, and more recovery. 'Personally, I thought O'Leary's stuff was better.' He paused again before sniffing: 'Much.' He walked away without congratulating me, and never said another word to me about it.

A year or so later, he came over to me while I was hammering on the old-fashioned typewriter (thanks to Gageby, *The Irish Times* adopted new technology somewhat after Malawi), and with a deadline approaching. 'You fancy a drink?' he murmured gruffly.

'Sorry Douglas, not when I'm working, and I'm behind here.'

He blinked and walked away. This didn't mean he had abandoned any further attempt to make me conform with his view of what sort of columnist I should be. He came over to me one afternoon soon afterwards and asked me to write about why one could never get a half-bottle of wine in a Dublin restaurant. I did my normal nameless column, and finished it with the question: 'A final unrelated thought: why it is impossible to get a half-bottle of wine in a Dublin restaurant?'

Next day, he came over to me and said: 'I didn't mean like that. That's not what I wanted at all. I'm editor of this newspaper. You don't seem to understand that.' Shaking his head, he walked away.

However, what I really admired in him was that he was a genuine patriot in the way that many of his generation, especially soldiers, really and passionately were. The Army shaped him, and exposed him to an ordinary Irishness which never left him. He loved the Army, and I think regretted not becoming a professional soldier after the Second World War (I refuse to call it by the E-word). He would have been an outstanding general. One day, I came into the newsroom having seen soldiers clearing packed snow from O'Connell Street. I was enthusing to a few journalists about the fact that officers—lieutenants and commandants—were clearing the snow alongside the ordinary soldiers. Gageby overheard me and his eyes lit up as he asked: 'What else did you expect of our Army? Best fucking bunch of men in the world.'

So I admired him for his patriotism. But he was still a crook, as the creation of the Irish Times Trust suggested. Did Gageby feel guilt that he had encumbered the company with debts that took 20 years to pay off, in order to buy his shares, while he remained in control of the newspaper through the Trust? Possibly—and perhaps that is why he allowed the constant expression of Lefty sentiments in the news and comment pages. How could a newspaper which tolerated such socialist thoughts possibly be at its heart and soul corrupt?

But it was, and instrumental in that process was Douglas Gageby, who had enriched himself to the tune of £325,000 in 1974. (To put that figure in perspective, a house that was sold that year for £14,500 was sold in 2002 for the equivalent of £800,000.) There are many disgusting aspects to this entire saga, but the most nauseating was Gageby's triumphalist editorial that morning which declared that if you were scared of the truth, don't buy *The Irish Times*: but it made no mention of the truth concerning how much he was benefiting from the deal. Nor did he mention the benefits the deal attracted for some by being rushed in immediately before capital gains tax became operative.

So I saw the negative side of him. Others saw his good side and were devoted to him. His deputy was the charming and erudite Bruce Williamson—the last of the Protestant old guard, complete with English public school accent, grey cardigans, and false teeth which fitted into his mouth like badly made bin-lids. He wrote poetry of which even he, on due reflection, had a low opinion, smoked incessantly, and was as fat as a water-balloon. One morning at around eleven I popped into Bowe's pub across the road for a cup of coffee, and Bruce arrived alongside me at the bar. He signalled wordlessly to the barman, who promptly poured him a triple gin, iceless, and served it alongside a little bottle of Schweppes. Bruce poured a gnat's bladder worth of tonic into the triple gin and downed it. Another gesture, another triple, another gnat's wee, and Bruce was now braced for the day. In his drawer at work, he kept a bottle of gin, from which he refreshed himself regularly, but he never seemed drunk.

Douglas Gageby rescued Bruce from his alcoholism. I don't know how he did it, but he managed to get his deputy on the wagon, from which Bruce never alighted until he finally retired. Moreover, Douglas was physically brave. A former sub-editor with profound psychiatric problems—Brian, for the sake of this narrative—once walked into the newsroom and started shouting manically. Those who had seen him in action before backed away, as if from a dog with foam dripping from its lips. Less experienced at Brian-watching, I stayed at my seat until our visitor lifted a huge, heavy typewriter and hurled it in a flat trajectory towards the newsroom window. It missed, hit the wall, and exploded in pieces like an artillery shell. I slid with serpentine alacrity under my desk, and watched through the small gap between my vertical partition and the desk surface as Gageby—twice my age—emerged from his office.

'Here. What are you doing with our typewriters?' he asked in a gruff but kindly voice. 'Does your doctor know you're out and about? You'd better come inside with me before you do some real damage.' He then led poor Brian into his editorial den. I remained crouching under my desk until our unfortunate schizophrenic was finally gone from the building, after which I sauntered the broad acres of the newsroom, quite the heroic war veteran.

Douglas Gageby helped change and improve the face of Irish journalism. He feminised it and softened it. He allowed subjectivity to enter news reports, often for the better. He was not unique in either regard—and it could be argued that a far more vigorous friend to Irish women journalists was Tim Pat Coogan, of the now defunct *Irish Press*. But on the other hand, Gageby helped create an ethos in which we did not seek to understand the predominant Catholic opinion of Ireland. Gageby was party—as was I, in my infinitely lesser way: we almost all were—to the creation of a system of cultural apartheid, in which a self-regarding metropolitan elite spoke to itself, without seriously attempting either to address or understand the feelings of the majority.

Moreover he had no interest in or knowledge of sports, the mainline connection to that majority, with the result that our sports pages were truly dire, in every area save the GAA, where Paddy Downey—no doubt unbeknownst to Gageby—maintained consistent standards of sporting knowledge and literary skill. Withered ancients of 50 years' standing could retire from sports and Gageby would be neither present for their farewell party, nor even be represented.

It barely matters now. Ireland has moved on to an era where almost none of the foregoing has any relevance, save as an incomprehensible footnote to an incomprehensible history. The great tragedy of Douglas Gageby's life was that the horrors of Charles Haughey occurred on his watch; he had his duty to do for law, decency and democracy, and he failed lamentably. And I think I know why: the tainted fruit of the Trust. That was where he proved fatally weak. He was ambitious for wealth, and his ambition was rewarded, but purposelessly. For Haughey knew where all men were weak and, I have no doubt, ruthlessly used that weakness. 'Fling away ambition,' was Cardinal Wolsey's dying whisper in Shakespeare's *Henry VIII*. 'By that sin fell the angels.' By that sin did Douglas fall.

Freedom of expression

Andrew O'Rorke

'Who is that man?' I asked my father as an eleven-year-old watching a politics programme in the very early days of Telefís Éireann. I got a simple answer for one who was born into a traditional Dev-idolising Fianna Fáil family. 'The first editor of the *Evening Press*.' But what followed intrigued—a Northerner, a Protestant, a member of the Defence Forces during the Emergency, in fact of 'the Intelligence'. I knew my Wolfe Tone—Protestant, Catholic, Dissenter, in the common name of Irishman. So there actually was a believer from the North! Unashamedly I own up—he immediately had a disciple. In the years that followed, when he referred to the Rev. Armour from Ballymoney in a leading article, that first introduction rekindled.

I grew up, *The Irish Times* came more regularly into our house. In the way of his times my father regarded journalism, which might have enticed me, as a profession that might not be as profitable as the law, so the law enveloped me. On qualifying I joined Hayes & Sons, the first step to meeting Douglas Gageby.

Hayes & Sons is the oldest solicitors' practice in the country, dating back to 1840. One of the 'Sons' was admiral of Dublin Port in 1916 and is said to have directed the *Helga* up the Liffey to bombard the GPO in Easter Week. In those days the firm acted for many merchant princes and represented leading business associations. The Walker family acquired an interest in *The Irish Times* in the 1950s and one of them, Ralph, was a solicitor and senior partner of Hayes when I joined. From his time, if not before, we advised *The Irish Times* on defamation matters. When the Irish Times Trust was created (as described in Conor Brady's recent book *Up with The Times* (Dublin 2005) he and Gageby were among the shareholders whose shares the Trust bought.

In the 1950s and 1960s the Irish were not litigious. *The Irish Times* was involved in very few cases. The principal issues arose from 'Backbencher' columns, whose author, John Healy, had impeccable sources in Ministers Donogh O'Malley, Charles Haughey and Brian Lenihan, revealing the thought processes of Taoiseach Jack Lynch's government. This gave rise to some concern. Sam Crivon, a senior counsel, was asked to read the column every Friday evening before publication—perhaps the first serious, continuous pre-publication advice sought by a paper in Ireland. After some years of this Ralph said to Sam: 'I'm thinking of buying *Gatley on Libel*,' which was the defamation bible. Sam, stunned, replied: 'Do you really need to?'

Epitomies of the establishment sued the paper in the turbulent 1970s, Peter Berry, secretary to the department of justice, and William Philbin, bishop of Down and Conor. Mr Berry, whom many would have regarded as a defender of the state, given his central position as secretary of the department at the time of the arms trial, sued over publication of a photograph that showed a placard being brandished by Sinn Féin members identifying him as a 'felon setter'. The bishop sued over an article written by Conor O'Clery about his attitude to confirming children who did not attend Catholic schools.

Berry lost and Philbin won, but I mention these cases not only for their historical interest but because Gageby, backed by his board and chairman Major T. B. McDowell, supported his journalists in conflicts where others sought to diminish his perception of freedom of expression.

Our's had principally been a reactive service—advising when a complaint was received and representing the paper if proceedings were issued. These matters were handled on a day to day basis by two perfect gentlemen, Ken Gray, editorially, and Dermot James, the company secretary. It was in the 1970s that the giving of pre-publication advices commenced on a regular basis. The principal catalyst for the change was Dr Conor Cruise O'Brien, who had become a regular weekly columnist. Given the sharpness and frequently controversial nature of his writing it was decided to refer his columns to us for clearance. He was not aware of this, but my senior partner, Adrian Glover, then the first port of call for advice, placed him on our Christmas card list. His departure to write for the Independent group was waked, again unbeknownst to him, in our old offices in St Stephen's Green.

The practice slowly grew of referring articles of a contentious nature to us in advance of publication. The contact point was invariably a duty, features or departmental editor but not the editor himself. The preference was for us to deal not with the journalist author but with a senior person who might be more receptive of advice and not necessarily regard it as conservative or defensive.

As solicitors advising on copy before publication we were somewhat removed from the work of journalists and editors, who every day in a matter of hours produced, through some unknown and even mysterious process, a newspaper which revealed and analysed the world, albeit at times from a particular perspective. Concepts of freedom of expression jostled nightly with the protection and vindication of the good name of the citizen.

Back then our advices were sought by telephone. The questionable piece was read to us. Copy that was too long to be read over the phone was sent by hand (pre-fax, pre-courier days). We were in St Stephen's Green, remote by half a mile from *The Irish Times* in D'Olier Street.

The developing use of pre-publication advice and the manner in which it was sought was not only highlighted but forever changed by the conviction of one Malcolm MacArthur for murder. I was asked for the first time to attend D'Olier Street to vet numerous pieces relating to the prosecution and conviction of MacArthur and the outcry that followed the entering of a *nolle prosequi* in respect of a second murder charge. This was novel, and because of the intensity of the pieces I attended at the engine of the newspaper, the news desk, where I sat reading many court reports, analyses or opinion pieces, some of which caused concern. At one stage I took a taxi from D'Olier Street to the home of a senior counsel in the suburbs seeking confirmation of our advices on one piece of copy.

The MacArthur story (grotesque, unbelievable, bizarre and unprecedented, as described by Haughey and GUBUed by Cruise O'Brien) demanded examination and care at a level that had not been sought or required until then for libel or contempt of court. Subsequently there were many similar long nights involving the reading and approval of copy but this was the first time we advised on site. It reflected Gageby's and his colleagues' acknowledgement of the changing reality in providing defamation protection. I don't know if other newspapers developed a similar approach, but subsequently some of the Sundays required, and still do, that all copy for publication is vetted in advance by lawyers.

Gageby resigned as editor shortly after the foundation of the Trust and delivery of ownership to it in 1974, the year after I started in Hayes. We had little or no contact with him for a number of years. On his return to the editor's office contact was still minimal. It was only in the early 1980s that I seriously engaged with him.

One autumn evening in 1982 I arrived home to be told Gageby had been looking for me. This was a first. Why had he phoned? We had spoken from time to time over the years but he had not been hands-on regarding advice, and certainly not by way of a home call. He did not participate directly in any High Court matters. They were largely handled by Ken and Dermot under the supervision of the chairman. I returned his call and found that he was seeking my advice on a piece by

John Healy. I was a little bemused—this editor by whom I was enthralled as a child some 20 years earlier was consulting me on a piece by John Healy, who was not now regarded as overly controversial.

The call went on for a considerable time with Gageby speaking affectionately of Healy, their long association and the fact that Healy was not really an '*Irish Times* type' but that Gageby had engaged and retained him because of his feel for Irish politics and his ability to write persuasively about it. I think it may have been during that revealing conversation that we touched on the occasional short columns that both he and Healy wrote under the pseudonyms 'H' and 'Y' regarding wildlife, and which gave him great satisfaction.

If that night reflected a gentle protection of a friend and fellow journalist—I am not sure which came first—the steel and determination that was Gageby was demonstrated shortly afterwards.

Olivia O'Leary's position as a leading political journalist in the early 1980s was long since established when, during a Garrett FitzGerald government, she wrote a story on cabinet deliberations concerning a sensitive topic. The wrath of the government, or at least some of its members, was unleashed on Olivia in the form of a directive to the attorney general to carry out an inquiry under the Official Secrets Act to ascertain the source of the leak. This led to a high ranking garda being dispatched to D'Olier Street to interview her.

I was asked by Gageby to attend at the 'interview' to ensure that it was monitored by a lawyer and Olivia was given legal protection. What would have happened if she was arrested on the spot for an alleged breach of this act was unclear to me. Olivia was her charming self, concerned that the superintendent had to carry out such a demanding and sensitive investigation, would help if possible, but knew that he would understand she could not possibly reveal the story's source.

Nothing came of the investigation but Gageby was furious that the government sought to use the Official Secrets Act to require a journalist to reveal a source. I cannot imagine that Peter Sutherland as attorney general was keen to have Olivia prosecuted or indeed jailed under this somewhat arcane act, but Gageby's outrage at the government which, in seeking to protect cabinet confidentiality, instigated an official investigation of one of his journalists, was palpable. Quite clearly O'Leary was doing her job and in circumstances where the source must reasonably have been a member of the same government that directed the investigation. (Although representing Olivia and the newspaper I did not know then and do not know now who the source was.)

Around the same time an internal Garda disciplinary inquiry took place in Kerry. Ger Colleran (now editor of the daily tabloid the *Irish*

Star) was news editor of the *Kerryman* at the time. He and another young journalist in *The Irish Times*, Michael O'Regan (now the paper's parliamentary correspondent), reported on the inquiry. The Garda authorities were furious and commenced a separate investigation as to how the fact of the disciplinary process was made public. They also sought to establish an evidential link between another garda and the journalist. They summoned Colleran and his editor, together with O'Regan and Gageby, to an interview in Crumlin Garda Station.

Gageby was somewhere between apoplectic and incandescent with rage on two counts, firstly that the Garda would seek to censure journalists for reporting on the matter and secondly that they sought to use the same journalists to condemn a garda whom they believed to be the story's source. Again I was asked to attend to 'protect' the journalist.

We went out to the Garda station and were brought into a depressing interview room. At the time Gageby was on crutches and he had some difficulty in accessing both the station and the interview room. The atmosphere was tense on this occasion and after the formalities were completed we were let know in an authoritative tone about the seriousness of the matters being investigated. It appeared the investigators may have thought O'Regan and Colleran would reveal their sources, given the seniority of those questioning them, and that appropriate interview techniques would readily achieve their aim. Gageby was having none of this. He let fly, denounced the Garda for seeking to use the journalists to sanction a garda who in turn was representing a colleague in difficult circumstances. His journalist O'Regan—and the young Colleran was not unhappy to nestle under the Gageby cloak of protection—was doing his duty reporting on the issue of public concern, neither sources nor other information would be given and it was time we left. We did. I chalked down another great personal success in defending journalistic rights, without actually having said much more than good morning, and informing the Gardaí of my name, address and occupation, and of course maintaining a serious composure.

The raw anger expressed by Gageby that morning at what he perceived as an abuse of power and position was genuine. We adjourned for coffee during which his contempt for what occurred was further expressed in unrepeatable and very uneditorial but unforgettable language. I understood fully the strength of his convictions on right and wrong and the extent to which he was prepared to go to protect proper journalistic standards in the interest of fairness and good reportage. I also observed the respect and awe in which he was held by two young journalists, whose editor's support far exceeded that anticipated. Twenty-five years on, both of them still allude to that encounter in the Garda station and the manner in which Gageby extended his protection to them.

Gageby's contribution to Irish journalism continued after his retirement as editor. He was asked by the National Newspapers of Ireland, a representational group, to lead a campaign seeking reform of our defamation laws. It is not for me to painstakingly recount the failure so far to amend a statute enacted over 40 years ago and which defines unhelpfully the relationship between the public and media. I heard Gageby speak frequently at seminars and meetings on the proposed reform. He was at his best outlining the position of the written media in contemporary society—the obligation to report and challenge, to protect and question and to do so fearlessly but not unquestioningly. I confess to having plagiarised and paraphrased one observation of his, and use it when speaking on defamation: 'Journalists write history on a daily basis, they have only a few hours to do so, mistakes will be made—that is inevitable.'

He saw it as the duty of editors and proprietors to protect and support journalists who are professional in their writings and approach and conscious of standards and obligations. He always readily acknowledged that he was not alone in *The Irish Times* in giving the support. The chairman made available all necessary resources to defend cases where appropriate, a fact confirmed by Conor Brady in *Up with The Times*.

Brady in his opening paragraph recalls Maeve Binchy's observation of her editor coming out of his office, pointing at something in the paper and demanding to know 'how the hell did this get in?' I was aware that the standards he expected of those in authority were equally demanded of journalists. He despised lazy journalism, the journalism of the handout. The spin of Ireland 2006 would be anathema to him. It was not the function of journalists or papers to merely publish the words of those whose words should, he thought, also be investigated. He spoke about his perception of the effect of press releases on good journalism in depressing tones.

Invariably, given we were speaking of defamation, he would deride journalists who sought to sue newspapers. He was suspicious of public people who use the media for advancement and then readily threaten to sue for alleged defamation. He believed that journalists were more difficult than most to appease when allegedly defamed; and he found it galling that they would not accept mistakes can happen, or in the light of their vocation be more understanding of the pressures of publishing a newspaper six or seven days a week.

He contacted me sometime after his National Newspapers of Ireland appointment and sought my comments on a detailed draft report prepared by Professor Kevin Boyle and Marie McGonagle of Galway University on defamation reform. He was excited by the report, as was I, but my written response disappointed him. However, if I knew my Wolfe Tone in the 1960s, I knew my politicians (of all parties) in the 1980s. I suggested to Douglas that notwithstanding the fair and considered approach adopted by Boyle and McGonagle to the need for reform, any presentation to government might be no more welcome than a story breaching cabinet confidentiality, that he must be conscious of the torrid relationship between politicians and media and that I did not see the then government or members of any other government contemplating easing the burdens of the media.

He expressed surprise and disappointment at my perception. He suggested that the relationship was not as I had outlined it. Subsequently he worked closely with Frank Cullen of National Newspapers of Ireland on the proposals. Boyle and McGonagle expanded on the initial report and in a formal ceremony presented it to then attorney general, now chief justice, John Murray, who in turn invited the Law Reform Commission to review the law of defamation, who in return published a report . . . and . . . !

Almost 20 years later another indication of reform, the fifth since 1987, is sliding perilously close to non-consummation. What Gageby worked for—to benefit not only media but society—has yet to be achieved. Such reform might have been easier 20 years ago but with the arrival of the tabloids in Ireland, perceptions and views have hardened.

So Gageby's last great venture on behalf of Irish journalism failed to unravel mutual layers of political and journalistic suspicion, which some on both sides would identify as healthily democratic.

It was but a minor irritant in contrast to his achievements with two of our great newspaper groups.

At the outset I posed the eleven-year-old's question as to who was that man? The beguiling answers lit up a child's beliefs. The subsequent reality, developed through a professional relationship and friendship, albeit not too close, expanded on those answers; a more intimate relationship was not necessary. His working colleagues knew him better but they may allow me a final question: 'Who could replace that man?'

Fishing for pollock, Blind Sound, Inis Mór, Co. Galway, in the early 1960s.

Mapping a new prosperity

Paul Tansey

Economics was not a subject that greatly excited Douglas Gageby. It languished down towards the bottom of the lists, somewhere between horse racing and golf. There were two exceptions to this unstable equilibrium. The first was when economics stories forced themselves to the top of the front page: the first oil crisis of 1973–4 or the tax marches of 1979–80. His nose for news always sensed that economic dislocation usually provoked deep political reverberations. And, in editorial terms, politics was Gageby's game.

Second, prevailing economic conditions played a decisive part in dictating the commercial performance of *The Irish Times*. A growing employed population of working age provided the necessary base for an expanding circulation. Rising real disposable incomes spurred advertising volumes. In this second instance, Gageby's interest in economics was commercially driven. And Gageby possessed strong and well-developed commercial instincts.

It is not generally realised that he arrived at *The Irish Times* not as editor of the newspaper, but as its joint managing director. In many ways he combined the roles of businessman and newspaperman in equal measure. Though editorial concerns were always pre-eminent and never compromised he rarely neglected commercial considerations. Unlike many editors, he never railed against budget constraints nor regarded the newspaper's current financial performance as beneath him. If, on a given day, the advertising was light, he would not hesitate to cut the size of the next day's paper. Few ads, no quibbles; cut the paper back by two pages. (Readers don't seem to realise that you can't cut it by just one.)

He was no mean hand at marketing either, as the growth in the newspaper's circulation testified. In his second incarnation as editor, he became highly innovative in marketing the newspaper, both generically ('If you miss *The Irish Times*, you miss part of the day') and editorially. In the latter case, along with Conor Brady who succeeded him as editor, he pioneered the use of radio advertising to support series of articles that ran through the fallow days of the week, where the journalists themselves voiced-over the ads. The objective of this novel marketing tactic was to convert more occasional readers of the paper—typically those who purchased it only on a Friday or Saturday—into more regular readers. It worked.

Gageby's successful blending of the editorial and the commercial aspects of management shaped *The Irish Times* in two ways. On the practical level, his commercial acumen safeguarded the newspaper's future, not once but twice. By dragging *The Irish Times* away from the periphery and into the mainstream of Irish life during the 1960s, he increased vastly the size of the market available to it, both in potential newspaper sales and in additions to advertising revenue. His second coming in the late 1970s acted to restore a sense of both editorial and financial stability to the paper at a time of great uncertainty.

On a political level, by temperament and by commercial necessity, Gageby was a moderniser. He understood that what was good for the Irish economy was good for *The Irish Times*. He saw the Ireland of the future as evolving into a quintessentially European liberal democratic state, less dependent on Britain and shorn of domestic authoritarian tendencies. While this characterisation sounds commonplace now, it must not have seemed so from the vantage point of the suffocating insularity of the late 1950s and early 1960s.

By the early 1960s, political and economic modernisation had become an imperative for the simple reason that, in the preceding four decades, Ireland had failed to find its future in its past. The economic nationalism of Sinn Féin, the *fons et origo* of most subsequent economic policy, centred on the fostering of indigenous and 'infant' industries behind tariff walls and a fragmented agriculture based on small family farms. But no country can expect to leverage sustained economic development on the back of a domestic market that is both small and poor. By the 1950s, the inevitable result was stagnation and a rate of emigration that had reduced the Republic's population to just 2.8 million people in 1961.

Yet the seeds of the late-20th-century boom were sown in this barren soil. And those seeds were intellectual. The traditional Irish world view was turned upside down. Protectionism was jettisoned in favour of free trade. Foreign industrial capital, once shunned, was attracted with generous grants and tax concessions. Education became an imperative. This revolution was led by T. K. Whitaker, secretary of the department of finance, but Gageby was in the vanguard. Through the 1960s and into the 1970s, *The Irish Times* under his editorship provided the platform and much of the cartography for the mapping out of modern Ireland.

As an editor, Douglas Gageby was simply the brightest and the best. His outstanding characteristic as an editor was his understanding of the limitations of the job. Editors of quality newspapers can determine their editorial direction, set the tone of the coverage, but they cannot write the papers themselves. In this, editors much resemble football managers. He understood that as captain of the editorial team, his principal task was to pick the players. He saw that recruiting and developing journalistic talent—not only writers, but designers, specialist editors and photographers—and refreshing that pool of talent at regular intervals, was the key to defining the character and personality of the newspaper.

Along with his chief scout and news editor, Donal Foley, Gageby was an assiduous creator and poacher of journalistic talent. And not only did he lure talented people to *The Irish Times*, but he managed to retain many of them. He retained them because he was genuinely interested in them. He praised them, criticised them, excoriated them, listened to them, encouraged them. Above all, he read what they wrote, looked closely at the pages they designed and sub-edited and the photographic prints they presented. In my experience, these apparently self-evident editorial functions are not universally exercised by editors. And they are centrally important to running a successful newspaper.

Gageby also mooched around a lot. He was an early exponent of 'managing by walking around'. And as he did so, he dispensed reassurance and encouragement—laced with occasional doses of criticism. In return, he earned the intense loyalty of almost all who worked for him. That personal loyalty to the man usually remained even amongst those who eventually left the paper.

When I worked in *The Irish Times* during the 1970s and early 1980s Gageby was considerably older than most of his journalistic staff. Yet he was avuncular rather than paternalist and surprisingly collegial in determining the newspaper's editorial line on major political issues. This collegiality was demonstrated clearly in the stance adopted by the paper during the general election of February 1982.

Charles Haughey had been elected leader of Fianna Fáil and taoiseach in December 1979. In a television address in January 1980 he had delivered a masterly, if in retrospect highly ironic, analysis of the country's economic plight, centring on the contention that we were living beyond our means and would all have to tighten our belts. In his succeeding 18 months in power Mr Haughey failed to follow his own advice. He lost office in the general election of June 1981 to a Fine Gael–Labour coalition headed by Dr Garret FitzGerald. The coalition was full of clever plans and good intentions, but little else. Its 1982 budget, proposed in

January, was defeated and a general election was declared for the following month.

For whatever reason, at that time Douglas Gageby had a soft spot for Charlie Haughey. And he had no time at all for the 'Blueshirts', as he habitually called members of Fine Gael. Against this background, it seemed certain that the newspaper would counsel a vote for Fianna Fáil in its election-day editorial. At the time, sentiment amongst the editorial staff of the paper ran strongly against Haughey, though not necessarily against Fianna Fáil. Gageby was well aware of this, knowing also that the majority of the paper's readers were equally suspicious of the Fianna Fáil leader. He was urged to publish an editorial backing the return of the coalition. He did not denounce this impertinence out of hand. Instead, he called for a draft. And another. And yet another. The fifth and final draft embodied a lukewarm endorsement of the Fine Gael–Labour coalition, criticising their ineptitude but praising their honest effort. It was published on election day.

Not that it made any difference. Fianna Fáil scraped back to power, forming an ill-starred government that lasted only from March to November 1982.

To my mind, that February 1982 election was Douglas Gageby's greatest triumph as an editor. Such was his character and authority that he allowed the publication of an election-day editorial which, while reflecting the majority view of those working within the newspaper, did not necessarily mirror his own opinions. With this, he taught us all a lesson: the publication of a serious newspaper is an inclusive and collegial activity, where the views of readers, writers and other staff deserve a hearing in shaping the paper's perspective on the world.

'The essential thing is curiosity'

John Bowman

This is a shortened version of an interview with Douglas Gageby on RTÉ television in 1998.

John Bowman: Do you believe journalists are born or can they be made?

Douglas Gageby: Well, there are a lot of colleges running courses in journalism now. I think the essential thing is curiosity and if you haven't got curiosity and an interest in people you might as well be doing something else. I think that to some extent the very good journalist is born, not made. I would instance John Healy,[1] a natural; and several others in my day, Donal Foley,[2] an absolute natural.

J B: Were you a newspaper reader as a child?

DG: I started very early reading newspapers. I had a lot of bronchial trouble when I was young and my father used to always bring me home a different paper at lunchtime, throw it down on the bed. And one day he came in, threw this newspaper down on the bed and said: 'De Valera has just brought out a new newspaper in Dublin.' And that was the first number of the *Irish Press*.[3] And I

---

1 John Healy (1930–91), worked for the Irish News Agency and the *Irish Press* before becoming editor of the *Sunday Review* (1959–63). That he was the author of the anonymous 'Backbencher' political column was the worst-kept secret in Irish journalism. He brought that column with him to *The Irish Times* in 1963 where he became one of the highest profile reporters and columnists.

2 Donal Foley (1922–81), worked in the London offices of the *Irish Press* and *The Irish Times* before becoming news editor of *The Irish Times* in 1963 and deputy editor in 1977.

3 Launched on 5 September 1931, the paper was the brainchild of Éamon de Valera; he had raised the money, much of it among Irish-Americans and had ensured personal and family control; supportive of Fianna Fáil—partisan rather than propagandist—its arrival in 1931 corrected a gross anti-Fianna Fáil bias in Irish newspapers. Decades before its rivals it had news on its front page and quickly won a reputation for being more than the 'kept paper' of de Valera.

read it and I continued to read it on and off. I read it right through college; through the Army. I actually wrote a few pieces for it when I was in the Army, and approached William Sweetman, the editor, towards the end of the war, would he have a job for me and he said: 'Well, I suppose we have to take some Army fellows in. So we'll give you a month's trial.' And I joined on the day that Seán T. O'Kelly was inaugurated [as President] in June 1945.

J B: You were born in Dublin, but grew up in Belfast, you were educated there and your father was a Belfast man who'd come to Dublin. So the two cities are both home to you. Aren't they?

DG: Yes, indeed. Yes, indeed.

J B: The border, in a sense, is invisible to you.

DG: I just think of myself as an Irishman, whether north or south or east or west.

J B: What was Belfast like growing up as a boy?

DG: Well, we first lived in a house on the edge of green fields, miles of green fields with a couple of lovely little streams running through them. Chaps would come with bird lime to catch linnets or whatever. And I led a rather wild life then. We had a very big garden for some reason. I think somebody had to get out in a hurry. And I enjoyed myself enormously; couldn't even be got to go to school or church for a long while. But my father would come home in the evening and there was always a rumble on. He would say now and then: 'There was a pub burned out in Agnes Street yesterday'; or he would come home and say: 'I was talking to a couple of policemen outside the library; a few shots fired there.' Now this wasn't every week but I remember it constantly through my life there, really until I went to Dublin in 1937 and the link was broken to some extent. But my memory is of Belfast as a potentially violent city. I never saw very much action at all. But if you walked across the city and you weren't known, people would say: 'Who are you looking at? What are you doing here?'

J B: And was there an important teacher in your boyhood?

DG: The whole school was very good, the Belfast Royal Academy as it was called. It started off as the Belfast Academy right down in the city. The headmaster, Alec Foster, a great chap, announced one day to our amazement that Wolfe Tone's brother, Arthur, had spent at least one term in the Academy. And Justice Hanna of the High Court [in Dublin] came to give out the prizes at the annual prize day and he startled all of the parents by saying: 'In my time Irish was very well taught in this school. But it stopped suddenly in 1912'; which was of course the hard year, the Carsonite year. It was altogether a very good school in that most of the people were in business—their fathers and mothers. And if you wanted to work . . . if you had to work hard to get scholarships and wanted to go into the universities which not many did—about one or two a year went into university in those days—they let you coast, go at your own speed; and they gave you great help if you needed it. We had for three or four years as a history teacher, James Beckett. He had just finished his degree and he was working on for a PhD. And he was wonderful, hands in his pockets, walking up and down, university style.

J B: Later professor of Irish history for many years at Queen's University Belfast.

DG: Yes. I don't remember a bad teacher. I don't remember any unpleasantness at all. They were very easy and very good.

J B: Why did you choose Trinity in Dublin rather than Queen's?

DG: Well, I didn't particularly want to stay in Belfast and my mother had always said to me: 'You go back to the Free State. Or whatever you like to call it', back to Dublin.

J B: What did she call it?

DG: Back to Dublin was what she said, I don't think she was particularly politically minded; again the border wasn't prominent in her mind. But she thought that Trinity College was the greatest educational institution in the world. Her brother had been there; her elder brother whom she so admired and who was killed in France. So you go back and take up and make your life in Dublin, which I had intended to do myself.

J B: And did you enjoy those years in Trinity?

DG: Oh, wonderful, particularly the Boat Club. I think it cured me of all my bronchial troubles. Being out there in little skinny vest and shorts with the rain pelting down on you, rowing out as far as Poolbeg Lighthouse sometimes when we were doing a long hard programme. I loved that. And we used to go up on days when there was no rowing and help to paint the boathouse. We then got a licence and we'd have one beer which is all we could afford anyway. And there was a lovely social life. And there were things called 'At Homes', that is small dances at the end of each term which were notable and indeed my wife-to-be was warned off them. Don't go up to it, that's a bad place to go, a rough place, drinking, all sorts of things go on. But she came. She came.

J B: When the war came, you joined the Army. You were in Intelligence in neutral Ireland. What did that entail?

DG: Well, I was very far down the line. When I first joined, they said hold on. When I first applied, hold on. There's a job for you but it's not coming up yet. And they sent down to interview me a chap who had been at school with me, Captain Robert Boyd. He took down all the details. And I said the only use I can be is that I speak German very well. I was studying it at college; I had been there three times for a month or two months as a schoolboy and when I was a student. So they said 'Hold on. We have a job.'

The job turned out to be in the end, German censor in the Curragh, after doing preliminary training. And I had to read the letters coming in to the German internees. And I had to read their letters going out and give a short report each day to the Command Intelligence Officer. I also had to clean out his fire and dust his office. And when I was finishing—it was only for about a four months' stint I think—and when I was finishing, one morning I was down on my hands and knees and ashes all around me, a very smart young man in uniform came in. I think he was a corporal or a sergeant and said: 'Where's the German censor?' And I looked around and said: 'I'm the bloody German censor.' 'Good luck to you, chum!' And went off. It was interesting to read the letters. There were various accounts. They shot this plane out of the sky and that plane out of the sky. And the next fellow told the story accurately what had happened. But anyway . . .

J B: They were permitted to write home provided they gave away no military secrets or anything of strategic or military importance?

DG: And we were trying to see what were they up to in between the lines. And I once had to go down, there was a bad fight and I had to go down and translate for the commanding officer.

J B: And Dan Bryan[4] was your immediate superior.

DG: He was the colonel. He was OC and an awful lot of it was in his head and Fred Boland's head.[5] They seemed to work together. I was invited a couple of times to the Monument Cafe at the top of Grafton Street with the pair of them for tea, six o'clock—not dinner! —we didn't rise to things like that in those days.

J B: But Irish neutrality was substantially benign towards the Allies, wasn't it?

DG: It started out in May of 1940. There's a very good book *Seven*

4 Dan Bryan (1900–85), soldier; director of military intelligence 1941–52.

5 F. H. Boland (1904–85), pioneering diplomat in the Irish foreign service, secretary of department from 1945, ambassador to Britain 1950, Ireland's first permanent representative at the United Nations, 1956; president General Assembly UN 1960.

Assignments by Brigadier Dudley Clarke. He has seven different secret assignments. One of them concerns us; they don't mention Ireland. It's just 'Our friends over there want you.' It's about five or six pages only. But he gives a wonderful picture.

He was told to stand at the staff entrance of the Piccadilly Hotel [in London] and to look as little like a British officer as possible and he would be picked up there. And there was a man waiting for him there who said: 'Yes. You'll do. You don't look the least like a British officer.' They went straight out to Hendon Aerodrome. No formalities. Got onto a plane. Flew over here. Parted. Were to meet next day at a certain hotel. Your man goes to the hotel. Sits there. Waits. And along comes not just his contact but another man with him who said: 'You haven't locked your case. Have you?' 'No.' 'I'll just go up.' And he went up and he came back with a bundle of stuff. And he said: 'You leave your case unlocked and these things will be returned to you when you're going back.'

And Dudley Clarke said: 'I was surprised. Even the laundry marks could have been a giveaway. These men had lived a life where security meant life or death.' And then he talks of two meetings. Again just the friends and he went away with everything sealed up. That's his story and I think it's true.[6]

J B: After the war you joined the Irish Press Group.

DG: Yes.

J B: What was the culture of the Irish Press Group; what was the ethos there in Burgh Quay?

DG: The ethos was to be a very good newspaper. It was a bustling, lively place with endless people—don't call them characters—of intelligence and verve. The joke was that when you went into the *Irish Press* you were told immediately three things: 'Éamon is spelt with one "n". Éamon de Valera. There is no such place as Navan, County Meath, it's *An Uaimh*. There is no such place as Kells, County Meath. It's *Ceannanus Mór*.'[7] You had to be very careful about political things. But basically the number of party members was small.

The journalists came from all over the place. Matt Chambers[8] had come from the north. Donald Smyllie[9] was there before my

---

6 Dudley Clarke *Seven Assignments,* London, 1948.

7 Attempts were made to Gaelicise some town's names, notably Navan as *An Uaimh* and Kells as *Ceannanus Mór* but local popular usage never adopted the Gaelic names.

8 Later news editor of *The Irish Times.*

9 Later chief sub-editor of *The Irish Times.*

time; that's old Bertie Smyllie's brother. They had an American called Carson who was brought in to redo the place again before my time and he had fights with everyone and buzzed off suddenly sending a telegram: 'My address in Paris is so and so, send on my screw [salary cheque].' Amazing people. Geoffrey Coulter a poet, a lovely fellow and Brian O'Neill: they were both foreign sub-editors. And above all, what we would now call the night editor, Arthur Hunter. A lovely man. He did all the work.

But Sweetman the editor I enjoyed immensely; slightly caustic style and his assistant editor was Paddy Kirwan, likewise. They were two barristers. The adversarial thing prevailed. And Sweetman would call for about three or four people each night to bring in their copy and read it out to him. And it's very salutary to read out your copy. And you'd say: 'Oh Jesus, why did I say that?' They listened always in silence. And then Sweetman would say: 'I don't know Kirwan, I think Gageby's got this all wrong.' And Kirwan would say. 'Oh, no, no, no; the beginning is not good.'

J B: And you were in the room?

DG: Yes. You were standing there like an eejit with your copy. And Anna Kelly called them 'Lo and Behold'. Anna Kelly was a great columnist then, a wonderful woman, 'Lo and Behold'. And they'd argue this out. Sometimes forget your presence practically. And then in the end they'd say; 'Kirwan is right; change the beginning there and anyway give it to Hunter, Gageby.'

But Sweetman gave me my best chance. I was going out to Geneva in 1946. Dorothy and I and our young child, and I said: 'I speak German. I had been in Germany before . . . what would it be like if I went into Germany from Switzerland and walked around and met people possibly that I'd known before . . . went to see them and just listened to see what the man in the street is saying?' And Sweetman said: 'Oh, I don't know. Cost an awful lot of money.' And I said: 'I don't know. I've got about £150 from my gratuity. I'll put up the money.' 'Oh no, needn't do that.' But I went. I got by luck an interview with Cardinal von Faulhaber[10] who had had a very hectic stormy career and Sweetman was at once impressed and sent me a note saying 'Stay as long as you like, congratulations and I'm sending money to you.' What he

---

10 *Irish Press* readers were told at the time that Cardinal Michael von Faulhaber (1869–1952), had been archbishop of Munich-Freising from 1917, and that his book *Judaism, Christianity and Germany* defended the principles of racial tolerance and called for respect for the Jewish religion.

didn't know at the time was that the London office anyway was
sending money all the time. Their manager there, Albert Crossley,
was an Englishman and knew that correspondents there had to be
paid for all the time. You had to pay the Foreign Office or
something. But I had a great time.

J B: Germany after the war must have been an astonishing place. . .

DG: It was appalling. It was appalling and I went to see people I'd
known, you see and it was very moving and touching. The first
glasses I ever got were from a German called Rudolf Zade in
Heidelberg. Now I had to go to him at night. He was a friend of
the Tobler family with whom I stayed . . . had to go to him at
night because he wasn't allowed to practice and then I suppose
the person who made the glasses, likewise, worked undercover.
And there were people like that with a half life and Frau Tobler
was very distressed.

Her son, Achim was in the SS—quite high, very high in fact—
had been put in charge of a foreign workers camp down in south
Germany. She didn't like this SS modern business. 'Achim, in these
democratic days, Achim has to go and have a beer now and then
with his men. But one does it, you know.' Anyway I went down
to the French zone where he was in jail and spoke to him. The
prosecutor told me that he wasn't one of the big fish. I never
found out what happened to him. But I talked to him in a corner
of a big room, the man [guard] was over there and I said to him
. . . the first thing I said to him was: 'Achim, what happened?' And
he said: 'That man misled us. That man . . . Hitler, misled us.'

Now he was a very, very bright fellow. He was a doctor of
laws; he had actually travelled a bit before the Nazis came into
power. But that was what he was saying: 'That man misled us.' I
don't know what happened to him later. I wrote to the mother
and said Achim was in good hands and I'd been told by the
prosecutor that he wasn't a major offender; that's all.

But while I was there I went down the country . . . do you
know, people without an income. It's like the time of the inflation
[after the First World War]. They'd go down the country to get
food, bringing their silver and I went down on one expedition
with them to a farmer who was very decent because he gave us a
meal as well. And I had my rucksack and friends had rucksacks
filling it with potatoes and turnips in return for—I've forgotten
what—vases or silver. It was a very painful time and the streets,
(not in Heidelberg because it wasn't touched) but the streets of
Berlin, absolutely, as you see them, like rabbit warrens. Terrible.

J B: When you came into the mainstream *Irish Press*, you were part of the launch of the *Sunday Press* which was very successful commercially; and later in the 1950s of the *Evening Press*, you were first editor of the *Evening Press*.

DG: Yes.

J B: Was that important to you, the challenge of a new frontier, a new title, carving out the market?

DG: Well, I liked it. You see in the *Sunday Press*, Matt Feehan was the editor. He hadn't been in a newspaper at all. Seán Lemass[11] appointed him as a political man to keep these damned fellows straight—myself and Dick Wilks—there were three of us altogether in there. I enjoyed the launch of the Sunday paper, the excitement of it, the fun of it. But, you know, when you're used to daily newspapers to have to wait a week for the paper to come out; it's a bit much. And while I'd been there about three years, I think, Conor Cruise O'Brien[12] came to me and said that the editor of the Irish News Agency—which remember Seán MacBride[13] had set up—was ill, very ill, didn't feel that he could come back as editor; but didn't want to leave the agency. But they were looking for a new editor and I think they had advertised but I was asked would I come. So again I thought, this is a change. I don't know anything about news agencies and you learn a lot. You learn, for example, that one man can sit through the night and put out tens of thousands of words, stuff coming in from everywhere. I enjoyed it very much. And Conor kept the politicians off our backs, he was very good but then the smell of ink . . .

---

11 Seán Lemass (1900–71), 1916 veteran, organising genius of the Fianna Fáil party and its second leader. Taoiseach 1959–66. Managing director of the Irish Press during Fianna Fáil's opposition years from 1948 to 1951, see John Horgan, *Seán Lemass: the enigmatic patriot* (Dublin, 1997), pp. 137–41.

12 Conor Cruise O'Brien (1917–), diplomat, writer, historian, politician; Labour TD 1969–77 and minister for posts and telegraphs 1973–7; as a diplomat was seconded by MacBride to engage in anti-partition propaganda, which he later found a matter 'not for embarrassment but for shame'. For his role with the Irish News Agency, see D. H. Akenson, *Conor: a biography of Conor Cruise O'Brien* (Montreal, 1994), pp. 135–8.

13 Seán MacBride (1904–88), barrister, politician, human rights campaigner. Briefly chief of staff IRA; founder Clann na Poblachta in 1946; led them to win 10 seats in the 1948 general election after which he became foreign minister; established Irish News Agency; co-founder Amnesty International; winner Nobel Peace Prize 1974.

J B: But was that not propaganda really on behalf of the government?

DG: It started off as propaganda but they got hold of Joe Gallagher from PA or Reuters, an Irishman, London born, his father was from Enniskillen, I think. Joe Gallagher said this is all nonsense. It will do the country good just to have a good news agency. And that's what we're doing. And that's what we did. Put out the news. And you could then do feature stuff and say Ireland was wonderful. But the news was the news was the news. Jack Smith had been in Reuters. We got experienced people as well as people like myself who hadn't been in a news agency. All the Dublin papers except *The Irish Times* were against it, unfortunately, because people had valuable correspondencies . . .

J B: They were stringers for other papers and they thought this was pinching their income . . .

DG: Joe wasn't the most diplomatic of people. It could have been worked out, I think, right at the beginning: this is good for the country; good for newspapers in general. I think so.

J B: But you came back, anyway, to the Press Group and the *Evening Press*, big launch and it was a successful paper, wasn't it?

DG: I came back, again by chance. I met Jack Dempsey in London for a few drinks. And he said, you know that we've been trying to get back an evening paper. They'd had one in the early days of the *Irish Press* which collapsed in a few months. Three papers: the natural trio, but it's coming back and Vivion wants to talk to you about it. So will you give us a ring when you get back? So we had a few more drinks, I think. And I thought it over and thought, yes, I would like it. And we couldn't say that the new evening paper was coming out. I was appointed as managing editor, I think—ridiculous title—and all the time Paddy Cregan and myself and advertising people were scurrying around the country setting up offices here and there. I think we had to wait for the annual meeting at the end of June to say that the *Evening Press* was coming out in September but everyone in the country knew it.

J B: What of the whole Palace Bar circle? Were you part of that?

DG: Well, no. It had moved by my time. But I was in the Palace Bar more than once—need I say?—and on one occasion I was there and only Smyllie[14] and myself were there. Smyllie said: 'Come and join me here.' I went over. He said: 'You should be working for

---

14 R. M. Smyllie (1894–1954), legendary editor of *The Irish Times* from 1934; major figure in literary and bohemian Dublin.

us.' And I said: 'No, I shouldn't.' 'What do you mean?' 'I wouldn't like to work for a newspaper composed of Gentlemen and Players.'[15] You know the Trinity graduates sit in here and then go and write their leaders. The men who produce the paper are Alan Montgomery and Noel Fee.' 'Hrgghh.' And he got up and went down to the other end of the place and didn't speak to me for six months. After that he relaxed. Great fellow.

J B: What was your estimate of Smyllie?

DG: He was a good editor, but he didn't realise that there was more to editing a paper than just writing leaders. I don't think he had a great concept of news. I don't think so. Otherwise he would have been bringing in news from more parts of Ireland. He was very much an east coast man, I think; nice fellow; agreeable fellow, full of fun. And he loved talking to Con Leventhal[16] and all these literati. But he wasn't in very good health—he had got very fat—when I knew him then. But he was a likeable, very admirable fellow. The newspaper game had changed. You mentioned a circulation of 30,000. George Hetherington[17] told me often it was much less, which was dangerous. And once the chairman went looking for a loan of £60,000 to re-equip and get new people in and he was just turned down flat. 'No, you mean?' asked the chairman. 'No.'

J B: In what circumstances then were you head-hunted by *The Irish Times,* because you went in there first on the management side, didn't you?

DG: George Hetherington asked me would I come in as managing editor. I said no, I wouldn't move unless I was put on the board. So he came back later and said 'Okay. I'm managing director. Most of my time is spent on Hely's different businesses. Come in as joint managing director anyway.'

---

15 A cutting remark since it refers to the practice then prevalent in many sports—cricket was a prime example—whereby the leadership and captaincy was entrusted to an amateur, a Gentleman, and the professionals were known as Players and used the tradesman's entrance to the clubhouse—if they were permitted in at all!

16 A. J. 'Con' Leventhal (1896–1979), Trinity don and writer, friend of Samuel Beckett.

17 Managing director of The Irish Times Ltd. Nephew by adoption of the newspaper's long-time chairman, Frank Lowe, who was head of the Hely's printing business. See Tony Gray, *Mr Smyllie, Sir* Dublin, 1991, *passim.*

I would like to have come in as editor but there you are. But that came about because in trying to build up the paper we hadn't enough money. We weren't sufficiently well organised for a real fight. And then Tom McDowell came in as business advisor, and then he decided and the board decided that it would be a good thing if he stayed on. So he stayed on as managing director, sole managing director. I took over the editorship because, fortuitously, Alan Montgomery[18] who was then editor was put on the board of a Guinness appointment committee for PRO, I think. And at the end of it they hadn't got anyone and Montgomery said: 'Well, the money's pretty good, so I'll take it if you'd have me.' So he was gone. It was wonderful; a miracle. I suppose. And I stepped into the editorship.[19]

J B: Now *The Irish Times* at this stage was a declining newspaper; it possibly was in terminal decline. It had 30,000 circulation, seen as an ex-unionist paper, Protestant paper, Anglo-Irish. It could be said that its circulation declined each morning by the length of its death column; that may be harsh.

DG: It is harsh. It was a good paper.

J B: But it wasn't commercially successful.

DG: It was a good paper; it was always a good newspaper. But it was under-funded and it was largely east-coast oriented and the first thing we did to move it—apart from getting some more money out of the banks—was to say this is going to be a 32-county paper; and one of the first things we did was to open an office in Belfast. We had a very good correspondent there but he worked at nights and could only send us stuff at night because he was working for the *News Letter* . . . very good fellow. But we opened an office and Fergus Pyle[20] was the first man there, I think. We said there are two parliaments sitting in this country, in this island; it may be nonsense that's talked up in Stormont but we're going to report it as we do the Dáil. And it is said that Fergus Pyle's accounts of the Stormont debates were longer than

---

18 Alan Montgomery was *Irish Times* editor from 1961 to 1963 when he was appointed chief information officer for Ireland with the Guinness Group.

19 See 'Bright, brilliant days' by Andrew Whittaker in this book for another interpretation.

20 Fergus Pyle, former Northern Ireland and European editor, edited *The Irish Times*, 1974–7.

Hansard. I don't know if that's true.[21] So we thought at first will people want to go and stay in the Belfast office. There was a queue. It was fascinating; because it was smaller then, the city. And everyone was easily reached, civil servants and politicians. Eileen O'Brien from Galway—mad about the place; Henry Kelly was there, two years and I think we had to take him out because there were some veiled threats made against him. It was a roaring success.

J B: But in the 1960s, Ireland was opening up; Lemass was in government; the Vatican Council was in session; you had John Horgan reporting the Vatican Council . . .

DG: Wonderful.

J B: The paper was becoming essential reading in a way that a lot of people hadn't read it before: isn't that so?

DG: Don't forget the opening up towards the west. John Healy, Mick Foy. The whole idea of the west being on the move and then we moved down to the south; it was a 32-county paper. That's what we kept saying to ourselves: and it was to reflect that in its reporting.

J B: And how do you think you turned its fortunes round?

DG: Well, we turned it round because we had splendid writers; we were a great community. A good newspaper is a community. And Donal Foley was an inspirational news editor. He was very much a *gaelgeoir* and he brought that side up too. But he also had a good eye for people. He picked Maeve Binchy for example. Mary Maher was there. Donal had a great eye for people and got on so well with them. He was a wonderful man. And a great deal of the success of *The Irish Times* was due to Donal.

J B: And what's the function of the editor in your view? What's your definition of a good editor?

DG: My definition of an editor is a fellow who sits on his backside in a chair and edits the paper. I used to say I was paid to edit the paper not to be the editor. At first it's a bit of fun to go round to these dinners and what not . . . after a while it's a waste of time. You're editing . . . I don't know how many millions of words

---

21 This could not be literally true since Hansard is a full record of the proceedings of parliament and *The Irish Times* could only report a news summary of the most significant exchanges. What seems more likely is that where the Hansard account took refuge in 'Interruptions' purporting not to have heard some of the more controversial heckles and interruptions, Pyle reported what had actually been said in the Stormont chamber.

must pass through the hands of any editor, I don't know.

J B: You then left for three years, Fergus Pyle took over. That wasn't a success, for whatever reasons. And you came back in.

DG: I was called back in, yes. I came back in 1977, had left in 1974.

J B: So had you thought that you would retire and look to other pastures.

DG: I was going to look for other things. One thing that came up was Louis Marcus. I did a series of six one-hour programmes on the heritage of Ireland.

J B: Television films.

DG: And I was working quite hard then with a group called Journalists in Europe, in Paris, run by a man called . . . I was going to say Beuve-Méry . . . he was just one of them. But anyway, I was very involved there. Philippe Vienney asked to see some of these and I showed him two of them.[22] And he said, 'I have friends in Brussels'; he had friends everywhere because of the old Resistance circle, he had been head of a Resistance group. 'I have friends in Brussels who think that the EEC'—as it then was, I think—'isn't getting the right sort of publicity. Could you apply that to the heritage of Europe.' So we were considering that at the time when I got a call. I was in Helsinki, at the time. Tom McDowell saying: 'Been thinking over what I said to you two days ago? Will you come back now?' So I came back.

J B: Was it difficult to come back in?

DG: No. It wasn't.

J B: Had you missed it?

DG: I had missed it, of course, yes, of course. But it was thought then that at the age of 55, all the business people were saying: 'At age 55 it's time to change course.' A daft idea. But I called a shout-in the first day I came back for all the editorial staff and anyone else who wanted to come.[23] And that's the beauty of a good newspaper that not only the editorial staff but the commercial staff, the circulation people, the fellows from the works, they all have a hand in it, you know. I used to like that at night, going off and you'd pass through the case-room. And the man in the box

---

22 Hubert Beuve-Méry (1902–89) was the legendary editor of *Le Monde* from its founding in 1944 to 1969. Journalists in Europe, a Paris-based organisation dedicated to encourage greater understanding of European politics among journalists.

23 A shout-in was when Gageby stood on a chair in the newsroom and invited all-comers to question or even denounce the management's policies.

would say: 'Good paper today.' And he meant lots of ads in it. Then you'd go down past the engravers. They'd similarly have something to say to you. And into the machine room; and Tommy Butler saying: 'Why the hell didn't you have it five minutes earlier?' Similarly going through where they were slapping the papers together, in the despatch. A few words of raillery from them. And then the poor fellows in the lorries: 'It's all very well for you up in your nice warm office.' It was a wonderful community. Everyone knew everyone else. I loved that about it. All the papers I worked on. It's a wonderful 'here we go' spirit.

A lot depends on the men at the top. Vivion de Valera [at the Irish Press Group] was very good to me. He gave me a letter at the beginning, saying 'I'm editor-in-chief.' So I said: 'I thought I was going to run this paper.' 'That's a formality, has to be gone through in the board. I'll never interfere with you.' And once he came through the newsroom, once in the five years, and it was one of the outbreaks in the North and it was the lead story and there was an off-lead story. And he said: 'hmph'; he was in a bad temper that day: 'Is that the best story you have for a lead?' 'Yes.' John O'Donovan said: 'Yes, by far the best story.' Jack Smith said 'Yes.' Silence. 'Are you telling us to change it?' I asked. And he humped off. And he rang from home and said: 'I'm sorry. I promise you I'll never do that again.' He was very good about that.

J B: And was Éamon de Valera a presence at all? Even if . . . I don't mean physically, but was he a *presence* in the Irish Press Group?

DG: He never rang me when I was there. I never met him. I never met him or had a word passed down to me from him. Vivion took over, you see. He came in just after Lemass and took over. I was quite happy with Vivion. And I think I told you earlier that when I was half way through the *Evening Press* and he'd known me for 15 years—actually I'd known him in the Army and done a job or two for him—he said suddenly, driving me home: 'Doug, that's what he called me, Doug are you with us? Or did we merely hire your sword?' I thought it was a gorgeous concept, hiring my sword.

J B: And your reply was?

DG: I said: 'I'm pretty well with you or I wouldn't have joined the *Irish Press*, 10, 15 years ago.'

J B: Yet if you look back on your career, the Irish Press Group has collapsed from being the leading Sunday paper, the leading evening paper. Both faded, and fell; and the *Irish Press* has folded.

And the group is gone.

DG: Terrible. Terrible.

J B: What are your thoughts on that?

DG: It's a hell of a shame and I don't know how that could have happened. And I don't know anything about that. But to go from the top to the bottom so fast, appalling, appalling. And it can't be entirely management and it can't be journalists. I just don't know. I miss it greatly, I must say. I miss it greatly.

J B: It's partly the market niche it had, too; isn't that so? Partly that and the way it filled that niche, and changing Ireland.

DG: Well, I think it was moving with the times. Tim Pat [24] was the last editor, wasn't he? Or second last editor. Tim Pat was very much with the times, very much. I was succeeded by Conor O'Brien [25] and then Tim Pat. I regret it because I had wonderful times there, wonderful times in all newspapers. It's a great life. You should try it, John.

J B: Broadly what changes do you reckon you've seen in Ireland over the past 50, indeed 60, years?

DG: Well, everyone seems to be a millionaire at the moment. And the house price thing is absolutely ludicrous. Daft, isn't it? I think it's very tough on young people setting out now, very tough indeed. In the past we didn't have money. For example from the *Irish Press* I walked home every night, bar there was two feet of snow, with two or three other people, Mick Brady a reader, Billy Holland, a printer; we'd walk up all the way to Rathgar, wouldn't see a soul, not a light in a shop. And look at it now, millionaires right left and centre. I don't feel out of it; I wouldn't know what to do with a million.

J B: But the social changes you've seen?

DG: Oh, enormous. I mean the universities are crammed full. It's incredible to walk through UCD or Trinity now. I don't know: is there such a thing as over-education. No? I suppose not in such a changing world. I'm, anyway, behind the times. I still have a portable typewriter and I work on it. And I can use fax but I can't . . . I have to get the grandchildren in from next door to fix various things for me.

J B: You don't use a computer?

DG: I don't use a computer. I was given one when I left but after 40 years of this, [mimes typing] I found I couldn't use its delicate touch.

24 Tim Pat Coogan was editor of the *Irish Press* from 1968 to 1987.

25 Conor O'Brien, later editor of the *Sunday Independent*. Not to be confused with Conor Cruise O'Brien.

J B: You need to hear the clickety clack, do you?

DG: Yes. And I've been asked several times to go into *The Irish Times* newsroom now; and it's all silent. And I said no, unless there's noise and dirt and paper all over the place, I'll leave it. Anyway once you're out, you're out, you know.

'Y'

Michael Viney

It was back in the 1980s that a cigar box arrived in the post. Inside, cushioned in damp moss, a dozen germinating acorns were sprouting their root-tips, ivory-white. The box was from Douglas Gageby, my editor for most of 20 years and a man who planted trees. 'Trees, trees, it's always trees,' he agreed, throwing in a quote from Walter Scott: 'When ye hae nothing else to dae, ye may be aye sticking in a tree. It will be growing when ye're sleeping.'

There were actually a pair of them—Gageby the hard-pressed, magisterial editor and John Healy or 'Backbencher', the acerbic, sometimes calculatedly uncouth, political columnist. They could seem a journalistic odd couple: one a quizzical Belfast Protestant and Trinity graduate, the other a professedly hard-nosed chaw from small-town Mayo. Part of the bond was that they really loved nature: it brought perspective to their work and gave them respite from its pressures. Through many political crises, what *The Irish Times* thought about things was distilled as the two men fished for trout on a midland lake or river.

'He had a broad view of life,' wrote Gageby of Healy, 'and trees became almost a passion with him.' Both men picked up seeds wherever they went—a Healy oak from Strasbourg shares my acre with the cigar-box dozen, while Douglas stuffed his pockets with wayside seeds in Provence. His stone pines now, in Co. Meath, bear cones as big as oranges.

The John Healy Forest Park, near Charlestown, commemorates the Mayoman's improbable tree-hugging, along with his totally unsentimental book, *Nineteen Acres*. Douglas Gageby has no such public memorial. While Jean Giono's mythical *Man Who Planted Trees* grew a forest by dropping acorns into holes prodded with his walking stick, Douglas's forest is all the thousands of trees planted by readers he prodded, for 15 years, with his daily corner-piece on the letters to the editor page.

The idea of 'In Time's Eye' was born when Healy and himself were fishing on the lovely River Borora, in Meath's Moynalty parish. A string of seven or eight hares ran across their green horizon—a remarkable sight. 'We should note that,' said Healy.

The title of the corner-piece came from Kipling:

Cities and Thrones and Powers
Stand in Time's eye
Almost as long as flowers
Which daily die.

Few readers, probably, caught the deeper message; even fewer knew who was writing the musing, colloquial commentaries on nature, signed simply 'Y', the last letter of his last name—all of a piece with his refusal to write in the first person.

This corner did, of course, have many more interests than trees. It found time to read widely: *The Countryman, Field, Country Life, Horticulture Week, The Dendrologist* (trees again), *Le Chasseur Français* from Douglas's beloved France. He was a dedicated foodie for things natural: honey, mushrooms, quinces, mulberries—herbs, above all.

> To make a lively salad you should add about a handful of good, spicy stuff. Say a mixture of winter savory (the king of them all, and an all-the-year-rounder), chervil, parsley, woodruff, salad burnet, borage, lovage, hyssop and some weaker element like lemon balm. . . Then, when some guest rolls a mouthful of salad around and asks just what the flavour is, you have a whole conversation in front of you. If they don't ask, you need not have them back.

He was a watcher of blackbirds and urban foxes ('How lightly they step across your lawn, forelegs lifted as elegantly as trotting ponies or those schooled horses from Vienna (Lippizaners, is it?).') The blitz against badgers could provoke a flash of anger: 'How long will it take us to work through and kill them all? And what animal comes next for the slaughter?' The assaults on our rivers by arterial drainage are followed now by fish kills from farm pollution. Talk of 'complete restocking' of a river was nonsense, said Douglas: the blow was to 'a whole unseen universe' of water life.

In all this, 'Y' occasionally gave way to 'H'—John Healy, watching hen-harriers in winter, perched on Achill fence-posts, or giving tips on casting flies upon the weedy rivers of July. To read *In Time's Eye* now (a collection was published by Town House in 2001) is to mourn the seeming lack of any personal feeling for nature at any level among Ireland's people of power.

In all the years of working for Douglas Gageby, I remained largely shy or in awe of him. His predecessor, Alan Montgomery, had a laid-back affability that was to make him a perfect fit as PRO for Guinness. Douglas's presence was immediately more challenging, with a depth and authority quite independent of any need to be liked. His cultural background seemed singularly distant from my own experience (in England, the gap could have felt like one of class). We had flashes of warmth and common feeling about nature and the Irish landscape, but these were rarely timely for corridor encounters or editorial conferences.

In the first years of his editorship, however, he gave me extraordinary freedom as a feature writer to pursue the kind of time-consuming social inquiry that, reared on the *New Statesman* and *New Society*, seemed to be my métier at that time.

I had spent a winter in Connemara in 1961, a writing-and-painting sabbatical from Fleet Street that edged into a strong desire to settle in Ireland. Lemass and Whitaker between them had sparked a sense of national emergence and self-scrutiny that I found exciting. Ireland seemed of the right size and intimacy for the kind of inquiring journalism ('investigative' now carries too much baggage) that might actually contribute to the way in which the country developed.

For Douglas, an outsider's eye may have seemed an asset in steering the newspaper into mainstream Ireland (an early series, 'Last Chance for the Language?' gave an opportunity for the first-ever *Irish Times* street poster in Irish). In 1964 he sent me to wander through the North: an assignment that, happily, 'discovered' Derry's John Hume for Dublin. But mostly I picked my own topics and took my time—sometimes six weeks or more—to research and write a multi-part feature series running to many thousands of words. Both parameters seemed distinctly shocking to Donal Foley, as news editor, for whom 1,500 words were more than enough to say anything that mattered.

Single mothers (then 'unmarried'), young offenders, the mentally ill, the alcoholic, the drug-addicted—so many of my subjects can sound wearily familiar today. But in the Ireland of the 1960s, where most academic sociology was bounded by the papal encyclicals, such researches often amounted to the raw material of social science; this was all a new approach. Reprinted in booklets, the series became student texts. They brought Catholic affairs and institutions into *The Irish Times* and its letter columns, and helped to show (I hope) the newspaper's determination to be fair. A series on Protestants in the Republic, 'The Five Per Cent', proved uncomfortable for many in that community, but Douglas, reading my copy, found it 'Great stuff!', which set me up for days.

He was less prepared, however, (and probably rightly) to trust my judgment about politics, always his central preoccupation. Even in the 1960s, the Haughey lifestyle evoked intense gossip. I rashly suggested that, with six months' assistance from a solicitor and an accountant, I might arrive at something safe to print, but Douglas rather doubted this. My attempt at a biographical series on Haughey was taken away by him and John Healy and largely rewritten by them: it must have seemed very naive.

Later, and with Douglas's assent, I reinvented myself as economic development correspondent. My hope was to bring entrepreneurial ideas and people into the news pages, the arena of daily life. But no, they 'belonged' in the business pages, to be read by businessmen. Eventually, tempted by money, I was recruited as director of public communications with the Irish Management Institute. This landed me in limbo in the corporate parkland of the suburbs, and within a year, upon the death of the splendid Lionel Fleming, I came back as environment correspondent. 'I never try to keep anybody,' Douglas had said when I went, but he knew a prodigal son when he saw one.

And there I've probably hit it: he was my father figure. I sensed when he was in the house, or gone away, was lifted by his excitement and scared by his glooms or bad temper. But the prodigal habit persisted. When we met one morning in Grafton Street in 1977, a few weeks before the Viney family went west, I had left him again a year before, to train as producer/director with Radio Telefís Éireann.

'Are you really going?' he challenged now. 'You won't be back in six months?' And then, generously: 'Write a column for us.'

'Another Life', initially a chronicle of self-sufficient misadventure, has paid the basic bills for almost 30 years. It was almost a decade old when 'In Time's Eye' began to appear on the letters page. When I discovered who was writing it, the distinctive style fell at once into place: tersely confident, idiomatic, not a word wasted—unliterary in the best sense and immediately engaging. Its determined anonymity (last letter of his last name) and avoidance of 'I' could make me feel quite embarrassed for my own first-person confessions.

Douglas's gift of acorns seemed like a present from home. The oaks that grew from them are as high as the wood-shed, and just now, in early spring, I wait on their bud-burst and canopy of green-gold leaves. In a muggy western summer they dust over with mildew, which doesn't look as pleasing. But: 'Mildew must be part of the scheme of things,' as Douglas reminded us. 'Be grateful that you have oaks, and growing well. They are survivors.'

Douglas Gageby and a liberal republican ideal

Martin Mansergh

'Liberal' is not the association that immediately springs to mind in connection with Irish republicanism in most of its manifestations. Volunteer professional armies of a democratic state are not merely compatible with, but help sustain, a liberal political order. Volunteer militias that helped to bring that state into being in the course of a national independence struggle with popular legitimation, exercised a discipline and ruthlessness that was minded to leave liberalism till later. Modern paramilitaries without that legitimation, having invested themselves with a metaphysical quasi-state authority, while in reality being an anonymous and unaccountable military junta, without recognition of established democratic institutions or procedures, are the antithesis of liberal democracy, though they may claim to aspire to it under their own conditions eventually.

Even in a purely political and democratic context, 'liberal' is a description that may arouse suspicion and hostility, and be an accolade that many politicians would prefer to avoid, even where it might be well deserved. In American Republican politics, to describe a person or party policy as liberal is not a recommendation, but rather an indictment intended to be politically damaging. As a result, most Democrats even are chary of the label.

In Ireland, some members of Fianna Fáil the Republican Party might be happier to describe themselves or be described as socialist than as liberal. Particularly in the past 25 years, liberal has been taken as applying primarily to one side of the socio-moral debate, those in favour of permissive legislation in relation to contraception, divorce, legalisation of homosexuality and civil partnerships, integrated if not secular education, and even in some cases the right to choose, with reference to abortion. While it has been claimed that, with legislation long since enacted in many of these areas that disregards the preferred norms of the Catholic Church, the liberal agenda is substantially complete, it is more the case that most remaining fences are too steep at present to be jumped. In the case of Fianna Fáil, which prefers to move forward by consensus rather than by ideological confrontation, there is in most cases no enthusiasm to jump them, or any particular belief in the desirability of doing so.

That is why the question of an alliance with the Liberal Group in the European Parliament, which might have had something to recommend it in terms of being a substantive pan-European political alliance, even if of less importance than the two main groupings in the European Parliament, the Christian Democrats and the Socialists, met with such a negative response from most of the party's MEPs before and after the elections of 2004. It was agreed that they could not promote or defend themselves on the doorsteps as 'liberals', the word conjuring up the image that they might be pro-abortion or in favour of embryonic stem-cell research and gay marriages.

Paradoxically, most European liberals belong in fact to quite right-wing and conservative parties, especially in relation to economic policy. The British Liberal Democrats are a notable exception who, being more observable from here, would have much more influence on Irish public opinion.

The use of the term 'neo-liberal' to describe Thatcherite and pro-globalisation and privatisation policies does not make the original term any more attractive.

If one points out to a politician realities that contradict or run counter to the routine rhetoric currently in use, he or she is apt to reply that that may very well be, but they have to deal with public perceptions.

II

Within Protestantism in Ireland, there are two political traditions, and in recent decades probably three, the third being the largely apolitical both North and South. This is not a reference to the different denominations, beginning with Presbyterian and Church of Ireland, nor to contrasts in cultural tradition between Anglo-Irish and Ulster-Scots. It is a political, not a religious or cultural, distinction.

Much of the history of Ireland since the time of the Reformation can be viewed as a struggle for hegemony between minority and majority in the island as a whole, but latterly concentrated in Northern Ireland, where in 1920–1 majority and minority changed places, giving unionist resistance to incorporation into a united Ireland for the first time a plausible democratic justification. For 50 years, the bulk of each community had the part of Ireland where their strength was greatest largely to themselves, politically speaking, despite very different demographic situations. The small minority in the South posed few real obstacles compared to what might have been posed by a more substantial one in the island as a whole. For other reasons, the much larger minority in the North until the late 1960s, potentially and in the end a much larger obstacle, did not for a long time get much in the way of unionist one-party rule.

Historically, Protestantism divided politically between those determined as far as possible to maintain the conquest, at least in its most basic essentials, not excluding some limited form of political accommodation, and those who had the vision of a united people and of the potential strength that this would give to the country as a whole and all sections of it.

Douglas Gageby was inspired by and a proselytiser for the ideals of an inclusive nationalism, as expressed by the United Irishmen, William Drennan, Wolfe Tone and Jemmy Hope; the 'new light' Presbyterianism that lost out by 1840; Thomas Davis; Parnell; the Literary Revival; and Northerners, like Samuel Ferguson and the Rev. J. B. Armour.

Ulster unionism post-1968, struggling to survive a heavy and unexpected onslaught, was not disposed to listen, even assuming his message reached them. He may on the other hand have provided valuable support and encouragement for constitutional nationalism, also struggling to survive against atavistic revolutionary forces. His editorials certainly contributed an idealistic, feel-good factor to the renewed and enforced Southern engagement with the North, but sadly missed its real target almost as much as the sterner rhetoric of earlier official anti-partition campaigns.

The outbreak of the Troubles, coming on top of a cautious ecumenical rapprochement, helped bring Southern society closer together and out of its earlier post-colonial mode. Southern Protestants, with some possible exceptions close to the border, identified with their Catholic fellow-citizens in the South rather than their co-religionists in the North, and distanced themselves from the injustices of Stormont and the bigotry of Paisley and loyalist and Orange manifestations. This largely apolitical small minority did not necessarily become strongly nationalist, but identified their interests more firmly with the South, to which they belonged.

Though in adult life very much of this state, Douglas Gageby brought with him from his background in the North and his early career in the South an intellectual and ideological framework that both preceded and transcended a partitioned Ireland.

The Irish Times, which had been evolving since R. M. Smyllie's editorship from being a newspaper for a mainly Protestant and ex-unionist readership, moved centre stage, and transformed itself into a national newspaper in the full sense of the term, despite some mild old-guard resistance. Indeed, it could be argued that the best fate for minority institutions in the South is in many cases to expand their mission and serve the people as a whole, even if in so doing their original character has to be transformed.

A meal has been made by a left-wing school of thought of an offer of assistance by *Irish Times* chairman and shareholder Major T. B. McDowell to the British ambassador in 1969 (only revealed in 1999), where he complained that his editor had gone native. Douglas Gageby more than once expressed utter contempt for British Intelligence, and there is not the slightest evidence that he was deflected from his editorial line by any intervention by McDowell.

Unionism survived the Troubles. Their ability to manage the peace still remains to be seen. The Provisional IRA campaign left Protestant nationalism in the North virtually stone-dead. In the South, the emphasis was more on liberalism and pluralism rather than nationalism, with the driving force coming from an influential and more liberal section of the majority Catholic community, with *The Irish Times* constituting itself its champion. As time went by, it became less and less necessary to invoke hypothetical unity arguments or references to the supposed views of Northern Protestants, who are in fact very evenly divided between liberal and conservative camps on moral issues, to justify change.

III

Douglas Gageby in retirement wrote a biography published in 1999 of his father-in-law Seán Lester, a Northern Protestant who joined the independence movement, later becoming a diplomat. He subsequently became the last secretary-general of the League of Nations organisation, which tried and failed to stop the overrunning of mainly small new independent countries by Fascist Italy and Nazi Germany, which in August 1939 enlisted the collaboration till 1941 of the Soviet Union. In March 1939, with the elimination of Czechoslovakia, Lester wrote: 'It is sickening to see a decent little country wiped off the map. And without a blow. Freedom shrieks again.' In one *Irish Times* editorial in 1969, thinking back to this time, Gageby wrote that Derry was known around the world better than Danzig in the pre-television age where his father-in-law served as League of Nations High Commissioner from 1934 to 1936.

Lester, having observed and dealt with the Nazis at close quarters, had the clear view at the outbreak of war that 'the Nazis must be beaten, if there is to be any decency in such life and civilisation as may survive'. Equally, however, he supported Ireland's decision to remain neutral. He wrote of the 'American note' of February 1944 from the

US and British governments, which demanded the immediate closure of the German and Japanese missions in Dublin: 'It might be a pity, but it was true that the Irish had not learned to accept ultimata. There is nothing there of the spirit of Denmark.' He took the view that to have entered the war Ireland 'would in the circumstances have been doing something utterly exceptional and amazingly generous and heroic', in contrast to the abject failure of larger powers to uphold collective security from 1935 to 1939. Indeed, his retrospective comment in 1945 that 'the League did not fail; it was the nations which failed to use it' has a contemporary ring to it, particularly when large powers criticise the United Nations. It was a new situation at the outbreak of war for Britain to have an independent Ireland as a friendly neutral on its flank, and he considered that there was a close identity of interests. Lester's position, which he spelt out privately in detail, represents a reconciliation of viewpoints. Despite having little choice but to remain neutral, Ireland's interest was in the Nazis losing the war. Gageby's views were probably heavily influenced by his father-in-law and were virtually identical.

Gageby, who was engaged in Army Intelligence (G2) in the Second World War, later regarded Irish neutrality as an act of self-preservation by a country not even two decades independent, even if (very debatably) a possibility of unity had been missed. He understood the security of the state, and was not as indignant about the censorship, which he briefly helped to exercise on the letters of German prisoners, as Smyllie, one of his illustrious predecessors, had been. Gageby once referred to the American minister during the war, David Gray, as having probably, among American envoys to Ireland, 'the highest profile as a disturber of the peace, but wartime censorship may have spared us the worst of it'. Gageby shocked his admirers when he admitted that he would probably not have published the stories about the Garda 'heavy gang' in the mid-1970s.

Gageby supported UN peacekeeping missions, and, in his opening editorial for 1966, the 50th anniversary year of the Rising, urged that the state not evade its responsibilities under the Charter. A few months later, he made the point: 'We are not likely to become an international busybody, but we could still be more aware of the world around us.'

Working in G2 probably gave him a greater awareness of the considerable identity of interest between Britain and Ireland, even during the Second World War, despite the more public political stand-offs over neutrality.

Irish foreign policy, even though operating now in a mainly European Union context, is still based on the principles of liberal internationalism, with its emphasis on the rule of international law, collective security, and the exercise of 'soft power', political and economic, but with a pragmatic recognition that force, particularly when sanctioned by the UN, may sometimes be necessary as a last resort.

IV

Douglas Gageby stood by the Republic. Long before the Proclamation was read out on the steps of the GPO in 1916, it was a republic conceived at McArt's fort on the Cave Hill overlooking Belfast in May 1795, where Wolfe Tone, just before leaving for America, took a solemn obligation with his friends Thomas Russell, Samuel Neilson, Robert Simms and Henry Joy McCracken 'never to desist in our efforts until we had subverted the authority of England over our country and asserted her independence'.

Gageby was strongly critical of those who had misread Tone's famous dictum, putting all the emphasis on the end, but entirely ignoring the means, which was to unite the whole people of Ireland, and 'substitute the common name of Irishman in place of the denominations of Protestant, Catholic and Dissenter'. Instead, the means was downgraded from an essential to a by-product of achieving the end in modern republican ideology, which of course was never going to work. Gageby was equally keen on Davis' pluralism of race, religion and culture. Arguably, Davis was a closet republican. Gageby heartily endorsed Parnell's statement, 'we cannot afford to give up a single Irishman.' He would make no concessions to the two-nations theory. He deprecated in 1969 voices in Dublin referring to 'our own people' in the North: 'The right view in all cases is in the old republican tradition as set out again in the phrase "cherishing all the children of the nation equally". Note cherishing, not just recognising.'

As editor of *The Irish Times*, Gageby was not bound to party. He supported critically those who did the most to fulfil his ideals at any particular point in time. His conception of republicanism was firm but liberal, inclusive, in no way racist, xenophobic or sectarian, and based on the belief that British–Irish relations would be best served by Ireland being a self-governing country on an equal footing to Britain. He quoted Bulmer Hobson, a founder of the Irish Volunteers, on the success that the Dutch people had made of Holland, despite their more limited space.

He appreciated de Valera as someone who had 'stood firmly on the honourable non-sectarian platform', and who had shown consistency and steel, when required. In certain fundamentals, he would have been close to Fianna Fáil up to the end of the 1960s. Gageby's republicanism included a much greater public role for women. In the pursuit of the liberal agenda he would have passed the baton in the 1980s to Garret FitzGerald and even the PDs at their foundation, before finding its champion in President Mary Robinson.

He praised Brian Lenihan for reforming the censorship ban. He contrasted former diplomat F. H. Boland's appointment as chancellor of Dublin University with the 'pathetic' ban of Archbishop McQuaid on Catholics attending Trinity, though adding that Protestants should not waste their time on affairs not strictly of their own agency. He greatly approved the Lemass–O'Neill meetings, but by 1969 was critical of the government's lack of preparedness and familiarity with the North.

While sympathetic to attempts to modernise militant republicanism in the late 1960s, he deplored the arson attacks on German-owned farms, which had echoes of 'the infamous Kristallnacht', commenting that 'the socialist-republican bigot is no more useful to Ireland than the Orange bigot or any other bigot'.

While he could understand the nationalist need for self-defence in 1969, his heart was with the civil rights movement and the leader who came out of it, John Hume, whom he supported through thick and thin as the nearest embodiment of his constitutional republican ideal. In 1981, he argued that 'the IRA will not blow the unionists out of it, no matter how many policemen they may kill'. But equally unionists would fail to persuade any considerable number of Catholic nationalists in the North that their future must lie outside an independent Ireland.

He welcomed the constitutional crusade, cheering, 'Hurrah for Garret FitzGerald', adding that for a long time Fianna Fáil had stood as the party that most nearly approached the ideals of Tone and Davis.

He supported the Anglo-Irish Agreement, but was also conscious of how far away it left the goal of Irish unity and how far short it was of a serious political settlement. 'It may be dawning on us that perhaps all our expectations of movement towards the national goal have been too optimistic in terms of time span. We have allowed politicians to go on talking as if unity were something on which we might stumble or have suddenly thrust upon us.' It was depressing to have to ask: 'Do no unionists or Protestants feel that a further opening of doors, notably eastwards towards Europe and southwards towards Dublin, can be not only spiritually satisfying to nationalists but even something of a liberation for ourselves?' Unionist reaction to the Agreement was even more dispiriting: 'One of the saddest things for Ireland, and not just for the North, is the fact that leadership of the Protestant people in the Six Counties seems to have been taken over by hysterics.' He protested:

'Must the North be permanently ghettoized . . . ?' but conceded that 'for the first time, Irish nationalism is aligned with sectarianism through the actions of the Provisionals.'

His editorship ended on a fairly bleak and disillusioned note at the end of 1986. The following decade would see considerable liberal advances, and also the advent of a peace process, that was in broad conformity with pluralist republican ideals. While his editorials on the North fell on stony ground as far as unionism was concerned, he helped foster and support a strong democratic consensus in the South linked to the SDLP in the North based on a liberal republicanism which does not find complete expression in any one political party, but which is one of the inspirations of the Good Friday Agreement.

Financial and production constraints in *The Irish Times* of the late 1960s

Derek McCullagh

Are you mad?—was one of the milder questions addressed to me when I told my friends in early 1968 that I was leaving my job as assistant accountant in the Merchants' Warehousing Company to join *The Irish Times* as accountant.

The Irish Times was a company just about keeping its head above water, not very profitable even in its better years and having survived the trauma of closing down publication of the *Evening Mail* and the *Sunday Review*. Nevertheless my brief earlier encounters with it when I was assigned there as junior audit assistant had sparked a fascination for the newspaper and I accepted the job after Louis O'Neill rang me one morning and asked me to have a coffee with him in Bewley's. I had seen when working on the audit of the circulation figures that they had started to rise following the appointment of Douglas Gageby as editor and had reached the dizzy heights of 37,000 a day after many years of languishing in the low 30,000s. I was hopeful.

The year 1968 marked a considerable change in the Irish Times—the use of a computer bureau to process monthly statements for customers, the start of the 'Tele-ad' sales department to do the unthinkable and actually sell classified advertising for the first time, new non-contributory pension and life assurance schemes throughout the company, the first posting of a staff correspondent in Europe when Dermot Mullane went to Paris in time for the riots of that summer, increases in circulation, which now rose into the 40,000s. A new group of senior managers had been appointed by the managing director, Major T. B. McDowell—Louis O'Neill to the traditional position of 'manager', Brian Dawson in charge of advertising and Colm Campbell in charge of production.

I had to learn fairly quickly the routines of accounting in a newspaper. I recall vividly the experience a few days after I joined of meeting Donal Foley, the news editor, for the first time to discuss budgets—not a topic for which he had a great deal of time or interest.

At the time we had a basic though workable system of budgeting which produced quarterly accounts. It was a couple of years later that Pat Gillen of PA Management Consultants came in to help us to set up a modern system of monthly reporting, which set a base for the systems which worked for many years. Irrespective of the system the preparation of budgets and the monitoring of monthly accounts remained a tug-of-war between departments and accountants, which generally ended in a draw.

The growth in circulation in the late 1960s and early 1970s, combined with a phenomenal growth in advertising, both on the news pages and in the newly developed classified pages, brought increased profitability. The paper grew in size with increased editorial content and the additional advertising, making for papers of a minimum of 18 pages up to the maximum possible of 32 pages, compared with a range from 14 to 22 a few years earlier. The mini economic boom of the early 1970s resulted in profits for the three years 1971–3 totalling £1 million—unheard of prosperity.

In April 1974 the formation of the Irish Times Trust was announced. I will not try to add to the acres of space filled by various pundits on this subject except to say that it achieved its primary objective—the independence of *The Irish Times* by insulating it from a predatory takeover which would almost certainly have happened without it.

Through the winter of 1973–4 we had endured long queues for petrol with the Gulf crisis but it seemed to have little effect on the economy as reflected in the volumes of advertising. In the second week of June 1974 the bubble burst with a suddenness that took everyone's breath away. Liam Healy, then accountant of Independent Newspapers, told me that when he went on two weeks' holidays everything was going well, when he returned it was to a crisis. Advertising fell sharply in all newspapers in the country. *The Irish Times*, in common with other quality papers with lower circulations than the 'popular' papers, got a higher proportion of its revenue from advertising and thus was more vulnerable to fluctuations in advertising revenue.

Three downturns of varying depth and length have hit newspapers in the last 30 years but the 1970s was the first such experience. A strong profit for the first half of 1974 turned into a loss for the year and losses continued to mount as advertising fell further. Losses for the three years 1974–6 totalled £1 million, cancelling the profits of the previous three years and putting the company under severe pressure.

Douglas Gageby had announced his resignation from the editorship before any of this was known and Fergus Pyle became editor. Within a short time he had to contend with cost cut-backs, which applied throughout the company, and rapidly rising cover price due to soaring annual inflation, which reached 20 per cent—a monumental task. When Fergus moved on, Douglas returned to steer the ship for some ten further years.

In 1973 *The Irish Times* had installed its first commercial computer (an IBM System 3 with 8K memory, rather less than the modern watch but state of the art in mini-computers at the time) and in 1976 the change to photo-composition and cut-and-paste began using new computers, which also provided an upgrade of the commercial systems. Training for this major change was substantial and was aided by the semi-state organisation AnCO, and the European Social Fund.

By the early 1980s the continued circulation growth was putting severe pressure on the 30-year-old Hoe Crabtree press, which had a top speed of about 26,000 copies an hour and had to stop every half-hour to change paper reels. With print runs over 90,000 its capacity was stretched close to breaking point. It had to be replaced but funding was a problem, because not enough profits had been made to build up the reserves for such an investment. Then the miracle happened—Reuters announced its flotation, with all the member newspaper companies, including us, to receive substantial payments for their shareholdings.

Choice of a new press was limited not only by the money available but also by height restrictions in the site of the old press. A Uniman 4/ 2 was selected: this would give us not only increased speed of output but, most important of all, the ability to print colour, for which there was a growing demand from advertisers.

Through all of this Douglas Gageby was a larger than life character—not perhaps in stature but through the aura which he radiated. He had brought *The Irish Times* circulation from the low 30,000s to the high 80,000s and had seen it through a technical revolution which changed utterly a production process unchanged for 100 years. To all of us on 'the other side of the house' he was a man to be respected and admired but also to be liked.

The board of Irish Times Ltd in the early 1960s. Left to right: Douglas Gageby, then joint managing director with George Hetherington (on his left), John A. Robertson (who resigned in 1962), Arthur Burgess, company secretary, with a minute book, Ralph Walker, chairman, his brother Philip Walker and Howard Robinson, acountant and banker. Despite the confident bonhomie, the group's problems were exemplified by copies of the ill-fated Sunday Review *on the table. The portrait on the wall is of Lawrence Knox, who established* The Irish Times *in 1859 as one of the penny papers made possible by the abolition of stamp duty in 1855, of which the most successful was the London* Daily Telegraph.

The Bank of Ireland and *The Irish Times*

Andrew Whittaker

On Wednesday 23 March 1977 I walked from *The Irish Times* to the office of Ian Morrison, managing director of the Bank of Ireland, and asked him to remove the editor of the newspaper, Fergus Pyle, and to reduce Major Tom McDowell from chairman and chief executive to non-executive chairman. The changes were needed to secure the finances of the newspaper and its journalism, I said.

Morrison knew me from my time as business editor in 1970–74. At the end of that period the bank had advanced a loan to finance most of the £2 million purchase of *The Irish Times* from its then owner-directors by a new body, the Irish Times Trust. Three years later we were rocking in the aftershock of an international stock market slump, the end of Prime Minister Ted Heath's lax UK monetary policy (to which Ireland was tied by the umbilical cord of sterling) and the 1974 OPEC imposition of soaring oil prices. The Irish economy rode all these badly. *The Irish Times*, which had enjoyed a decade of unparalleled circulation growth under Douglas Gageby as editor, nearly capsized. National inflation was 17 per cent in 1974 and 21 per cent and 18 per cent in the following two years. Interest payments on escalating bank borrowings burdened the newspaper with compounding losses. Given the inflation rate, wage demands from staff were strident and incessant even though understandable.

Gageby had retired soon after the purchase of the newspaper by the trust. Circulation fell under his successor, Fergus Pyle, whom Gageby and McDowell had chosen. Pyle was a friendly, burly, tousled individual—keen and bustling and full of good intentions but hopelessly unorganised. He arrived for his first editorial conference looking bemused and taking off his bicycle clips. He was a wretched choice, he hadn't a chance, we all knew it, poor Fergus, it wasn't his fault.

As circulation and advertising figures fell in the recession the editorial managers became confused. They felt undermined. They were out of their depth. For the first time their editorial decisions were being questioned over the sliding circulation and they had no solutions. Nor had they solutions for the Pyle crisis, as they had not been consulted

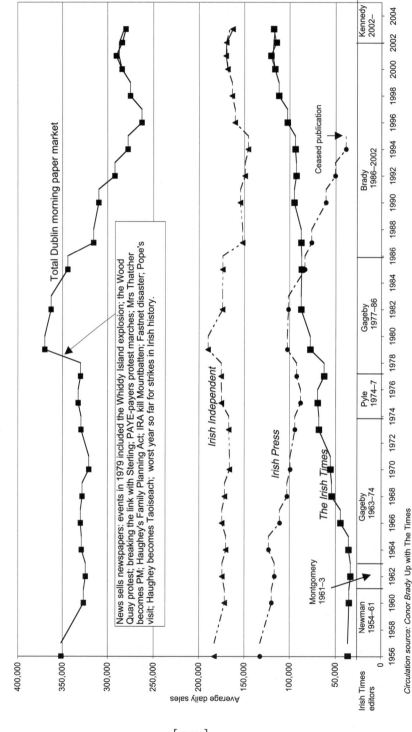

Irish morning newspaper circulations 1956–2004

News sells newspapers: events in 1979 included the Whiddy Island explosion; the Wood Quay protest; breaking the link with Sterling; PAYE-payers protest marches; Mrs Thatcher becomes PM; Haughey's Family Planning Act; IRA kill Mountbatten; Fastnet disaster; Pope's visit; Haughey becomes Taoiseach; worst year so far for strikes in Irish history.

Total Dublin morning paper market

Irish Independent

Irish Press

The Irish Times

Ceased publication

Average daily sales

Irish Times editors

Newman 1954–61

Montgomery 1961–3

Gageby 1963–74

Pyle 1974–7

Gageby 1977–86

Brady 1986–2002

Kennedy 2002–

Circulation source: Conor Brady Up with The Times

about his appointment and had no mechanism to remove him. The journalists behaved as an insulted army unused to setbacks and became truculent.

I had resigned my job as business editor and was working for Peter O'Hara, a long-time management consultant to McDowell. O'Hara had started with projects in what was called 'new technology' and went on to help McDowell formulate the trust. McDowell appointed him an initial trust member then made him group managing director. When I met him O'Hara was cobbling together a budget and projections to satisfy the board and the Bank of Ireland in desperate times. He taught me (a non-accountant) how to do cash flow projections: the iterations were carried out in pencil and re-pencilled and re-pencilled until he considered the inputs and outputs acceptable to show to the directors and the bank. He was simultaneously trying to design a new group management structure.

In the summer of 1976 *The Irish Times* had hired a remarkable new management accountant, Patrick Lyons. He had previously lectured in accountancy in University College Cork. That autumn he began to look through the company's monthly reports. He used the backs of envelopes and only if necessary lined paper to do his analyses. He became puzzled and inquired into the circulation figures. He suspected that they were being inflated by the traditional attempts of the distribution department to improve sales by pushing more copies into the shops than the shops had ordered, a procedure known as a 'box-out'. As the returns of unsold copies arrived weeks or maybe months after outgoing copies had been logged, box-outs, which in a time of underlying rising sales would produce greater sales, in times of underlying lower sales produced not increased sales but, after a delay, higher returns. When the delay was factored in, Pat found that our circulation, which we knew was dropping, was dropping faster than we knew.

He looked at both the annual management projections or 'budget', and our monthly financial reports, which together were used to report how we were doing. He found that in a time of declining financial performance not only were the projections out of date, but the accumulating rate of under-performance was not taken into account in projecting the outcome to the end of the year. Only under-performance up to the reporting date was accounted for. Eyes were not lifted from the real performance to the real horizon.

Time and again Pat expressed to me his scepticism of the company's departmental budgeting assumptions and forecasts. He dug deeper. He was in a race to discover our true situation as the true situation deteriorated faster than the management accounts showed. He looked at what would happen if the rate of deterioration in our performance continued to the end of the year. His conclusion was devastating. He estimated that we would record a loss of about £477,000. The figure available to O'Hara, made up in the traditional way, was a loss of about £200,000. The budget approved by the board had foreseen a profit of £110,000. Pat came to his conclusion in early November 1976.

From about three months before that, in mid-1976, I had advised McDowell that Pyle must go. He had seemed to agree; but he did not act. Both aspects of his behaviour were characteristic. When the reality of the financial crisis hit him through Pat's figures he would choose to let O'Hara go, who was working on solutions, rather than remove Pyle, who was a problem. The best that can be said of McDowell in this respect—and it should be said—is that he was attentive enough to hear what he must have found dislikeable, that the company's management and controls, which he had been in charge of for 14 years, had failed in their purpose at this time of peril.

Ever-more deplorable circulation, advertising and cash figures kept coming in. With Pat's figures I projected the timing of the company's decline (unless corrected) into insolvency—that condition in which un-less something were done it would be unable to pay its bills as they fell due. It already wasn't paying its tax bills on time, so far as I recall, for the Revenue was a complacent creditor in those days. The company's finances were slaloming to a condition in which the directors would become liable at law if they continued trading. I wrote to O'Hara pointing out that the company's net worth would soon be zero. Pat pressed for action to raise our income.

In mid-February 1977 the journalists thought of holding a meeting at which they might vote no-confidence in Pyle as editor. Ken Gray, a respected but by then jaded assistant editor in charge of administration, told me fatuously: 'There is a need to reassert Fergus's authority.' It would be done at a meeting on Friday 11th by himself, personnel man-ager Des Bury, and long-time general manager Louis O'Neill, who had been deployed to a loss-making subsidiary building-up a chain of news-paper and tobacco shops. The journalists, said Gray, 'would be given firm negative replies to their arguments for more money, more staff, and representation on staff selection boards.'

I sent a note at once to O'Hara, saying that discontent with the editor 'is to be found right through the editorial staff. He is personally disliked and distrusted, and the loss of authority that he has suffered is not of a sort that firm (or any other) action by management can help him recover . . . The gravest problem is the actual editing of the paper, and I remain sure that only Fergus's replacement can now help us . . . Little or no long-term good will come out of actions designed to "beat" the union in a case where the union is right. We should concede, if we have to; and fight the worthwhile fights.'

In mid-March 1977 Pat wrote ten longhand pages to McDowell. He summarised: 'The pattern of rapid sales growth followed by decline after the peak is the standard life cycle of a product, which indicates that some renewal or revitalisation of the content or the image of the paper is required. The form which it should take would follow the establishment of the needs of those identified as the marginal potential customers to be satisfied.'

He went deeper. He had picked up an understanding of what Gageby had done during his first editorship (before Pat joined the company). He forecast what should be our editorial policy now:

'The basic and most long standing type of customer is the older person formerly part of the unionist tradition; other types of customers of more marginal commitment would include those middle-aged people seeking truth, serious comment and high standards of journalism, and younger people who are anxious for liberalisation, justice and economic development of society and the social systems. The primary need is probably to develop the paper in a way to increase the commitment and regularity of those marginal yet potential customers.'

Within the fortnight McDowell threw off his torpor. I have been told by a colleague who liked and respected O'Hara that it was on the basis of Pat's analysis that O'Hara confessed to McDowell that he had provided duff information to the board. McDowell let O'Hara resign. He kept Pyle as editor. It was the reverse of what the company needed. After thinking about it, I asked Morrison to see me.

In the Bank of Ireland's big black brute of a building on Baggot Street I told Morrison that the bank's financial and management support was needed to ensure that *The Irish Times* continued to trade legally and drew management lessons from the crisis. I set out Pat's analysis and projections. Morrison was tall, bulky and filthy rich by my standard. He was a chartered accountant by training and ocean racer by passion. He had merged his accountancy practice into Coopers & Lybrand and was plucked from there in 1966 by Don Carroll, governor of the Bank of Ireland, to be made the bank's first modern managing director. Previously it had been run by an 18th-century system of governors and a court of 'after you, m'sieur' directors. Three years later he oversaw the acquisition of the National Bank and the Hibernian Bank.

Morrison was puzzled but outgoing. He said he did not know how newspapers were run, and I dare say I told him. I told him that McDowell should be a non-executive chairman, unable to hold up decisions or interfere with subordinate managers. Control of managers should be in the hands of an attentive managing director who would study their targets and their reports, quizz them about staff performances, problems, the state of the market and the competition. He should check on their implementation of agreed policies.

Morrison said that he and Douglas Gageby had talked 'about 17 or 16 years ago' about buying *The Irish Times*. The idea was of 'buying out the Walkers', who were shareholders and directors. They had talked to 'old John Arnott, he was an alcoholic.' However, 'the bank asked me first.'

Morrison said that he did not like McDowell. They had had a row years ago. He said that the bank would have to write off £0.8m in that year (1977) on account of its *Irish Times* loan, plus £0.3m of interest unpaid. It was the first decision on the matter that the bank had made. 'It's embarrassing,' he said.

I asked why the bank had financed the Irish Times Trust in 1974. He replied that McDowell 'is a good advocate.' McDowell had put the trust plan to Bill Finlay, a senior counsel who was then governor of the bank. The bank knew it was 'not a normal business investment' but had not expected things 'to go so badly wrong so fast,' said Morrison. He added that the paper had always been in financial difficulty with the bank: when he joined its debt had been about £80,000. Morrison said that he had supported the loan to the trust with his board for short-term advantage. The directors had feared the conjunction of high inflation rates and the activities of the IRA. They had wanted *The Irish Times* to be there as 'at least one voice of sanity', even though the paper was not controlled by the bank.

I told him that the newspaper's management needed stiffening with a new régime adequate to future risks. I asked him whether Don Carroll, already a member of the trust, might act as a catalyst, since at present neither the trust nor the board was able—and perhaps were not even permitted—to grasp the broad range of inadequacies we suffered. Morrison replied that he was aware that the trust felt 'ill informed' and that the board felt 'under utilised'.

The newspaper's circulation had fallen below 60,000 copies a day, I said. That was a drop of 14 per cent from the second half of 1975, or about 1 per cent a month. It was a tough comparison because newspapers had all benefited from the sensational kidnapping of Limerick-based businessman Dr Tiede Herrema by IRA sympathisers in October 1975 and his release following an 18-day siege by the Garda.

Morrison said that McDowell was vain. I said he was uncertain and dallying about what to do and deeply committed to what had failed; the company's managers and their organisation were largely his appointees and creation; his judgment of people was poor but in the past

Gageby had saved him by his success; his leadership had been indirect in good times but became direct in bad, without being better directed or consistent; a lot of his attention went on secondary matters or mere meddling.

Morrison listened, made a note, replied that the problem with making changes was 'the Major's contract'. He meant the nature of the trust, which gave McDowell dominance of trust and board. 'We may not be able to remove him,' he said. He spoke with finality, even resignation. He said that the bank had had 'no part' in the recent changes in which Peter O'Hara had left and that it was 'not particularly pleased' to see Louis O'Neill come back to the paper.

Would Gageby come back, he asked? I replied: 'Don't ask him as editor, for you can't play history twice. He might do as chairman.'

What about James Walmsley as chairman, Morrison countered? Walmsley was a trust member and I knew him slightly, for I had been in Trinity with his son Malcolm. I said that I had tried to open the problem of the trust with Walmsley, but I thought, now, that a perceived clash of interests must rule him out: for Walmsley was chairman of Eason's, the dominant distribution business for printed journals and for many newspapers who were rivals of the Dublin dailies—which ran a competing network.

Morrison disliked my simple idea that the bank appoint a receiver to *The Irish Times*. 'It would be the last resort,' he said. It would collapse *The Irish Times*'s credit. Suppliers, such as those of newsprint, would demand cash up front before delivering. Also it would raise problems with preferential creditors. It would cost a lot of money. Then there would be the problem of who to put in as receiver. 'However, it might be used as a threat,' he said.

I left after one hour and forty minutes and wrote up my notes in a pub.

Was the kidnapping of a businessman to seek a prisoner-exchange for IRA men a consideration in Morrison's mind when he and his board reviewed the bank's attitude to *The Irish Times*? It must have been.

In those difficult years it was Morrison's policy to help the bank's ailing customers correct their own faults. Our newspaper was a small item in his large portfolio of non-performing loans, but it was what he had just described to me as a 'voice of sanity'; so I think caution and leniency were his approach.

In some months' time Pyle was removed. Gageby returned as editor for nine years. McDowell continued as he was for 24 years. So far as I know *The Irish Times* still deals with the Bank of Ireland. It wasn't a bad outcome for the bank.

Ian Morrison died in September 2004, three months after Douglas Gageby.

The editor as countryman, crossing the road outside his old college, Trinity.

Putting flesh on an icon

Patsy McGarry

There is a wonderful story which says as much about the sort of man Douglas Gageby was as any account of hero-courageous achievements. For years he coveted a painting in the home of Donal Foley, that other remarkable man who as news editor at *The Irish Times* was a central figure in the success story which was Gageby's era at the newspaper. While living and working in London, Donal befriended Belfast painter Gerard Dillon and bought one of his works. Titled 'The Falls Road on a Saturday Night' it hung in the Foley home in Dublin. In September 2006 when I talked to her, Mrs Pat Foley, Donal's widow, said: 'Every time he (Gageby) came to the house he made a bee-line for that painting.'

With some humour she remembered that in 1980 she and her husband had been on holiday, driving around England.

> 'Donal was a very nervous passenger and he said we ought to make a joint will, which we did on our return. The solicitor asked about leaving personal items and I hadn't really thought about it but I said something about leaving jewellery to my daughters and the books to my sons. I was surprised when Donal, who was from a very large family, said he wanted to leave things to other people. He left Smyllie's desk to Maeve Binchy and the [Dillon] picture to Douglas Gageby. A year later Donal died.'

On the day of her husband's funeral 'Douglas was there looking at the picture again, but I didn't say anything.' A week later she rang him.

> 'I had the feeling he thought it was "the widow wondering about her pension" or something like that. He arrived on his own and I sat him down with the usual brandy and told him the story of the will. I had it wrapped in brown paper and handed it to him. "Here's your picture," I said. There were tears in his eyes. All he said was "I'll never forget him."'

Many years later, she went on, Gageby met her son Michael and asked whether she would be very annoyed if he were to give the picture back, as it had gone up a lot in value. 'Indeed she would not be a bit annoyed,' Michael said; but nothing happened. Then, as Gageby declined in health, his family rang Michael to say Douglas had asked to see him. 'Which he did. He [Gageby] was very weak. He gave Michael back the painting. It was 21½ years since he got it. I was very, very moved,' she said. Gageby died soon afterwards.

Ten years after Donal Foley died, in 1991, Gageby wrote about that painting in an article on Belfast, for *The Irish Times*.

> 'I remember Belfast by gaslight in the 20s and 30s, as painted by the great artist Gerry Dillon in "The Falls Road on a Saturday Night". It could have been the Oldpark Road or many other roads, with its pale light, its girl swinging on a rope around a lamp post, a woman in a shawl and the lads leaning against a shop, two cats in the middle of the road. This was left to me in his will by that most generous and lovable of men, Donal Foley.'

He loved Foley, (probably more afterwards than in life, as happens so many of us where an early death occurs); he loved Belfast; and nearing his own death gave back the thing he loved to those with whom his decency said it rightly belonged.

What he owed Foley was immense of course, and it was acknowl-edged. The day after Foley died, and clearly grief-stricken, he wrote a generous and loving appreciation in *The Irish Times* of 8 July 1981. The newspaper 'today bears indelibly the imprint of the mind and journal-istic skills of Donal Foley,' he wrote. Foley's part in shaping the newspa-per 'went far beyond anything that appeared under his name in these columns'.

> '[He] poured forth ideas. He early had seen the significance of the tide of new thinking in religion . . . and all religious news was a major feature of the era. He recognised talent with the sureness of instinct and was the first news editor to hire on a generous scale women reporters—not women to write about women's affairs, but women who covered events day in day out as did their male colleagues.'

Foley 'ran the newsroom as a family; sometimes he was the father ruling the roost, often the indulgent uncle; always a powerhouse of ideas, always demanding the best in journalistic standards.' And 'he had collected pictures from his London days, when George Campbell and Gerard Dillon were his friends, and went on doing so through his later years,' he wrote. That picture again, though at the time he didn't know it had been left to him.

Then the emotion.

> 'There was not a scrap of hate in Donal Foley's make-up, not one mean or sore spot. He loved life and enjoyed work and leisure as if they were

the same, which to many journalists they are . . . Donal Foley was a peerless journalist; he was life and joy and high spirits. Above all, he was to us, his colleagues, the most lovable man we will ever meet.'

Such deeply-felt emotion is not the first quality that comes to mind when people of my generation think of Douglas Gageby. But in going through the files it is evident, if at some depth. He was not a man for the social gathering and tended to shun such as editor. Indeed it is significant that most of what he said and wrote in the files is from the period after he retired and when he began to accept invitations to give addresses and interviews.

Probably Tim Pat Coogan, the former *Irish Press* editor, got him most accurately. In an obituary prepared by Donal O'Donovan for *The Irish Times* in 1987—17 years before Gageby's death!—Tim Pat was quoted saying:

'The caustic manner, the flint-edged public personality, that kept the world at arm's length were part of the public armour of a very private man, highly intelligent and deeply sensitive. This sensitivity was part of what made him a great editor.'

You might say it was that intelligent sensitivity that helped him 'create' that other major figure in journalism most associated with Gageby in the public mind, John Healy. He spoke at Healy's funeral in 1991 in the Church of the Three Patrons in Dublin's Rathgar, his bearing stately, upright, the Army man in command, his words clear, calmly expressed, warm. Healy, he said, was

' . . . irreplaceable in our world of journalism and in the hearts of his many friends and colleagues. He was individual and entirely original. He was the heart of corn and a caring and responsive friend, and we will miss him always. As a journalist, he is a loss to this community.'

He finished: 'Farewell, friend of *Irish Press* days, of Irish News Agency days, of *Irish Times* days and of the many hundreds of hours spent out along the river banks and on the lakes of this country. You will never be matched.'

Gageby was, it seems, a man with a gift for deep and loyal friendship. His affections also extended to place, particularly to Belfast. At the Yeats summer school in Sligo, in August 1988, he said:

'The country that Yeats knew was different in one major respect from the state we know today, in that it contained the mighty industrial city of Belfast, at the height of its prosperity and self-confidence or arrogance. . . . . Ireland is not Ireland without that part of the island, given that Belfast, the supreme centre of loyalty to Britain on this island, was also the fount of Republicanism—and where the movement that eventually led to the foundation of this state flourished. And this state, based around Dublin, needs Belfast and its environs. It needs its scepticism, its vigour, its brashness. And Belfast and the North could benefit from the qualities fostered in this state: tolerance, easy social attitudes, and an awareness of the wide world around us.'

But his feeling for Belfast was more deeply rooted than the political. In a 1991 article in *The Irish Times*, he wrote:

'Belfast is in my bones. I love the warmth of the people, their generosity, and their fine scepticism, a quality from which we, in our republican public life could benefit: scepticism not cynicism. It is a passionate city, vengeful at times, maddened often by outrageous preachers; also a city of intrepid entrepreneurs and diehard proletarians. There is not much "sirring" around. And always of suffering . . . there were no "rare ould times" in Belfast. I love Belfast. I have family graves there and I know streets, now being recreated under urban renewal, where members of my own family sweated and went hungry. My father left his father's house in the 1890s because there was never enough to eat in the house, and six children to feed. Belfast people don't give up. They are Yeats's indomitable Irishry and they are great fun to be with.'

Yet he was, as he wrote in the same article, 'a born Dubliner and [I] have, by choice, lived most of my life in Dublin, but Belfast is in my bones.'

He returned to the theme at the Parnell summer school in August 1993, asking:

'Is there some terrible inhibition among our politicians or public people here that prevents them, once in a while, from saying loud and clear, a kind word for the people of that great city of Belfast?'

But there was indeed that political element to his affection for Ireland's second city. 'For God's sake, we must stop talking about two traditions [on the island of Ireland]. There is only one tradition, the Irish tradition of Robin Flower. There are variants, maybe four, maybe five, all under the one umbrella of Ireland,' he said in an interview with Liam Robinson of the *Irish Press* in October 1986. On the North, and in words with as much resonance today, he told the Merriman summer school at Lisdoonvarna in August 1987: 'Reconciliation is a big word. Let us say that to live side by side in peace is a fair start.' And that was now down to each one of us, as

'. . . we will probably never again see and follow a great political leader, a chief like Dev or Parnell, a liberator like Daniel O'Connell. I think that day has passed. People are now too sophisticated, too educated in some ways, too wary.' (He said that at the launch of a pamphlet on Brian Friel, by Ulick O'Connor, in Dublin, March 1989.)

His felt patriotism too had changed. 'Patriotism [in Ireland] used to be seen as a lively interest in speeches from the dock. Now we see patriotism in a wider sweep, in respect for the soil and rocks of Ireland, the wildlife and trees and herbiage,' he said at the launch of *The Way That I Followed—A Naturalist's Journey Around Ireland*, by Professor Frank Mitchell, in Dublin, November 1990.

That Gageby had great love for this island and its people is evidenced further in a report of an interview he did with then German information minister Hans Klein, in *The Irish Times* of 21 June 1989, just six months before the Berlin Wall fell. Klein told him, following a leading question from Gageby on German attitudes to the Irish:

HK 'There has always been in this country an admiration for this tremendous will to freedom with the Irish. I say there are—now this is my very personal assessment—there are three absolutely crazy people in this world, and they are freedom-hungry to the degree of craziness—the Afghans, the Poles and the Irish.' (laughs).

DG 'The Poles and the Irish are frequently linked, yes.'

HK 'So are the Afghans. Now if you look into Afghan history you will find parallels, lots of them. Now the other thing is the Irish way of life. They like to sing, they like to drink, they like company.'

DG 'The Germans love singing, too, don't they?'

HK 'There are a lot of similarities in our own character.'

He had a fascination with Germany: 'That amazing, crazy people. What a culture! What a literature! I'd love to write a book on Germany,' he told Eileen Battersby in an interview in *The Irish Times* in September 1999. He learned German at school and at Trinity, and had been to the country as a student in the late 1930s. He used his German as an intelligence officer in the Army during the Second World War and visited the country as a reporter after the war, as he explained in the same interview.

'The place was in ruins; the people were depressed, defeated. I went around asking questions. Of course, it all depended which zone you were in. The French were particularly bitter, and it showed. The Russians were paranoid.'

For people of my generation Douglas Gageby is more legend, icon and symbol than the person emerging from the stories and quotations above. I did interview him once for the *Irish Press* in the late 1980s but was too junior and awestruck to get any further than softly, softly 'my-days-at-the-*Press*' type of stuff with him. And he had great lines about his days at the *Press*, as I discovered recently. 'It was peopled by enormous talent, eccentrics galore and rare men of many disciplines who proffered pure comradeship. You could say it made me,' he said of the newspaper during an RDS address in 1987.

I heard him speak at John Healy's funeral. Healy's sister June Egan is a neighbour of ours at home in Ballaghaderreen, and I had been reading Healy for years, but my acquaintance with and knowledge of Gageby was very limited. People of my generation would tend to see him in terms of journalism and what he did for and with *The Irish Times* and, through it, for Irish society. He took a niche newspaper with a narrow tradition and made it an indispensable instrument for those who wished to be informed in mainstream Ireland. There were other such 'indispensable instruments' media-wise in Ireland at the time, but they—Radio Éireann, the Press and Independent groups particularly—had always had a mainstream role. But not only did he successfully reposition *The Irish Times*, there was the manner in which he did so. He insisted on the very highest standards in journalism and writing and established those exacting aspirations which remain integral to the tradition of the newspaper and a constant challenge to all of us who work here. Even in his absence what he put in place continues to shape and stretch those of us following in the steps of the extraordinary generation of journalists he and Donal Foley recruited and shaped.

And, apart from those standards put in place, there was his deep-seated commitment to those liberal values of tolerance and respect, particularly for minorities, which has been pivotal to the newspaper's role in helping open up Irish society and, hopefully, in making it a 'warm house' for an increasingly diverse population. In our globalised world what Douglas Gageby imbued in his journalists has as deep a relevance today, and on a grander scale, than in his halcyon days as editor of *The Irish Times*. The values he espoused are timeless. So, therefore, is his legacy.

His views on journalism are of course of most interest for those of us coming after. At an adult education course in University College Galway in 1970 he said: 'The duty of the journalist is the same as that of the historian—to seek out the truth above all things, and to present his readers not such things as statescraft would wish them to know, but the truth as near as he can attain it.' In an interview with Deirdre Purcell in the *Sunday Tribune* in March 1987, he said: 'Fairness is the best you can hope for. There's no such thing as objectivity in journalism.' At the RDS in December 1987 he said of journalism: 'It's thrilling, stimulating, frustrating and demanding. And, in case you get uppity, there are all your mistakes in print, daily, for everyone to see . . . including solicitors and others with an eye to litigation.' The prime function of journalists, he said in the same talk, is 'to give as accurately as possible, as fairly as possible, as fully as possible, the facts of what is going on—the word picture. And the documentation.' Newspapers, he said, were 'not just the property of a family or a company to use as they want. They are a public service. Socially they do not make enough profit to be able to stay in existence and to help re-equip. They are for comforting the afflicted and afflicting the comfortable.'

And he had views on the then rising generation, views probably as relevant today. 'Young journalists today want to be instant commentators. But as every editor knows, the genuine, old-style, if you like, reporter, fired with a desire to tell it as it is, is the pride of our calling, trade, craft, vocation, call it what you will, journalism,' he said in an address at 'Power of the Press' advertising awards in Dublin in October 1987. Gentle words too. 'I do believe in trying to see people content. If a journalist, and by the nature of the game so many are sensitive and vulnerable, is not happy in what he or she is doing, it is damaging to the personality and doing little good for the paper,' he said at the same event. He 'always liked strong reporting. Working on a provincial paper is the best training you can get. You get to cover everything,' he said in that 1999 interview with Eileen Battersby.

And for those of us who worry about the future in an age of increased competition from electronic media, he was most reassuring in that interview. 'There'll always be a newspaper. When people see something on the television news they will want to read about it in the paper,' he said. And maybe that's because 'newspapers play an important role, not as pillars of society but as a necessary Lucifer element,' as he said at the launch of the book *Paper Tigers* by Hugh Oram, in Dublin in November 1993.

Gageby was indeed, as Donal O'Donovan wrote presciently in that *Irish Times* obituary, prepared in December 1987, 'the most remarkable Irish newspaperman of this [20th] century.' A citation 12 years later, when the still-very-much-alive Gageby was being presented with an honorary doctorate in laws at Trinity College in December 1999, described him as 'an outstanding figure among the dedicated journalists who have chronicled our epoch.' And who could, or would, dispute that?

Douglas and Dorothy Gageby in Switzerland, 1946.

Appendix 1
Douglas Gageby's despatches from Germany, October and November 1946

The Second World War in Europe ended with the surrender of the German forces in May 1945. At the Potsdam Conference of August 1945 the Allies—USA, Britain, France and the USSR—divided Germany into four military occupation zones; each was to be governed in characteristic national style.

The German economy was shattered, as was the physical infrastructure—food and clothing were scarce, and in some cities as much as two-thirds of housing was unsafe. Millions of Germans were refugees. Exigent rationing and black market activity were daily experiences. (This was very much the world of The Third Man.*) Facing the winter of 1946/7, which was to be one of the coldest of the century, the shortage of fuel was dismaying.*

For the Allies, the preoccupations were firstly to feed the people and then to establish the controversial denazification programme. The themes of the Nuremberg Trials echoed through court-rooms across the country. The first of this long series, dealing with the major war criminals, ended with the execution of ten of the defendants on 16 October 1946. The second, the trial of 23 Nazi doctors, began a few days later.

This was just as Douglas Gageby, then employed by the Irish Press, *took the opportunity of a visit to his father-in-law in Geneva to make an extended tour of occupied Germany, sending back to Ireland the following remarkable despatches, all of which were given front page prominence.*

Irish Press Saturday 19 October 1946
HUNGER AND DIRT ON TRAIN RIDE IN GERMANY

Frankfurt

Take a long ride in a German train, preferably at night, and you have a month's experience condensed into a few hours.

You see the hunger and dirt of life in Germany today, the every man for himself quality of it, and you realise how the burden of immediate daily problems is so great that the people have little time to think of anything but keeping alive, clothed and housed.

I was brooding over this as darkness came down on the train bringing me from the Swiss border through the French zone and into the US zone of Germany.

Several hours before I had eaten a meal in Basle the like of which none of these people would see for years. Now all around me hands were groping into rucksacks and bags for food they had got by barter in the country parts.

While it was light no one dared to eat openly. Anyone who did eat turned away from the envious and curious glances of the rest.

Now I could hear, right up against my ear, the slow methodical crunching of an apple or pear, and that tug as a mouthful was torn from a slice of bread.

Welcome cigar

Across the way a man lit a cigar—a good thing, for people who have to pay anything from two pounds on the black market for a cake of soap don't smell well when packed tightly in the space at the end of a train corridor.

I could only see dimly for the train had no lights.

Later that night I saw a crowd of happy American GIs lolling in beautiful first-class carriages, pull out of Karlsruhe station while I waited six hours to connect with a train even more draughty and gloomy than the first.

An occasional station light was the only outside relief on our gloom. House windows that had been blown out by bombs are now simply boarded or shuttered up by night, and so you get the impression of passing through a countryside where there is no life at all.

But light comes at last as we pull up at the station, and with it a babel as people wrestle along the corridor to the exit.

It's often a fight to get onto a train here. It can be even more difficult to get off. For that reason, people anxiously crowd in corridors, often leaving seats empty.

Shouts of 'Let us out' from behind are met with a yell from outside as the door is thrown open and the two-way assault begins.

One or two people get off, and as the aching mass sways and groans a man scrambles up from the platform, balances for a second on the top of the steps, and then plunges in, like an ancient film sequence of going over the top. A dozen follow him and mill through our midst to the peace of the lower corridor regions.

Handicapped

A man with a rucksack on his back is awkward in a cramped space. When he is carrying bags or boxes in his hands as well, as were most of these, and when he has to make his way through a concentration of people who refuse to be shifted from their precious possessions, the result is chaos.

As the door slams shut, three old women come up the corridor to us, 'More to get out,' one gasps, but everyone is consolidating his position, and no move is made to make way.

'More to get out,' says someone half-heartedly, and a few make a pretence of shuffling. But it is too late. The train is on its way and, weeping, the old women retire. 'Have we all gone mad?' I hear one of them say.

All are tired and weak around me. Most of them have been out on the land all day. This is the French zone still, where the rations are much worse than either of the other Western zones.

On these barter trips city people bring out mostly tobacco, also household goods like cooking utensils, blankets, clothes, too, or whatever happens to be in demand in the particular area.

One man told me that his wife and he had gone out in the US zone with a pound of sugar and had returned with over a hundredweight of potatoes, a quarter pound of butter and some fruit.

The journey continues. A middle-aged man whose grey face I had noticed in daylight is slowly stirring, trying to shift his bag for more comfort. After five minutes' painful work, he gives up, slumps down with head in hands, and does not move until the end of the journey.

A baby is crying in the compartment next to us. A boy of about 20 years, clad in the remnants of military uniform, who, since the beginning of the journey, has stared blankly out in daylight and darkness alike, is muttering distractedly to himself and hammering on the carriage walls.

Hitch-riders

As we slow down before the next station I hear a thud, and looking out, see a man racing across the grass. Hitch-hikers are a daily feature of German travel now.

At the last station in the French zone many get out, and in the dim light I look at some of my fellow-travellers for the first time.

At least half are wearing some sort of military dress—women in old jackboots and re-made army coats, some in battle-slacks and jerkins, and many of the men have the peaked cap that first became familiar to us in the day of the Africa Korps. All are drab and dirty, if not actually in rags.

As they stumble off with their awkward burdens, I feel that I must have seen some of the worst aspects of life in this part of Germany.

So much of the country we passed through looked neat, orderly; crops seemed good.

Townsfolk agree that country people have a reasonable existence, and after I have lived a few days on German rations I will be able to judge for myself.

Irish Press Wednesday 23 October 1946
CIGARETTES FOR WHAT—? NEW BARTER IN GERMANY

Frankfurt

You can no longer buy a country mansion and six racehorses for a few cartons of cigarettes in Germany. In fact, the day may not be far distant when cigarettes will once again be things to smoke and not articles of currency.

Latest blow to the value of cigarettes is the opening of a barter centre in Frankfurt-on-Main.

It works like this: Germans badly need cigarettes, soap, chocolate and other commodities the American GIs can easily get. Of course, they need meat, butter and nearly every other article of food you can think of, but for the moment we stick to cigarettes, soap and chocolate.

GIs on the other hand, want cameras and many kinds of luxury goods. So bring them together and make the deal open, says the US Army.

Our GI writes home for the goods he is going to trade in, mostly cigarettes, which he can get in unlimited quantities for about a dollar (or five shillings) per two hundred. For this number of good cigarettes he gets 55 barter units.

Our German wipes the dust off his best camera, or parcels up the cut glass decanters, and presents himself to one of the appraisers at the store.

Camera estimate

I went myself yesterday to see how it works and asked for an estimate on my camera. It cost £60 in Dublin during the war, and in America would be somewhat less.

I was told I could get 1,170 barter units for it, so a GI, getting his 55 units for a carton of cigarettes, could have had my camera for 21 cartons or about the same number of dollars—a £60 camera for £5 isn't bad business.

Of course, if I had been a German I wouldn't have paid half that sum for it pre-war. Maybe that consoles the GI, who must just now and then feel a pang.

The US Army authorities hope that if the soldier can get a £60 camera for a twelfth of its value in the legalised deal he would do it rather than go to the black market and risk getting into trouble, perhaps losing his camera.

Of course, if the German could take all his thousand odd units and cigarettes in one go he would start off on the black market roundabout again. He'd go straight out into the street and make a fortune, but is only allowed to take 400 cigarettes at a time. He can store up his units and take 400 every day.

Among other things he can get are soap at about four units per bar, coffee at eighteen per pound, and chocolate at the same figure. This is serious for the black marketeer, who has been getting 350 marks for the coffee and 80 for soap.

An idea of what some Germans are earning will show what it costs to go on the black market better than quoting the pre-war value of the mark. The man or woman behind the counter in a shop will have about 250 marks per month, not enough for a pound of black-market coffee; a telephone operator about 50 less; and one of the senior journalists on a good paper may have eight or nine hundred. An unskilled labourer has about 100.

So while this barter market is heavily weighted on the side of the GI, some Germans who could hardly afford to buy much on the black market nevertheless are for the first time getting things that were out of their reach.

As yet there is no real food available, but it is hoped there will be soon. The US Army people make a point of not allowing persons to trade in articles they really need for themselves.

They will not take carpets, for example, if they feel that the house is being stripped of an article necessary for warmth and comfort in the winter, though a rug whose use was purely decorative would be accepted.

Special money

This barter system is the second blow to the trading between GIs and Germans. The first was the introduction a short time ago of a special currency for Allied personnel in the zone which can only be used in army canteens, etc. Germans may not use it and Allied personnel may not use marks.

If this barter system becomes widespread it will cut down the black market in many commodities to manageable proportions.

The impressive stack of cigarettes I saw at the centre yesterday made it obvious that in a few days the cigarette will come down from its present black market value of two marks.

But the black marketeer is resourceful. Already he is quoting mark prices for barter points, and, no doubt, cigarettes and other articles bought in the Frankfurt barter centre are on their way to areas where they would fetch higher prices.

Irish Press Monday 28 October 1946
GERMAN FAMILIES COUNT POTATOES—GRIM LIFE IN HEIDELBERG
Heidelberg

After a few days in one of Germany's most bombed cities, Frankfurt-on-Main, I went to look for the other side of the picture. I wanted to find some place the air raids hadn't reached and landed in Heidelberg, which had suffered no damage beyond blowing up of bridges in the last phase of the fighting

Heidelberg should be fairly well off, I thought. It is small, easy to get out of, and in the fertile country round about there should be enough surplus food to allow the townspeople to supplement their rations.

A cold but sunny autumn morning. Heidelberg promised all these things. The shops were bright and their windows well dressed, whereas in Frankfurt, almost all were boarded up. The trams were brilliant and sky-blue and white and ran frequently.

Gaily-coloured villas dotted the russet, tree-covered hills which surround the town. Heidelberg looked really good.

But not until you sit down at a German table, as I have done, and share their meals do you realise that even for those who were not bombed, even for those who can afford to supplement their rations, life is grim.

In this, the US zone, people get 1,500 calories per day. This is what it means bite for bite.

Breakfast in this family I visited is usually a thin soup and bread. Coffee and tea are non-existent and the coffee substitute hardly drinkable.

The bread ration allows four slices per day of a loaf about 3 inches square, and on two of these you may have a smear of butter or margarine. If there are children in the house, as there are in this case, the grown-ups will have to give up some of their rations, for children have very much less bread. If you use much fat in cooking you will, of course, eat your bread dry.

So breakfast, and the children use up the daily bread ration here.

. . . *of old fish*

Dinner yesterday started with soup. It was thin and tasted strongly of old fish, but had no other indication that it really was fish, and I didn't like to ask. A few pieces of macaroni floated in it. The daughter of the house, who is mother of four children, was able to have a second helping.

Then we had potatoes and vegetables. This family assures me that it is fortunate in knowing some very kind people in the country who sell them vegetables a couple of times a week.

Note that it is a favour to be able to buy from the country people, who usually insist on exacting household goods in exchange.

The potatoes were, on the average, the size of a large egg. I took two, as I saw the others do, and started in with a knife to peel them. When I had made rather a mess of one, I noticed the others deeply absorbed, as if in a ritual. There was no cutting with the knives, just the making of a small incision and then a gentle flailing so that no one particle of edible matter was left on the skin.

They looked with satisfaction at the job well done and began to eat slowly, chewing each mouthful many times. There was something very sobering in the sight of four adults and one boy of four eating a few potatoes as if it were to be their last meal for days.

The vegetables which we were so lucky to have were plentiful this time, and I was encouraged to take a very big spoonful. It was a mixture of spinach and some unknown quantity.

After the first helping we each took another potato, and later the mother and her child finished some small ones at the bottom of the dish.

For supper there was salad instead of spinach and not quite so much potatoes.

As for meat, I helped choose the week's ration for the family. It was a piece of veal which will give them a dinner today and a little left over for the most deserving tomorrow.

They explained that they have a few ounces left over on their ration cards. With this they buy a sausage to send to the son of the house, now in a prison camp waiting to be 'denazified'.

I had expected fruit to be plentiful here. Before the war I remember buying peaches, apples and pears by the half-stone for a few pence, but so far I haven't seen any. Neither have the Heidelbergers.

I am told by American officials that not one person dies of hunger in their zone. I am told by elderly Germans that some people can even get used to eating like this.

The woman of the house where I have been visiting is about 60 and looks much as I remember her before the war, but two other members of the family, one about 60, the other 30, are so changed, so thin and yellow, that I wouldn't have recognised them had I not met them in the familiar setting.

The children, only two of whom are here at present, look well, but it is at the expense of their parents.

I arrived at this house unexpectedly. If they had known I was coming, they might have had different meals for me. They might have coaxed some countryman into giving them an egg or two to celebrate my coming, but I just walked in and took what came.

People in many parts of the world may live on even less food than this. I cannot argue with the official who tells me that the number of calories is enough to keep the people from actually falling down dead in the street from hunger. I am simply telling what one German family ate yesterday.

Irish Press Wednesday 29 October
GERMANY IS RIFE WITH RUMOURS

Heidelberg

The American zone of Germany is rife with rumours, because the people have little faith in the controlled Press. When they know you are a foreigner, people come up and say: 'Tell us, is it true that British bread rationing was brought in to conserve stocks for the next war?' or 'Is it true that the Americans burned a lot of food last week near such-and-such a place?'

There is no end to the fanciful tales you will hear in a half-hour's conversation with a German to-day, and he will end up saying: 'You see, we still can't believe what we read in our papers.'

This is unfair to the controlled Press, which is doing a reasonably good job, within the limits laid down by the occupiers, but it illustrates the difficulty of convincing the Germans that they are being educated for democracy, when one of the basics of democracy, a free Press, is lacking.

There is no Press censorship of newspapers, but a lot of news comes through the Agency Dana, an American creation which has just passed into German hands nominally, but is still under strict survey, and all papers are similarly scrutinised carefully. Raps over the knuckles are administered to those who cross the line.

There are three matters about which German editors must exercise particular care—maintenance of military security, dissemination of Nazi and militarist propaganda, and criticism of Military Government and personnel.

The phrase 'maintenance of military security' is so interpreted as to make it impossible for the Germans to raise any criticism of the occupying soldiery. If a GI commits a crime of a particularly revolting nature, the facts may be noted, but no comment or reproof is allowed.

May not criticise

The driving of American transport has given me many bad moments, but German writers may not suggest that it is about time that something was done to make the roads safer. Again, the military police are, in my experience, often—to put it very mildly—uncivil, but I have yet to see any thing about this in the press.

Of course, the Germans have ways of getting round this. A GI misdemeanour, though given only in the barest terms, may be made pointed by being placed beside, let us say, a speech by a General congratulating the men on their splendid morale. But these are dangerous tactics, and most editors would probably prefer to continue in their present limited sphere rather than have their licence revoked.

The second head 'Dissemination of Nazi and militarist propaganda', including racism and pan-Germanism, is not one that a German editor of to-day is likely to transgress. The third head is the one which gives the most difficulty. It concerns, mainly, what a directive calls efforts to disrupt unity among the Allies, or to evoke the distrust and hostility of the German people against any occupying power.

This means, in practice, that the papers must go very warily on news reports about the expulsion of Germans from the Eastern territories now given over to Poland and anything that might be in any way read as criticism of Russia,

They may not compare Russian administration of German territory unfavourably with that of the Americans or vice versa. In short, they may not do what many American papers are doing. Even when quoting approved foreign news sources, editors are not relieved of responsibility under this head.

Editor's grievance

The sense of this is, from the Allied viewpoint, quite obvious. There are many Germans who would gladly play off the Russians against the Western Powers, and the military authorities mean to see that this is not done.

Yet, at the same time, it is easy to see how these regulations affect the German's faith in the credibility of his Press, for one of the great topics of conversation to-day is this question of the Eastern territories, which, the Germans like to tell each other, are to a great extent lying fallow, but the Press can only handle the matter in the most delicate way.

The requisitioning of German houses by the Army is a thing which particularly irked one editor with whom I spoke. 'How can we write that the Allies are bringing democracy to us,' he said, 'if every day we see them act as the Nazis did?'

He told me that an American officer arrived at his house with a requisition, and ordered his family to get out in six hours, taking only personal effects. As he was regarded as politically acceptable to the Army he was able to get in touch with a senior officer and have the period extended to 48 hours, by which time he got a requisitioned flat.

He complained that no list of his furniture had been made out, and fears that the officer who has taken over his house may give away, or lend, a lot of the furniture, while he will have no possibility of recompense. He complained a lot about this, but most of all complained that he wasn't able to air his grievance in his paper.

You get very weary of listening to the everlasting complaining that goes on in Germany to-day. It is rather like the grumbling which soldiers the world over indulge in because they can't argue when the officers say 'No'.

Problems of staff

The German Press can't argue for the people and until it can it will not cut much ice. How to get suitable personnel has been a big problem for the Americans. No one who has ever written for the National Socialist Press may be a journalist to-day, which means, for all practical purposes, that anyone who worked between 1933 and 1945 is automatically excluded from the profession.

Staffs, then, are mostly chosen, on the one hand, from those who had retired before the National Socialists came to power or who were rejected by them, and, on the other hand, from young men without any experience.

The Americans who ran the Dana Agency trained a great number of these recruits. Still another type of person coming into journalism is the would-be politician, without any newspaper experience, who sees in the profession a good stepping stone to his ultimate career.

The running of each paper is in the hands of several licensees who are, in fact, joint editors. The Americans try to have every viewpoint represented in forty odd papers in their zone so, while one licensee may be a Communist, his colleagues may belong to the Social Democrats or Christian Democrats, according to the local representation.

Those licensees have an unenviable task. They have, in many cases, been in concentration camps or have, at least, been workless for years because of anti-Nazi activities, and they are writing for a public which, for the greater part, supported this party.

One editorial I read just after the Nuremberg executions was written in best atrocity style and probably lost that paper a good deal of support. The question then arises as to how these journalists, who are now working hand in hand with the occupiers, would fare if the army were withdrawn in a few years? Would the German people turn on them as collaborators?

I have asked several journalists how they feel about this and one admitted that he had received letters warning that the day of reckoning would come when the Allies moved out. Few of them feel that this need be worried about, yet.

While paper and facilities are in short supply, allowing newspapers to appear only every second day, blame for the small amount of straight news appearing in the German Press must also be attributed to the editors, who give a disproportionate amount of space to essays and *belles lettres* of all kinds.

There are many reviews which cater for this and the newspapers might, with profit to themselves, give more space to the reading matter for which they are primarily intended. There are signs that the restraints on the German Press in this zone are being relaxed, but that has still to go a long way before it will be free, and able to convince its people that its opinions can be taken without reservation.

Irish Press Thursday 31 October 1946
'DENAZIFYING' GERMANY—PARTY MEN HAVE TO JUSTIFY THEMSELVES
Heidelberg

Yesterday I sat through one of the German 'denazification' Courts. On trial was Karl Muller, of Mechesheim, near Heidelberg, a factory owner, who had been a member of the National Socialist Party from 1930 to 1945.

I came into the small room where the case was being heard to find Muller speaking. He sat with his Counsel at the front of the dozen rows of chairs which held the public, and facing him, in a semi-circle, were the members of the Court; the Chairman—who was a lawyer—and four lawyers, each representing a different political party.

Muller, a prosperous looking man of middle age, clean-shaven, and with grey, neatly brushed hair, spoke in a strong clear voice, jutting out his determined chin at every pause. He remained sitting, having an infirmity which compelled him to use a crutch when walking.

He was explaining that, although he had been a member of the Party, he had many friends among the anti-Nazis, and even Jews. His relations with both Catholic and Protestant churches were of the best. He had joined the Party? Yes, but soon became disillusioned. Already in 1933 he felt that something was wrong. He had never hesitated to say so. The dossier in front of him, he said, tapping it, fully documented that.

The Chairman, an impeccably dressed and unusually handsome young man, is becoming impatient. He fingers his white tie and smooths his glossy black hair. At last he interrupts. 'We are still only at 1934,' he says. 'Will you get on a little quicker?'

Muller speeds up. He gets to the period when his disillusionment

brings him into open conflict with the Party; how he came to be regarded as the black sheep in local political circles. He relates how he
was twice disciplined by the Party. Soon he is at 1943 and is helping a
Jewish family, the father of whom had been killed in Buchenwald Camp.

He tells of a visit from the Gestapo and a fine of a thousand marks,
later reduced to a hundred. He tells of his care for his workingmen and
of his many friends in every party from Communists to Christian Democrats.

The prosecution has a few questions to put to him: As well as being
a member of the Party, did you not hold office in the local organisations? Did you write the following letter in your official capacity? A
letter is read out down to the final Heil Hitler.

Yes, he wrote that, but he was only in those posts as a deputy, the
local leaders not being very literary men. 'Does this letter not refer to
you?' And we hear Muller described, in glowing terms, as a good organiser and propagandist.

There is a wrangle as to what posts he did actually hold, but Muller
maintains that in 1934 or 1935 he withdrew from active participation.
'So in thirty-five you were finished with active work for the Party?'
'Yes.' 'Then how do you explain this letter of 1936, saying how much
you are looking forward to the Nuremberg Party Festival?'

The witnesses for Muller come in one by one. The first is a local
Burgermeister, a solid red-faced man with a big moustache that twirls
at the end. He gives the Chairman his name, age. Is he married? Yes. Is
he related to Muller? No. 'Tell us what you know of his political activity,' says the Chairman.

The Burgermeister testifies that Muller never was a Party man in the
real sense of the word. He was never radical, and treated everyone
fairly and considerately. He, that Burgermeister, was on the Party's black
books for having been a Social Democrat, but that never made any
difference in his relations with Muller. Muller was straight. Another witness gives similar evidence.

Big impression

The testimony of the next witness, obviously, made a big impression. Professor Welther, formerly of the *Frankfurter Zeitung*, one of the
best-known newspapers in the world in pre-war days, now bombed
out, took the floor. Whereas the previous two had gone right up to the
table where the Chairman sat, the Professor, a trim figure in a dark suit,
stands well back, obviously perfectly at ease.

He is forty-six, of medium height, with a keen intellectual face and
long grey hair, brushed straight back and neatly trimmed behind, just

short of his collar. He met Muller in 1941 as a result of an extraordinary letter Muller wrote to his paper. The Professor has his back to me most of the time, but his flying hands and swaying shoulders are as expressive as his face.

'Extraordinary' is the word he uses again and again. He was surprised at the extraordinary critical tone of the letter. Extraordinary to get such matter through the usual post. When he got to know Muller, he had to admit to himself that he had seldom met such an independent, critical, outspoken man.

The Professor's eloquence is not halted even by the cross-examination. If Muller was so clever, why didn't he see through the Nazi theories earlier? he was asked. The Professor gave us a long examination of Muller's social conscience, and explains his tremendous energy, which would never allow him to stay out of the swim. Finally, he points out that although Muller did join, he got out for all practical purposes in thirty-five.

The Professor was followed by what were probably the most decisive witnesses in proof of Muller's good faith. Mother and son of a Jewish family told, in almost inaudible tones, of Muller's help to them after their father had been killed in Buchenwald and they had been bombed out of their homes.

She is a very elegant woman of fifty-one; white hair carefully done; wearing a well-cut suit. She stands with her hands folded in front of her lowered head and almost breaks down in relating her tragic story. Muller had helped them in every way—with money, with advice, with protection. The court is impressed.

Prove two things

After two more witnesses have spoken, the Chairman point out that, to clear himself, Muller has to prove two things. First—that he resisted actively; and secondly, that he suffered loss thereby to show active resistance. Muller and his counsel again quote letters to the papers, including one to the *Voelkischer Beobachter*, the official organ of the party. 'Not so hard to do that when you're a Party member,' comments a member of the Court.

A letter to Dr Goebbels is mentioned. Muller was a great letter-writer. We hear again of his disciplining by the Party, his visit from the Gestapo and his fine. Finally, there was the fact of his factory having been closed in 1943—being classed as luxury production.

Great stress is laid on this and there is much cross-questioning. It is pointed out that many people in his position were similarly hit and it may have had no relation to his political activities. Did he do anything to hinder the war effort? 'Sabotage? Never,' replied Muller, really roused.

The prosecutor sums up the case against Muller. He is a quiet, small man who has never once raised his voice. He has done his job conscientiously, but without enthusiasm.

In a brief speech he goes over Muller's history since 1930, stressing that, while he ceased to be active for the Party soon after it came to power, he did not resign membership. He points out that in Muller's district the membership rose steeply, probably as a result of the example given by Muller, who was a respected citizen. He asks that the accused be found guilty in class two.

Cleared of charge

The defending counsel makes a speech which clearly gets home. Muller, he says, was an enthusiastic Party man in the early days. He read another of the letters to show what great hopes Muller had that National Socialism would bring peace, prosperity and unity to Germany.

He read a similar sentiment expressed by a renowned academic figure. Neither of these men, he said were fools, and yet they were taken in. But when Muller became disillusioned he didn't grumble within the safety of four walls as so many did. He spoke up and wrote what he thought. 'We need men like this to help us rebuild our economy,' he summed up.

The Court leaves to consider the verdict. After about 20 minutes they return. Muller is cleared, and the State must pay the costs of the proceedings. They find that he resisted and that he suffered loss thereby.

'We need men like this today,' says the Chairman. Muller's friends rush to congratulate him. He is smiling.

Irish Press Monday 4 November 1946
TOBACCO SAVES A GERMAN FARMER

Frankfurt

Nearest approach to normal food conditions in Germany today exists, naturally, in the country districts. In the towns, people speak bitterly of the fine life that goes on out beyond the ruins and make heavy jests about farmers with Persian carpets in the pigsties, but after two days on the land it is my experience that, while much better off than the townspeople, the country folk are not nearly so well off as is generally believed here.

If their produce was not closely surveyed by Government authorities, they would have endless opportunities for exploiting their surplus food, but they are in fact so closely watched and their own share so accurately calculated that there is seldom much left over for outside dealing.

And while their rations are in accordance with the heavy work they do, much greater than those of most town dwellers, yet tremendous demands are made on their generosity by people on food hunting expeditions and by the refugees—who in this part of the country crowd every town and village.

In one village where I spent a few hours yesterday the pre-war population of 12,000 has now risen to 17,000 with the influx of refugees from the Sudetenland and the eastern territories, many of whom arrived without even the traditional vagrant's bundle.

I was told there of the constant stream of people who go from door-to-door, begging for potatoes not by the basketful or even by the pound, but potato by potato. Or they may ask: 'Spare us even a spoonful of meal.'

One of the most fortunate families I came across is that of—let us call them the Bauers of Bauersdorf. Willie Bauer is a successful man, and the secret of his success, as in so many cases in Germany today, lies in tobacco. He actually grows it.

As I sat over a glass of his home-made cider after dinner yesterday, listening to his farm chat, I offered him a cigarette. Willy, who looked at it as if the last thing he wanted to see was a cigarette then, obviously only out of politeness and in record time, smoked it.

Throwing away enough of the end to cause an unholy scramble on any town pavement, he went over to a cupboard and produced three large boxes.

'They take most of my tobacco from me, of course,' he said, 'but there are ways and means'; and he opened up the boxes to reveal dozens of cigars, dark brown, khaki, and downright green.

'Strictly illegal,' he went on, 'but what would we do without them?' He put his feet up on the table. 'I wouldn't have these boots if it hadn't been for the cigars, nor would my wife nor the girl.' This was a paradox. For when the townsman goes out into the country he can be more sure of getting food if he brings tobacco. A man then, who is not only a farmer with the relatively good feeding that means, but who is independent in regard to tobacco, is a king.

Comfortable

And Willy's place, like that of so many of his fellow tobacco growers in this district, looked very comfortable. He showed us over the massive wooden building, half barn, half cattle byre, that dwarfed his living house.

Its high, steep-sloping, red-tiled roof had eaves that projected several feet out from the wall, and from one end of the building to the other hung drying tobacco leaves. Out behind, the whole face of the building, open to the weather but protected by the long eaves, was covered with row upon row of bunches of the precious plant. Willie, ever puffing his cigar, gazed with pride at it.

Ducking low under beams from which hung maize, we were led to see his livestock.

From six fine cows, I guessed, he ought to get quite a lot of butter for himself. He shook his head.

'They took away our churns during the war,' he said, 'and we have to turn in our milk quota twice a day and draw our butter rations like the rest.' But as a substitute for butter they eat a lot of thick sour milk known as 'quarg'. Then we saw the pigs. Willy kept opening doors in the walls so quickly that I lost count of the pink snouts, and perhaps we looked at the same pig several times. It looked, at any rate, as if the family could get a little extra meal now and then.

'We get little enough,' he said, 'but you have to ask my wife the details'; and we found out from her that 1½ pounds per week was their allowance.

I had come out to Willy's place with Hans, a university professor who is out of work, waiting to be 'denazified'. It is his sole present occupation to make an expedition like this about twice a week, and he especially likes to come to the Bauers, because, owing to some family relationship, the Bauers sell him some food at a reasonable price instead of driving a hard barter deal, as many do.

This type of transaction was illustrated just after we arrived at the house. A knock came to the door, and Frau Bauer went out. There was a low buzz of voices for a minute, a rise in pitch, and finally from Willy's wife: 'Never come back again if you don't bring it.'

She came back, red with anger. It seemed her visitor had got some potatoes a few days before in return for a promise of floor polish, and now was back again for potatoes but still without polish.

Gift of sheet

Although Hans pays for the goods, it never does to arrive empty-handed, and yesterday he brought a sheet as a present for the daughter, who is engaged to be married.

Willy's wife looked at it without much enthusiasm, probably wondering if it was good value for the dinner she had promised us, and then threw it on to a pile of what looked like similar booty on the dresser. The previous addition to the pile was a case of cutlery.

I had also in my ignorance brought some cigarettes, which I didn't dare produce after Willy got going on his cigars, but some chocolate which we gave them smoothed the way.

It was certainly the best meal I had seen at a German table. It consisted of one dish only, thick broth or stew of potatoes, milk, vegetables and small shreds of bacon.

Along with this went a huge slice of dark brown bread containing a lot of rye, which gives a pleasantly sour taste, making it for me a lot more palatable than our own. The slices were enormous, the best part of the average German's daily ration.

Two full soup plates was my capacity for the broth, but Hans, whose once full pink face is now pinched and lined, went on to a fourth and even a fifth.

Later in the afternoon we were called in for something else before leaving, and again we had the enormous slices of bread, this time with a bowlful of thick sour milk. I reckoned that Hans at this meal ate almost two days of his normal rations at the sitting.

While we were eating, Frau Bauer told us of the various ways the country people have of supplementing their food, such as the raising of hens, which, though a certain quota of eggs has to be surrendered, can usually be counted on to give a certain surplus. Geese, being uncontrolled, are popular, and rabbits are kept by many people.

But, like every German, she again and again came back to the problem of fats. Here, at least, they were reasonably well-off for milk and had the 'quarg' to put on their bread, but to supplement ten grammes per day of butter they were forced, like the townspeople, to resort to devices like gathering beech nuts.

I was told that a couple of days gathering might bring enough to make a quart of oil which could be used for cooking.

Hans mentioned the shipping of Irish food to Germany, and she said: 'If we could only get some fats from you.'

Our train time was coming near. We went down to the cellars, where she filled our two rucksacks with potatoes and stuffed a few cabbages into a bag. Hans paid her five marks and a little of my chocolate, and we were on our way.

'A very nice family,' Hans kept saying, and I kept wondering what people do who know no families in the country like this. On our way to the station we met Willy returning home in his cart. He was still smoking a cigar.

Irish Press Wednesday 6 November 1946
IRELAND SWEETENS SCHOOL MEALS—GIFTS OF SUGAR PLEASE
 GERMANS

Wiesbaden

Even where it is only a trickle, little more than a symbol of goodwill, Irish food is appreciated in Germany today. In Wiesbaden this morning, one of the lesser bombed towns in this zone, I saw several hundred schoolchildren hungrily eat oatmeal and milk gruel supplied by American relief agencies and sweetened with the latest consignment of Irish sugar.

A small thing to us, the sweetening of gruel, but to these children, aged six to 14, it meant a lot, for until recently the last sugar they had got on their ration cards was a special issue last Christmas.

For two months, now, the ration has been coming through—half a pound per month for those over six and one pound for those under six—so that, even today, the few spoonfuls per week that each child gets from us is considerable in proportion to the rations.

At ten o'clock, I arrived at one of the schools as the first lot was being served. The children had been at work since eight o'clock, as is the German custom.

Led by the headmaster, Dr Broglie, an elderly man with a white goatee beard, his long grey overcoat flapping around his ankles, I pushed along a dark passage where the children stood in line, beating tom-tom music on their various receptacles—army mess tins, enamel bowls or, more often, plain tin cans.

'Children,' proclaimed the headmaster as he strolled down the middle of the classroom, 'here is someone from Ireland, the green isle whose people make life so sweet for us today. You all know of the green island, and now here's an Irishman to see how much we appreciate what they are sending us. We do appreciate it, don't we?'

But faces were deep in their gruel, and beyond a smile or a murmur here and there, there was no response. 'Of course, they do,' he said to me, and we went up to another room where the same concentrated lapping up was going on.

Thrice weekly

Our few bags of sugar help with this meal three times a week in Wiesbaden. It would be fine to think that we could help provide the small amount for all the needy children, but at present we cannot.

Before a child can qualify for one of these meals, he has to be medically examined, and only the most necessitous qualify.

In this school of about 900 pupils, only 420 can be fed, although, according to the headmaster, 80 per cent are undernourished.

How difficult it must be for those who are left behind when half of a class troops off to the meal and the rest are unfed, not because they are properly nourished, but because there is not enough food to go round.

In one other town, nearby Darmstadt, where cellar life is the normal thing, the authorities felt they couldn't make any distinction and fed all the children until the supplies ran out, which they quickly did.

'Don't think of the food value alone,' said a welfare worker to me when I deprecated the amount we could send. 'The food value is something, but you must also count the happiness units you bring to these children.

'German life today is mostly a struggle for food, but there are other miseries, and perhaps the greatest of these is the feeling that everyone hates the Germans. Gifts like these have, therefore, a double significance for us.'

Half to schools

Half of the present allocation of Irish sugar in this district of Greater Hesse—one of the three units into which the US zone is divided—goes to the feeding of schoolchildren and half to the Red Cross, which distributes it through other channels, some of it being used in homes for the aged, some to feed the refugees which cram the houses everywhere in South Germany.

In Frankfurt, too, 160 doctors can give certificates to very necessitous people, which allows them to draw a pound of our sugar.

The stock being used at present in Greater Hesse consists of the merest 330 bags, each containing about 200 pounds—or rather, originally containing that amount, for even in a locked railway carriage supplies are not safe from thieves who, with thin steel tubes, bore through the flooring and drain away the grains.

Gratitude for this small amount is pathetic, and gratitude in the shambles that town life is in Germany today is a rare thing.

Irish Press Saturday 9 November 1946
IRISH SUGAR MAKES LIFE SWEETER FOR GERMAN CHILDREN

Darmstadt

Irish sugar is playing a considerable part in making life more bearable for thousands of children in this zone of Germany, but in at least one case that I have come across credit for it is going to the Americans, and especially to the Quakers of America.

If we are satisfied that the children are getting some benefit out of our contribution, then that is perhaps enough. To feed politics with the sugar is unthinkable.

But as the children in this particular case have tried to thank the donors, it is a pity that they cannot thank the right people.

In front of me I have a folder containing 'thank you' notes and drawings from children between the ages of six and fourteen. On the outside of the folder is inscribed: 'German children's home. Thanks,' and a line from Goethe: 'Let man be noble, helpful and good.'

Throughout the contents two words recur—sugar and Quakers.

Dr Schenck, head of the Red Cross relief section for Greater Hesse, one of the three divisions of the US zone, gave this to me yesterday to bring to Ireland and apologised for the mistake the children had made.

'The Quakers are so indissolubly connected in the German mind with relief work because of their efforts after 1918,' he said, 'that the mistake is understandable. But,' he went on, 'this sugar for which they are giving thanks really does come from your country.'

The fault certainly does not lie with the Red Cross local centre in Darmstadt, where all food is labelled according to its source—I saw there an invoice for this home labelled 'Irish gift'—but to people at the lower levels of distribution Ireland is a far off country about which no one knows much, and in this case easily became assimilated to America.

Are coaxed

The dossier was compiled by children in a home in the Odenwald, south of Darmstadt, called 'Rimdid'. I will always remember it as the place where children have to be coaxed to eat.

I spent about an hour there looking into the dormitory where they were having their after-dinner nap, looking at the toys they had made, talking with the sisters who looked after them, but during that hour I could not get out of my head what the matron told me—that most of the children have become so accustomed to semi-starvation that they can only with difficulty become used to even the modest diet provided for them there.

They have to be persuaded that the unaccustomed food is good for them, and can only very gently be introduced to it.

And the food is not so very much better than the average German rations. For example, while the normal ration of fats is 300 grammes per month, the home can only supply 60 more, and all the relief supplies do not bring the scale of feeding up to what is needed to make their stay here of any lasting value.

The average gain in the six weeks, then, is only three and a half pounds.

It is in the light of these conditions that we must judge our gift of sugar and not by our comfortable standards at home. That is what makes the 'Thank you' book such pathetic reading.

The home is perched on a hilltop about 1,200 feet above sea level, and in this autumn weather a piercing wind assails it. The first people I met when I arrived were two children lying on the veranda and wrapped up to the ears—asthma cases—who puffed their thanks when I handed one a bar of chocolate.

A sister who came along explained what it was and tore off the wrapping. For the children had never seen chocolate before.

The running of a home like this presents innumerable difficulties, for practically everything is in short supply.

There is a shortage of soap—the children use a cake of what looks and feels like sandstone. There is a shortage of mops and brushes to keep the rooms clean, a shortage of clothes to keep the children warm.

Here are some things from the 'Thank you' book. Gisela Schutrumpf, aged ten years, has inscribed in a page bordered with multicoloured flowers: 'We German children are very happy when the Quakers send a ship across the sea with good pure sugar, and we give thanks for it.'

Heidi Behr, aged ten, of Darmstadt, has a drawing of a ship with Sugar Ship written in giant letters across the side and sacks of sugar strung along the deck.

Another little girl has drawn a house against which leans a huge sack labelled 'sugar', which reaches almost to the chimney pots.

Six weeks in the home doesn't do much more than check temporarily the decline in the children's health. Every one of them could do with a year.

But relief sources are limited, and after six weeks the child must go back to the cellar life of Darmstadt or to the squalor of overcrowded rooms, which is universal here.

Later in the day I visited the Red Cross offices here, where I saw the sugar in pink bags labelled 'Irish gifts', each containing a pound [of sugar]. Every child between six and ten in this town gets one of these from the present supply.

This is quite apart from the free school meals mentioned in my last dispatch, and one worker told me of the enthusiasm with which the tots relate what they are going to do with it.

One will make a little jam, another thinks she will have some puddings, and yet another is determined to eat it spoonful by spoonful.

When you see in a ledger that 56 sacks, each weighing 200 pounds, are being distributed in a town like Darmstadt (pre-war about 100,000, now approximately 70,000 population) you think how little there is to go round, but a child with a bag of sugar in his hand makes nonsense of statistics, which seems to make our effort so small.

Irish Press Wednesday 13 November 1946
CIVILIANS 'JUST PESTS' IN US GERMAN ZONE

Munich

Vermin abounds in Germany, but to the US military authorities the most annoying type of vermin is the civilian. They hate this pest. They set up every type of barrier to protect themselves from it. Notices everywhere warn the pest: 'No loitering' or 'Entry forbidden to civilians'.

Military police push him in the face or at least wave disgustedly at him if he halts in front of them to ask a question, and the German police tend not to hear him unless he speaks in English. Officers lift one foot from the desk to keep him off while they shout for the sergeant to put him out.

If the pest carries a good camera, soldiers plague him with queries of 'How many cigarettes?'

For pest or civilian in the above paragraphs, read 'this correspondent', all are personal experiences.

In short, it is the lot of a civilian here, be he German or not, to suffer a score of pinpricks daily at the hands of officialdom—probably the lot of civilians in any occupied country.

Any type of uniform is invaluable for making life more easy, even to save one some of the endless showing of identity documents and encounters with watchdogs who have 'never seen one of those before'.

It's wonderful what even a single article of military type clothing will do. An American windjacket without badges of any type, borrowed from a fellow correspondent, saved me one whole day's fumbling with Press cards.

Incidentally, I've walked straight through a German police guard, simply by pointing to the Irish Army badge in my button hole and muttering inaudibly without having anyone stop me to enquire what was the significance of the words 'Óglaigh na hÉireann' or what unit had the sunburst as its emblem.

Raw police

The military police are the most difficult problem. It is one of the worst features of the American occupation that so many of the soldiers new here are extremely young men, totally unequipped to withstand the temptations that come to any garrison in possession of a foreign country, but especially to soldiers so well supplied as the Americans are with food, money, clothes and luxuries like chocolate, fruit juice and cigarettes, living among a population that is not only on the verge of starvation but has in many cases lost most of its possessions in the bombings.

Only the best troops could win through a situation like this, and it is hardly surprising that arrogance and indifference to anyone not in uniform is the most noticeable feature of the US military police who have the maximum opportunity for making their authority felt.

I stood in a queue one night at a railway station surrounded by American uniforms. Suddenly I became aware of a military policeman at my side. 'And who are you?' he asked ironically, smirking at the soldiers around. He was going to have some fun with the civilian and was probably hoping that I was a German.

But all my papers were in order, and I was able to go on standing, an isolated civilian figure among the khaki.

'Never heard of it,' is a frequent reply when you ask the way to some important building, perhaps not a hundred yards from where they are standing, and 'don't worry me, buddy', comes from the more outspoken.

Difficult job

Like all those who co-operate with the occupiers, the Military Government's German police have a difficult task. Keeping on the right side of the authorities means very often getting on the wrong side of German people.

For while all agree that it is all right to take a job with the US Army for the sake of the one free meal a day, becoming a policeman is going a bit too far. Hence the German police often tend to go right over to the side of the occupiers and treat civilians much the same way as the Army does.

Again this is a matter of my own, personal experience. I have been bawled at after addressing the police guard outside a Military Government building only to have them wave at me, all bows and smiles, when I asked them in English how dare they speak like that.

There is one type of civilian who does not come into the pest category—the pretty young German girl secretaries. They form one of the most privileged classes in the country.

I have heard other German women complain bitterly that the only way you can get things done in this country to-day is by getting on the right side of these girls.

Being a foreign civilian in Germany, however, has its moments. The other day, when riding in a borrowed car, I gave a lift to two GIs, and at the end of the run they each tipped me in the usual manner—two cigarettes.

Irish Press Tuesday 19 November 1946
GERMAN CARDINAL SAYS 'END NAZI PURGE'—GERMANY'S MAIN
PROBLEM TODAY

Munich

Cardinal Faulhaber,[1] in one of the rare interviews he has given to the Press, replied without hesitation 'Denazification' when I asked him: 'What is the greatest problem facing Germany today?'

It was difficult for many to keep out of some National-Socialist organisation, said His Eminence. The shoemaker who refused to join might as well close down his shop, for he would get no leather. The smith in a similar position might as well close his smithy, for business would be impossible.

In the academic life, the student who aspired to some official position had to join one of the Nazi organisations or throw away all the benefit of his previous schooling. Now all these people were classed as Nazis and were in many cases workless as a result.

Many who never in their hearts accepted the teachings of National Socialism are thus classed as active members, the Cardinal said.

A man was only a real Nazi when he had accepted certain doctrines which were basically anti-Christian, characterised, for example, by anti-Jewish violence.

His Eminence stressed that he was not referring to the main classes of the accused but to the broad masses of the people technically classed under the denazification laws as 'followers'. Here I may interject that the Cardinal's remarks on denazification come at a time when Bavaria is seething with excitement at the repercussions after Gen. Clay, Deputy Military Governor of the US zone, had criticised German officials' handling of the problem as too lenient.

The Bavarian minister entrusted with the task, Dr Pfeiffer, was attacked by the commentator, Herbert Gessner, over American-sponsored Radio Munich. Dr Pfeiffer replied at a special meeting. The US Military Government chief of Bavaria, Gen. Mueller, claims that Gessner spoke as a private German individual and not as a mouthpiece of the Military Government, and the fight goes on. The class about which there is most discussion are the 'followers', defined by the 'law for liberation from national-Socialism and militarism' as those who only nominally took part in National-Socialism or gave it little support, and who did not prove to be militarists.

That includes people who, though members of the party or its af-

[1] In 1951 Cardinal Michael von Faulhaber ordained the present Pope Benedict XVI as a priest.

filiated organisations, did no more than to pay their dues and attend compulsory meetings, also candidates who were never elected. Punishment for this class includes single or recurring fines, compulsory retirement, or demotion from official positions.

Germans unable to look ahead

After his remarks on denazification, I asked Cardinal Faulhaber if Germany would in the foreseeable future play a major role in world politics. He was silent for some time. Silence was in this case really eloquent. Even in 1918, who would have hesitated to answer this question with 'yes'? But His Eminence was silent. Then he said:

'We cannot look ahead. We are too busy with the problems of day-to-day living. In Bavaria, for example on top of all the distress of war, two million refugees have been added to a population of six million. Care for these millions of refugees from Silesia and other eastern territories, who have lost their home and all, is our second greatest problem.'

His Eminence went on to speak of the task that faced the Church in Germany today. In Munich, for example, out of 79 churches, 43 had been destroyed or rendered unfit for use, including churches in which he used to preach—St Michael's, the Cathedral and the Basilica of St Boniface.

Many who had fallen away from the Church during the National-Socialist regime were coming back, but they were being carefully scrutinised and put on probation first, he declared. Schooling was another great problem because half of the buildings were ruined and half of the teachers removed from their positions.

Speaking of matters in general in the zone, the Cardinal said that the American officials, apart from small incidents, put no difficulties in the way of the Church.

Irish Kilian was German apostle

The Cardinal smiled when I asked him if he had any connections with Ireland. 'As the part of Germany from which I come—Franconia—was Christianised by the Irish Kilian, I have a special feeling for your country and for Saint Patrick,' he said.

We spoke of Irish relief supplies, and His Eminence listed as the most important requirements, after food, medical supplies and footwear, especially for workers.

Of the medical supplies, he said that even the simplest remedies were lacking.

His Eminence, at 77, is strong and active and has a powerful handclasp. He speaks slowly and emphatically, and his smile, too, comes slowly but expansively.

He has been in Munich since 1917, when he became Archbishop of Munich-Freising, and not even the heaviest bombing raids during the war could shift him as long as one room remained habitable in the Erzbischofshof which is his residence.

Finally, the day came when not even one remained, and only then did His Eminence consent to move out for the few days required to get one room ready again. He moved to Freising, the original seat of the archdiocese, and on that day the town got a heavy raid.

Irish Press Tuesday 26 November 1946
GERMANS FACING FIRST GRIP OF WINTER

Munich

It is cold in Bavaria. Autumn has turned to winter with vicious suddenness and the people are face to face with the grimmest period of trial they have yet had. The first snow fell a few days ago and, though it vanished within 24 hours, the chill has stayed on.

For the first time in my life, I've realised what I've owed the Gulf Stream all these years for keeping me warm in winter. In two days' travelling through the Bavarian countryside I kept putting on more clothes until I finally decided that nothing I could do would be of any use.

I was staying in a lakeside village south of Munich from where we could see the Alps—in better conditions a glorious sight, but when you're cold and ill-fed only representing the place from where the bitter winds come.

These winds could pierce anything. In my case, they had to get through a heavy tweed overcoat, a windjacket, a tweed jacket, a woollen waistcoat, a tweed waistcoat, another woollen waistcoat, a heavy shirt and final layer of wool.

And they did get through. For those two days I stalked around like a Frankenstein monster, legs and arms swinging almost uncontrollably, frozen stiff.

This was probably due to a large extent to lack of acclimatisation, but also to the fact that German food was beginning to take its toll of whatever fat I had brought from Ireland.

Doctor's journey

It was cold in the morning when I got up and looked out at the brilliantly sunlit lake. Unlike the last German family with which I stayed, where five slept in one room and the only fire was in the room which served as nursery-dining-room, drying-room, kitchen, study—these people were not cramped, and I was alone. I threw off the stack of rugs, overcoats and miscellaneous garments that I had piled on, and hurried over to breakfast to keep in the night's warmth.

This family lives well above the average as both husband and wife have professions and they have relatives in Denmark, Switzerland and America who send them parcels. So on our bread we had a slice of Danish sausage (cold) and a little cheese.

'Will you have a little German coffee?' asks the hostess heavily emphasising 'German', and for the umpteenth time I think out a comparison for the smell. This time I make it old bones stewing.

This is the last meal we are to have for over twelve hours. The Herr Doktor and I are going off visiting, and in these days you don't call near mealtimes unless your hosts happen to be self-sufficient farmers. The Herr Doktor is in a gloomy mood to-day. 'Why do I bother to work at all?' he asks. 'With taxes as they are and money almost worthless, I could live better by trading my cigarette ration on the black market or collecting butts.'

The doctor, like so many Germans, is an expert on butts. When you offer him a cigarette be is likely to put it in his pocket and save it for the luxury of an after-meal smoke, in the meantime producing his pipe and feeding it with your cigarette ends.

Our journey proceeds erratically, always being timed so that our arrival does not coincide with mealtimes anywhere. In intervals of waiting we chew gum and chocolate.

One call, however, is outside the general rule. A. farming family the doctor knows to be well off is good for some milk and bread any time, so we call and soon a pint of milk and several slices of dry bread are before us.

When the doctor has eaten some, he asks politely if he may take the rest to his mother and carefully puts two slices of dry bread in his pocket. His mother, when we arrive at her house, is delighted with the present he has brought.

I have seen the same doctor, after a long, hard day, produce a slice of bread from his desk, bread that might have been a week there, so hard and grubby was it, and chew it with satisfaction.

Our visits are mostly business calls for the doctor, and I have plenty of time to reflect on how impossible it is to appreciate scenery, people, conversation or anything if you are cold and hungry.

Each succeeding house seems to get chillier. Night is already on when we call to see a professor friend of the doctor, and are in danger of being invited to stay and eat.

It takes a very heroic effort on the doctor's part not to accept. It is seven, and we have been eleven hours on the road, but we say that we are expected at home.

We are invited into the one room that is heated. Most of the heat appears to come from the electric bulb, for I am up against the tiled oven that is standard German equipment and feel not a glimmer.

Sometimes you wonder if everything is wrong in Germany, and the answer is, of course, nearly everything.

Two hours later we are back in the lakeside village to find that the central heating system is being replaced by a couple of stoves to economise in the little fuel they have. So Bavaria means one thing to me now—coldness.

There is a lot of the first person in this story. Instead of applying it to an Irishman who all his life has been well fed and clothed, apply it to any German to-day who has not had much to eat for at least a year, whose house is not properly heated, whose clothes are thin and shoes leaky, and you may feel something of what this winter is going to mean to the Germans.

Irish Press Wednesday 27 November 1946
BREAD RIOTS TALK IN GERMAN CITY—RHINELAND PEOPLE SEE WINTER
OF TERROR

Düsseldorf

This is the first place in Germany in which I've heard talk of food riots. People are not merely hungry, ill clad and ill housed, they are veritably starving. There is terror in their hearts, for they see only complete collapse in front of them.

How can you distinguish the line between the hungry and the starving? You can do it by spending a few days in the Ruhr and the North Rhine-Westphalia.

Is it not starvation when some people have seen no bread for 14 days? Is it not starvation when potatoes have run out and the next allocation is weeks or months away?

Is it not a sign that the area is at the edge of chaos when a medical examination in a university reveals that 30 per cent of the students are either suffering from tuberculosis or immediately threatened with it?

(These university tuberculosis figures are of Bonn, but it is stressed that they are based on only two days examination. There is a hope that final figures may, perhaps, fall to 25 per cent.)

Crisis is not over

It has been said that the immediate crisis in this area is over. As yet the Germans have little sign of it. I have actually spoken with people who have been without bread for weeks, and have seen families whose only food in one day was turnip, and not a lot of it.

I have found these conditions not only here on the fringes of the Ruhr, but as far south as Bonn. Not everyone is equally badly hit. Conditions vary from town to town, from district to district, and even from street to street; but the general picture is of a people on the verge of disaster.

The first thing that strikes you about this north Rhine area is the extent of the destruction. In about five weeks' travelling throughout Germany I have seen big cities like Frankfurt and Munich, where you were seldom more than a street away from ruins. I have seen industrial centres like Mannheim, where square miles have been flattened as if by a giant bulldozer.

But this place surpasses all. You can travel for hours and never be out of sight of jagged ruins, twisted girders and smashed rolling stock.

From Hamm through Dortmund, Gelsenkirchen, Duisburg and on to Cologne I had nearly a hundred miles of it.

Even in pre-war days the greater stretch of this journey must have been a drab experience. You feel that to these towns belong mist and drizzle and permanent twilight. Now there is just a vast slag-heap. There is a stirring in it, but it remains a slag-heap.

The next thing that strikes you is the number and size of the queues. There were orderly queues of people standing two abreast, and then there were shop doors where half a dozen were wrestling to be first in. I reckoned that in one street the eight or ten queues we passed had well over a thousand people in all.

Then there are many shops that had no queues—a fact explained by notices like one I saw: 'No bread baked today through lack of coal.'

Other shops displayed cards with 'Sugar on bread coupons today'. Again, dried potatoes were offered for the same coupons, and even biscuits.

Ration display

In a British Military Government office they display a week's rations with dummies. The chief thing to note about it is that you can get very little of it here at the moment. Without going into it too exactly, this is what it shows:

About 25 middle-sized potatoes.

A long loaf of bread, giving maybe three or four slices per day.

Quarter pound of meat, including bone.

Quarter pound of fish.

2 ounces of fats.

Morsel of cheese, smaller than the silver-wrapped sections in our boxes.

1 pound of vegetables, represented by a cabbage.

6 ounces of sugar.

Three or four tablespoonfuls of ersatz coffee.

One and three quarter quarts of skimmed milk.

A pound and a half of meal.

A footnote adds that a couple of ounces of jam may be had or more sugar.

If you could get all this—remembering that it is not just a basic ration, but all the food you are likely to get—and were to divide it into three meals a day for seven days of the week, it would make a sorry show. It is very important, for you have no hope of getting anything like it here today.

Take away the bread for even a day or two, and what have you left? Take-away bread or potatoes for a week or more, and you can see why there is terror in the hearts of the people.

As I said, this is the first place I have heard talk of riots. Men have sworn to me that if they see their children starve much longer they will take matters into their own hands.

British Military Government officials on the spot are fully alive to the situation and make no attempt to conceal their dismay at the prospects for this winter.

One welfare officer with whom I spoke had just made a tour of houses, getting at first hand the data on the day-to-day conditions, and confirmed many of the examples I have given above of families who have been weeks without bread.

But the remedy is not in the hands of these men. They can only do their best to inform their authorities in Britain of the realities of the situation and wait for moves for improvement from those at a higher level.

Fuel worries

There are other worries beside food. Fuel, for example. Some families have had two hundred-weights this winter and in other cases only people with doctor's certificates have been able to get any at all.

There is a complete lack of shoes and boots. Anyone who had not several pairs at the end of the war is now almost barefoot.

Not once but many times I have heard of young children who have never had a single pair in their lives. To buy a pair of shoes for an adult on the black market costs the pre-war price of one of the Volks wagons or 'people's cars'.

You keep on wondering if there is not somewhere a brighter side of things. I asked a Military Government official, and he spoke of factory production figures, instancing in one case the production of a million pairs of shoes.

'When will these be available to the Germans?' He didn't know.

Railroads and rolling stock are being restored in increasing numbers; coal production has been raised, so that in some months the effect of all this work may become apparent to the German in his day-to-day life.

But for the moment his plight in this area of the British zone is really desperate.

Irish Press Friday 29 November 1946
GERMANS STILL CRAM RAID SHELTERS FOR HOMES

Düsseldorf

It is 18 months since the bombers ceased to come over Germany every night, but the air-raid shelters or bunkers are still populated. No longer by packed crowds seeking escape from death, but by bombed-out or refugee families, who are trying to convert these chill, ill-lit caverns into some semblance of a home.

Not the worst off in regard to housing, perhaps, they at least have a firm roof over their heads, and are often not much more overcrowded than the mass of the people.

But the constant breathing of an atmosphere that is by turns chill and damp, or stuffy and thick, has given them a toadstool complexion and a staring listlessness that makes many seem little better than walking corpses.

The plight of the very young children is especially bad. Seldom seeing daylight, seldom breathing fresh air, they cannot even stray more than a few yards from their cubicles because of the danger of falling down the narrow winding stairs that characterise the sky-scraping shelters—at times 11 storeys.

The passages—and even the beds of their fellow-occupiers — are crammed with cooking apparatus.

Woman reading

I went into one of these above-ground shelters near Düsseldorf yesterday, stumbling along a maze of unlit passages before emerging into a vast gloomy hall, lit in one corner only by a solitary bulb. Under this bulb sat an old woman reading. I went up to her, thinking she was the warden.

'Oh, no, I'm just sitting here because there is no light in my cubicle,' she said, and went on reading. A drooping child clinging to a pillar was the only other sign of life, and my heels beat a loud tattoo as I went off to look for the man in charge.

Most of the wartime signs were still there—signs exhorting to calm and discipline and forbidding smoking. But most distinctive were the notices put up for the present occupiers, chief among which was the schedule for the weekly delousing parades.

In German it reads discreetly 'Pudern' or 'Powdering'—almost like a woman and her handbag operations.

These shelters are simply large extra solid buildings with several cubicles on each floor, but the only furniture provided consists of benches and built-in bunks, to which have now been added cooking apparatus.

Many of the occupants have brought their own furniture in, so that here and there you get the impression of being in a small cosy room in an ordinary house, except that there are no windows or fireplaces and that heating and ventilation is done through slits in the wall.

Young couple

The first room I went into was bright and cheery and belonged to a young couple who had obviously gone to great trouble over it. True, the cubicle was so small that you could hardly move between the table and bed, but the same held of many rooms I have been in here.

Then they began to tell of the trials of bunker life and to detail the maladies it brings on. There was scabies from over-crowding and dirt, not in evidence here, catarrh, sore throats and rheumatism from the atmosphere, and rashes, especially in the case of children.

One woman brought me to where her daughter of about eight lay with a bad throat. A pitiful, bare little cubicle, not even a shred of matting or sacking on the floor, and the child whimpering in a corner. 'All our furniture and clothes are going in exchange for food,' she said.

Her husband is a prisoner of war in Russia. Beyond the bare announcement of this fact, she knows nothing of his fate.

In another cubicle lay a woman who was to have a baby in a month. Her bed was the ordinary shelter bench, without even straw as a mattress. For her child she had not one single garment and very little for herself.

The warden was bitter. 'I was persecuted under the Hitler regime,' he said, and showed me a special identity card he carried to prove it. 'I was cured of Communist leanings when I saw the condition of our men coming from the Russian prisoner of war camps, and now I think I am cured of democracy.

'If these people could send guns and tanks across to Germany, why couldn't they now send us food and other things we need?'

Train story

A man cannot reason properly on an empty stomach, and when he went on to tell a story that I had heard with varying details in every part of Germany I have been, from Munich to Düsseldorf, without ever finding one first-hand witness, I didn't interrupt or question him.

It usually runs like this. A man loading potatoes onto a train which is supposed to be going to another part of his zone leaves his coat down in one of the trucks and, while he is busy elsewhere, the train goes off.

He tries to get in touch with the station to which the goods are said to be going but fails, and finally gives up hope of ever getting it back.

Some days later a train pulls into the station, bearing what is alleged to be food sent from overseas. A coat is found in one of the wagons containing potatoes, and, lo and behold, it belongs to our friend.

So not only do they take away our food, say the narrators, but the supplies which are supposed to come from abroad are really our own.

'Don't talk to us of charities,' said some of the bunker dwellers, when I asked if they got no assistance from anyone. 'People are always coming down promising us things, but we never get anything.'

In this case, at least, their self-pity was not justified, for shortly afterwards I came across a bunker from which several children had been sent to Ireland.

Irish Press Saturday 30 November 1946
GERMANS ANXIOUS FOR NEWS OF THEIR CHILDREN

Düsseldorf

Some parents of German children who left this area for Ireland in August are very anxious because they have not had any letters from them or the families with which they are staying, I was told by Dr Schwarz, head of the German Welfare Organisation in Düsseldorf.

The parents know that the children are in good hands, but the separation is a hard blow for them, and could be made more tolerable if they got regular letters. Dr Schwarz made an urgent plea to those concerned to get a few lines across to the parents.

I visited some of the homes in Düsseldorf from which these children come. First was that of Hans Brouemme, who is now in Dublin. His mother triumphantly produced a letter from the family saying that all was well. 'It's hard to let them go,' she said, 'but not so difficult when we hear that they are happy.'

'How are they going to manage about German?' I was asked. 'Do many in Ireland speak the language? Of course, he will soon learn English.' An awful thought dawned on her: suppose he forgets his German?

The mother, the grandmother, the two young boys and I sat in silent perplexity, but more important things were moving in the mind of the youngest boy of four. I could see it about to burst.

Finally it came. 'Any chewing gum?' he asked, and Hans was momentarily forgotten in a torrent of rebukes and apologies. He was lucky. I had some.

I called next to see the family of Ursula Becker, aged nine, who left with last week's party. Like the other families, the Beckers had all the details of the trip off by heart—the train to Calais, the boat across the Channel, the meeting with the Irish Red Cross officials in London, the few weeks in a camp, and final allocation to Irish families.

For child's sake . . .

Frau Becker, in spite of the break, was very glad for the child's sake that she had got to Ireland, as she had always been a bit delicate.

'There are mountains in Ireland, aren't there,' she asked, 'and plenty of open spaces where there is good fresh air?' You have to see a town like Düsseldorf with its miles and miles of ruins and its grey-faced inhabitants to realise what a picture the thought of Ireland must bring before them.

Among the most deserving children are those whose home is in one of the bunkers or air raid shelters. Several of them came from one of these bunkers at Kaiserwerth, on the outskirts of Düsseldorf.

I first went to look for the family of five-year-old Horst Kowalski, whose father is still a prisoner of war. This bunker has no doors on its cubicles, and after calling out the name several times the warden who accompanied me pulled aside the blanket that hung over the opening to find it empty.

However, nearby we found the father of Hannelore Hoenig, one of the last batch of children. He had a book in front of him and rose to the sound of our voices.

Only when I offered him a cigarette and saw his hand groping about did I realise that he was blind—wounded two months before the end of the war. The book, I then saw, was not printed but studded with raised dots in formation like dice, and he proudly explained how he had learned to read the system in six months.

He spoke with some emotion of how much he hated to be separated from his daughter, 'even though we have only this', waving his hand at the tiny cell, about twelve feet by six, which was now the home for himself, his wife and one child.

'Perhaps conditions will improve here soon, and we can have her back before the period is up,' he said.

On the floor above we came across Frau Hubertus, who had two sons in the last party to leave—Joseph, aged eight, and August, nine.

Husband missing

Her husband has been missing since Christmas, 1944. Frau Hubertus was patiently slicing some vegetables for the evening meal. She was tired, having stood for seven and a half hours in queues that morning, beginning at six o'clock. She spoke in a monotone, as if nothing mattered very much anymore, and all the time continued doodling with her vegetables.

Like almost every family I have spoken to in this area, they have sickness. One of her four remaining children is in hospital and another was just being x-rayed. The other two are working, which helps to eke out the 97 marks per month she gets in relief money.

The two young ones need all the fresh air and good food they can get, she said, and her own drawn, grey face showed that she needed exactly the same things.

After a few days spent in surroundings like this, after seeing the children that are left behind, you come to the conclusion that those who have gone to Ireland are being given a chance to live, and you hate to think what is to happen to the others.

At John Healy's funeral in 1991, outside the Three Patrons Church in Rathgar, Douglas Gageby (left) with Garret FitzGerald. Gageby's wife, Dorothy, constantly urged him not to smirk at funerals.

Appendix 2
Appreciations

Dynamic, tough and idealistic

Conor Brady

Douglas Gageby was our editor and our hero in the exciting, frenetic, idealised world that was *Irish Times* journalism in the late 1960s. He was dynamic, unpredictable, inspirational and he generated an energy-field around him that infected even the most cynical and somnolent in the editorial offices of *The Irish Times*.

His diamond-toughness was matched by a capacity for deep human compassion. His patriotism ran in parallel with a commitment to the great post-War experiment of a united and peaceful Europe. His mind was endlessly inquiring and eclectic. In the course of a drink or a meal it could run from religion to food to history to fly-fishing. He was utterly indifferent to sport of any kind—apart from rowing. When he had to focus on an issue, the intensity of his concentration could be awesome.

He had fixed points in his philosophy of life. He loved Dorothy and his family. He loved journalism—but not just the journalism of *The Irish Times*. He had a great love of country, expressed in his loyalty to the Army in which he had served, his admiration for the non-violent nationalism of the SDLP, and his fascination with the people and the countryside around Moynalty in Co. Meath, where he went in quiet times to read and fish and walk.

He and Dorothy shared with my Ann and our family an enthusiasm for that region of Catalan, France, known as the Roussillon. It often figured in his 'Y' column, when he extolled the produce of the Languedoc, the warm sea of the Côte Vermeille or the clear air of the Albères mountains.

His principles of journalism were at once simple and uncompromising. He prized accuracy and honesty. He abhorred laziness and assumption. He always acknowledged that ours is an imperfect craft, executed under strain and against deadlines. He was generally forgiving of a misjudgment but was implacable where he encountered arrogance or bias. He never thought that journalism could be truly objective. What he sought in writers who worked for him was detail, accuracy, curiosity and fairness.

There are myths about Douglas. One is that he eschewed the company of those in power. Not so. He would regularly meet with men and women in key positions of influence across Irish society, often through the 'Murphy Club'. But insofar as the political and power structure of this state was concerned, he remained in many ways an uncomprehending outsider. He relied almost wholly on his great friend and colleague John Healy to be his guide through the labyrinth of Southern Irish politics.

He was a republican. But in the tradition of Tone, McCracken, Emmet and his beloved Armour of Ballymoney. He held fervently to the conviction that one day, Catholic, Protestant and Dissenter would really rejoice in the common name of Irishman. Perversely, this gave rise to another myth, that he was soft on the violence of those who hijacked the republican label. In reality, he believed absolutely in the supremacy of the state and of its agents, duly appointed and answerable to its elected representatives. Once he told me that had he been editor in 1976 when *The Irish Times* investigated allegations of abuse by the Garda 'Heavy Gang', the articles would never have seen the light of day. Fergus Pyle, editor from 1974 to early 1977, took a different view, and to his great credit, courageously ran with the material.

Douglas had an extraordinary capacity for mobilising and stimulating those around him to give of their best. He recognised that a successful newspaper requires a multiplicity of talents. So he built around himself a team of disparate geniuses. There was Bruce Williamson, the supremely literate poet and classicist; Donal Foley, the Irish-speaking news editor with flair, instinct and imagination. There was Gerry Mulvey, the professional news editor, who watched every story and every detail with the eye of a hawk. And Ken Gray, the calm, imperturbable administrator.

His relationship with Tom McDowell, later chairman and chief executive of *The Irish Times* remains an enigma. Theirs was the partnership that anchored the newspaper's success. Gageby's editorial genius and McDowell's business acumen combined to make *The Irish Times* a valuable title so that in 1974 they were both able to become—by the standards of the time—rich men, when they sold their shares to the new Irish Times Trust.

Douglas could be blindly unreasonable and judgmental. Once, when his telephone line to Moynalty was disrupted, he penned an editorial headed 'Sack Jim Mitchell' (the minister for communications). Yet he could be infuriatingly indulgent. He took a benign view of Charles Haughey, mediated through the judgment of Healy, forgiving him almost everything.

His view of newspapers was at once idealistic and hard-headed. He sometimes made a point of grumbling about the commercial side of the organisation within the hearing of other journalists. But he knew well that a successful paper is a marriage between editorial and business talents. 'It's the hardest job in the world,' he said, 'trying to sell ad space in a newspaper. Journalists have it easy by comparison.'

If you asked him what makes a good journalist, he would say 'curiosity'. When I went for interview as a young graduate he asked me: 'If you were in my house and I left you to go and make a cup of tea, would you read the letters on my mantelpiece?' I said I would. 'Good man,' came the response. 'Be here on the 1st of October and there's a job for you.'

He had no formal training as a journalist or editor. None of us did in those days. But he understood intuitively the things that are now taught at university to would-be practitioners of the trade. He grasped the necessity for specialisation in journalism before anyone else in the country. He used to say that a newspaper was a bit like a Christmas pudding—it had to have all sorts of ingredients to appeal to the different tastes and preferences of its readers. Thus, to him, the features pages or the arts pages were as deserving of his attention as the front page. He spent countless hours with me in the late 1970s working on the design of a new television listings page.

Little was left to chance. Important things were planned carefully, even though he might represent it otherwise. It is probably 20 years since he told me over a drink one night that when he died nobody would know about it until four days later when his funeral would have taken place.

Behind his vital absorption in the world about him, there was a spiritual dimension. He distrusted organised religion and churches. But he was fascinated by the Polish Pope who came to Ireland in 1979. He joked that he had probably become the first Catholic editor of *The Irish Times* in spite of himself.

He oversaw the rise of women journalists through the newspaper and took immense delight in their successes and triumphs. In spite of the occasional volcanic outburst, he was limitlessly tolerant of human weakness. Once a particularly recidivist correspondent was summoned to his office for some unforgivable offence. He left with a raise.

He had a clear and firm view of what a newspaper's function should be in society. He shared with John Delane of *The Times* the certainty that its duty is to publish all it knows—regardless of the consequences. He would not be led into any acknowledgment that newspapers should be responsible, respectable or restrained. He knew when to hold back, to hint rather than bawl. He knew that a criticism expressed in sorrow is usually more effective than one vented in anger.

G. K. Chesterton articulated a view of the newspaper's role that might have been written to encapsulate Douglas Gageby's view of what is done in a good newspaper:

> A poet writing in the silence of his study may or may not have an intellectual right to despise the journalist. But I greatly doubt that he would not be morally the better if he saw the great lights burning on through darkness until dawn and heard the roar of the printing wheels weaving the destinies of another day. Here at least is a school of labour and of some rough humility, the largest work ever published anonymously since the great Christian Cathedral.

Conor Brady followed Douglas Gageby as editor of The Irish Times *from 1986 to 2002. This appreciation was published in* The Irish Times *on 28 June 2004.*

He moved our newspaper from the margins to the mainstream of Irish life

Geraldine Kennedy

The death of Douglas Gageby is a milestone in all of our lives, for the extended *Irish Times* family who have come here, for Irish journalism and, it is no exaggeration to say, for Irish society, which he helped to mould into the country we live in now.

I first met him in early 1973 when he offered me a job as a cub reporter, on the recommendation of the then News Editor, Donal Foley.

Like Maeve Binchy, he was always Mr Gageby to me—a hugely authoritative figure whose journalistic reputation long preceded my arrival in Dublin, in the Irish News Agency and in launching the innovative *Evening Press* in the 1950s before coming to *The Irish Times*.

One of the first things I wanted to do when I became Editor of *The Irish Times* on October 12th, 2002, was to meet Mr Gageby. He invited me to his home, though he was ill at the time.

'What have you done to your lovely long red hair?' he greeted me.

'I'm much older now, Mr Gageby.'

'And we have a Madam Editor. I'm delighted.'

'Being Editor of *The Irish Times* is the best job in Ireland,' he said.

'And how are you, Mr Gageby?', I asked him.

'Waiting to be with Dorothy,' he replied.

He moved our newspaper from the margins to the mainstream of Irish public life. It was a huge achievement and he made it appear so effortless. Essentially, he possessed the key component which makes a good reporter: he was curious about people's lives and the way they lived them and he was always sceptical of the spin doctors' arts.

He believed in fair and honest reporting and keeping the clear distinction between facts and commentary.

As a Protestant republican espousing the spirit of Armour of Ballymoney—who never featured on my school curriculum—he recognised the vision of the young John Hume, sent John Horgan off to Rome to cover the Second Vatican Council, introduced a Women's Page to give expression to the emerging women's movement and gave a young generation of journalists their heads.

Up to a point, that is. He was there to curb their excesses of enthusiasm, to bring perspective and superior judgment to bear on their exuberance. And his great motto about daily newspapers was that tomorrow is another chance to get it absolutely right, to produce the perfect paper.

It would be fair to note, on this platform, that he wouldn't have been the great Editor that he was without the insights of some of those who worked with him: Bruce Williamson, who told us never to forget that the plural of referendum is referendums, John Healy, and Donal Foley, all of whom predeceased him; and Gerry Mulvey, his hands-on News Editor, here with us today.

Mr Gageby guided *The Irish Times* through the most turbulent, if exciting, developments in modern Ireland. Through the hopes, horrors and uncertainties of the Northern conflict as well as through the slow and sometimes halting emergence of a pluralist society in the South, Mr Gageby's *Irish Times* became the medium through which the alternative Ireland emerged.

With the benefit of hindsight, it is easy to assume that these developments followed a preordained and inevitable course.

But they did not, during his first period as Editor from 1963 to 1974 when the outcome in either part of the island was far from clear.

He played no small part then—and again during his second period as Editor from 1977 to 1986—in ensuring that we ended up with the peaceful and generally pluralist country we live in today.

He engaged Ireland in a conversation with herself and, to adapt a phrase from political history, Ireland won.

Like all of us, he had his pet interests. The SDLP, whose formation and advancement he supported; the Army, in which he had served during the so-called Emergency; and trees, which reflected his love of nature.

Above all, he was a newspaperman to his fingertips. He loved the dirty big print page, to be on the stone where he knew every printer by first name. He loved the buzz of the big story. The pressure of the deadlines.

Mr Gageby left Ireland a great newspaper, a beacon of independent and trustworthy journalism in a world of media conglomerates, cross-selling and so-called synergies.

And he left us the tools with which to maintain that position—reliable reporting, fair commentary, freedom from any sectional interest, a platform for the voiceless, an endlessly inquiring mind, and a determination to go on trying to make tomorrow's paper more interesting, more revealing, more incisive than today's.   .

Geraldine Kennedy succeeded Conor Brady as editor of The Irish Times *in 2002. This sddress was given to a memorial event for Douglas Gageby, held in the Royal Dublin Society premises on 9 July 2004.* © The Irish Times *2004*

EDITOR OF *THE IRISH TIMES* FOR MORE THAN 20 YEARS WHO WAS REAPPOINTED IN HIS RETIREMENT BECAUSE THE BACKERS TRUSTED NO ONE ELSE

The Times of London obituary 7 July 2004

Douglas Gageby was Editor of *The Irish Times* from 1963 to 1986 (with a short intermission in the 1970s). He transformed the paper from being the organ of the ex-Unionist, largely Protestant, minority to being the upmarket paper of modern Ireland with more than double its previous circulation. This transformation replicated Gageby's own journey from an Ulster Unionist background to becoming an Irish nationalist deeply committed to the ideal of a united independent Ireland where the differences between Catholic, Protestant and Dissenter would be subsumed in the common name of Irishman.

His father, a Belfastman married to a schoolteacher from Westmeath, had moved back North to a minor post in the Northern Ireland Civil Service at the time of Irish independence. Robert John Douglas, their only surviving child, who had been born in Dublin, went to school at the Belfast Royal Academy and followed on to Trinity College Dublin, where he read French and German. He also rowed for the college.

Gageby was at Trinity when the Second World War broke out but he did not join the mass of his contemporaries who flocked to join the British Armed Forces. Instead, he enlisted in the Irish Army as a private. He was later commissioned and served in intelligence; one of his less congenial tasks was to read the letters sent to interned Germans. He met and married his wife Dorothy, the daughter of Seán Lester, an Ulster Protestant nationalist who had become an Irish diplomat, the League of Nations High Commissioner in Danzig and finally its last Secretary-General.

Gageby's happy years in the Irish Army and his strong levelling instinct helped him to blend in easily in nationalist circles. He was loud in professions of distaste for the English, although, ironically, Kipling was his favourite poet. He was employed in the *Irish Press*, the official organ of de Valera's Fianna Fáil republican party, and impressed by his reports from post-war Germany. He later worked under Conor Cruise O'Brien in the Irish News Agency, founded by Seán MacBride to campaign against partition and to counter the view of Irish events emanating from London. In 1954 the *Irish Press* group founded a Dublin evening newspaper with Gageby as editor, which proved remarkably successful.

The struggling ex-Unionist *Irish Times* saw the Protestant Gageby as a natural member of its stable and enticed him to become its joint managing director in 1959. He became a member of the board and a one-fifth owner when the Arnott family sold out. He was appointed editor in 1963. He brought to the post a capacity for leadership and a deep feeling for good journalism. Meeting his staff for the first time, he announced that anyone who came in drunk would be dismissed. Gageby imposed his will and the staff were in awe of him; quite a number suffered at the receiving end of his short fuse and blunt tongue. But his journalists appreciated that, short of a libel writ, he was unwilling to entertain outside complaints against them, something that may have bred within the *Irish Times* organisation a rather cavalier attitude to outsiders.

Gageby was an editor who stayed in his office rather than socialise and he was receptive to ideas proposed by his staff. Under him *The Irish Times* pioneered investigative journalism in Ireland with some notable pieces.

Journalists were recruited from a broader constituency than the Protestants and Trinity men who had once held most key posts; in a gesture to the growing Catholic readership Gageby sent a correspondent to cover the Second Vatican Council. He was especially encouraging to women journalists, among whom were numbered Mary Holland and Maeve Binchy.

In editorials, which he often wrote himself, he took quite a strident nationalist line on partition as the agitation against the Unionist regime in Northern Ireland gathered pace in the late 1960s. His sermons to Ulster Unionists to find their future in a united Ireland, which reeked of his own personal odyssey, reached few of them as *The Irish Times* was no longer much read in Northern Ireland. Neither his fellow proprietors nor the bulk of the paper's Dublin readership were all that pushed about Northern Ireland or shared Gageby's Anglophobia. In 1969 the managing director, an ex-major in the British Army, expressed regrets to the British Ambassador, Sir Andrew Gilchrist, that he could not get his editor to take a line more helpful to Her Majesty's Government. The ambassador reported to London remarking on Gageby's Ulster Unionist background and describing him as a 'kind of white nigger'.

But Gageby, by broadening the appeal of a paper that had been threatened with extinction, had made it a commercial success and had to be indulged.

He himself profited mightily from that success when in 1974 he and the other four proprietors sold their interests to a charitable trust they set up and had funded by a bank loan. It was presented as a means of preserving the independence of the paper. But the valuation put on the interests sold was such that it took many years for the paper to generate enough profit to repay the loan. Meanwhile, Gageby and his fellow former proprietors remained in complete control and the financial affairs of the business were effectively hidden from public view. It was a situation pregnant with possibilities of abuse and was anomalous in a newspaper that was vociferous in calling for accountability from all manner of persons and institutions.

Gageby himself retired as editor in 1974 but was recalled little over two years later when the paper got into financial difficulties under his chosen successor and only Gageby's return would satisfy its bankers. His second term of office coincided with the succession of Charles Haughey as Taoiseach. Gageby was impressed by Haughey's harder line on the North and said so. But he knew that *The Irish Times* readership was a broad church, much of which did not share his political views. He employed as a regular columnist Conor Cruise O'Brien whom he did not much like and whose hostility to Haughey and less nationalist line on Northern Ireland often infuriated him.

The Irish Times was also vocal in advocating reforms in family law and other areas that were opposed by the Roman Catholic Church; Gageby was anxious that the Republic should make itself a more secular society so as to be more acceptable to Ulster Protestants. If *The Irish Times* had wandered far from its traditional Unionist allegiance, it was still seen by many Catholics as displaying the old Unionist antipathy to their Church.

Outside his office Gageby was a bluff jovial kind of man blessed with a happy marriage and a successful family. He had a passion for fly-fishing.

After his retirement as Editor in 1986 he contributed an anonymous column, largely about nature. In 1999 he completed a biography of his father-in-law Seán Lester, whose background and aspirations so mirrored his own.

Gageby was predeceased by his wife and is survived by two daughters and two sons. His eldest child Susan, a judge of the Supreme Court, was the first woman appointed to that court.

Douglas Gageby, former editor of The Irish Times, *was born on September 29, 1918. He died on June 24, 2004, aged 85.* © The Times 2004

'IRISH TIMES' EDITOR WAS A JOURNALISTIC GIANT WHO CHOSE TO SHUN THE LIMELIGHT

The Irish Times obituary 28 June 2004

Douglas Gageby, who died on Thursday night [24 June 2004] after two years of ill health, was a key figure in Irish journalism during a career in editorial chairs which spanned a half-century, although he remained relatively unknown to many members of the public.

In the 1950s, he played prominent roles in the successful launches of the *Sunday Press* and the *Evening Press*. He was editor-in-chief of the less successful Irish News Agency from 1951–1954.

But it was his long association with *The Irish Times*, involving two stints as editor—1963–1974 and 1977–1986—which made him the most influential figure in Irish journalism as the paper completed its transformation from the newspaper of the Protestant, unionist minority to the national and independent newspaper of record of today.

With his Ulster Protestant origins and Trinity College education, Douglas Gageby was perhaps an unlikely figure to guide the evolution of *The Irish Times* to its position of influence in a predominantly Catholic Republic country.

But he recruited new writers, opened the newspaper's columns to all opinions and its appeal grew with the political and economic élite and the increasingly affluent middle classes, especially in urban areas.

During his first stint as editor, the circulation almost doubled, from 35,000 to 69,500. It also grew steadily during his 'second coming', as his later term was sometimes dubbed.

But, while the newspaper was extending its influence during the Ireland of the second half of the 20th century, Douglas Gageby remained by choice a behind-the-scenes editor who largely shunned the invitations to wine and dine with the great and good.

He saw himself as a working journalist who preferred 'sitting back at the office' to working the cocktail circuit. An editor should not have too much contact with the people in power, he would point out, as this could inhibit the writing of editorials, which he did almost every day as editor.

'A paper is no good unless it sparks and sometimes pokes people in the eye, as long as you can give all the information you can dig up fairly,' he told an interviewer. He summarised his aim for *The Irish Times* as trying 'to be a good and honest and sober and stimulating and occasionally jolly newspaper', but 'the news, the facts, are what matter'.

He was sceptical of the influence often attributed to newspapers, telling Ivor Kenny in an interview after his retirement for Kenny's book, *In Good Company*: 'I never see a paper as a power in the land, in shifting parties this way or that. I see it as giving information and, with our comments from all quarters, helping people to sift out information.'

Douglas Gageby was born in Ranelagh, Dublin, on September 29th, 1918, the only son of Thomas Gageby, a junior civil servant under British rule who had come South from Belfast at the age of 15, saying that he never had enough to eat in his father's house.

The father had been a mill worker whose discontent with unionist domination of politics led him to contest and win a Labour seat on Belfast City Council. He stood unsuccessfully in the general election of 1910.

Douglas Gageby's mother, Ethel (*née* Smith), from Co. Westmeath, had been a national-school teacher who had wanted to be a concert singer.

When Douglas Gageby was three, his five-year-old sister died of meningitis, so he was reared as an only child.

The family soon afterwards moved back to Belfast, where Thomas took up a position in the new Northern Ireland civil service. Douglas Gageby grew up in Belfast and always retained a strong affection for the city and an admiration for its people.

He spoke of a childhood spent exploring Cave Hill and MacArt's Fort. 'I was always out and about, covered in mud, looking at some newt or other. We had hundreds of acres on our doorstep. Now it's Ardoyne.' His passion for natural history stayed with him.

He was educated at the Belfast Royal Academy, where he excelled in languages, especially German. He was able to observe the rise of the Nazi movement at first hand during several visits to Germany in the 1930s.

In 1937, at the urging of his mother, he began his studies in Trinity College Dublin, although he had won three scholarships to Queen's University Belfast.

Douglas Gageby loved his time in Trinity, where he studied modern languages and later studied for an LLB. While there, he met his future wife, Dorothy Lester, whose father was Seán Lester, an Irish diplomat seconded to the League of Nations, who served as its last secretary-general after a time as its high commissioner in the then-free city of Danzig (now the Polish city of Gdansk).

The young Trinity student from Belfast who became an enthusiastic member of the university rowing club was enthralled by the turbulent political scene in Dublin, where Fianna Fáil under Éamon de Valera was installed in power and striving for increased separation from British Empire links.

'I was enraptured by the whole national thing and still am,' he told Kenny in the 1986 interview.

After the second World War broke out and 'The Emergency' was declared in neutral Ireland, Douglas Gageby decided to abandon his degree and join the Army—'because Dev asked us to'. It was a decision that alarmed his parents, who persuaded him to finish his degree first. He enlisted as a private in 1941 but was soon spotted as officer material and commissioned as a second lieutenant.

He served in the G2 military-intelligence branch under Col. Dan Bryan, whom he came to admire greatly for his handling of sensitive intelligence matters when Irish neutrality was under pressure from the British and American governments.

These years in the colours were to leave Douglas Gageby with a lasting affection and respect for the Defence Forces, and woe betide a reporter who made a mistake writing about military ranks.

With the war over, the recently married Douglas Gageby applied for a job in the de Valera-controlled *Irish Press*, where he worked as a sub-editor and a reporter. He later told Éamon de Valera's son, Major Vivion de Valera: 'My politics are in or around Fianna Fáil or I would not have looked for a job on the paper.'

During this time, he reported extensively from ravaged post-war Germany, including the Berlin airlift, putting his excellent German to good use. He would return to the country in 1989 to contribute a memorable series on the country's changed face to *The Irish Times*.

In 1949, he was appointed assistant editor of the new *Sunday Press*. Two years later, he became editor-in-chief of the Irish News Agency, which was set up by the coalition government at the prompting of the minister for external relations Seán MacBride, to supply Irish news material to the international press. Here, Douglas Gageby met journalist John Healy, with whom he was to establish a long collaboration and friendship.

In 1954, the Irish Press turned again to Douglas Gageby to help set up a new evening paper, the *Evening Press*, which would give the group a strong footing in the Dublin newspaper market. He was editor of the new paper for the first five years. It flourished after a shaky start. Vivion de Valera later showed him letters from Fianna Fáil ministers 'asking what the hell that bloody Orange editor was doing'.

Meanwhile, *The Irish Times* was in trouble, with a falling circulation and increasing debts. In 1959, Douglas Gageby was offered the post of joint managing director of the ailing newspaper by George Hetherington.

He also asked for a seat on the board and told the directors that 'I was a nationalist of a certain kind, largely in favour of Fianna Fáil'. In 1963, he was appointed editor, succeeding Alan Montgomery, who became head of Guinness's PR department.

It is revealing of Douglas Gageby's low-profile style of editorship that *The Irish Times* cuttings library contains only two items on him during this 11-year period. One is a talk he gave to an adult-education course in University College Galway on 'Newspapers in the world today'.

The other is an account of his evidence to the inquiry into the RTÉ 'Seven Days' programme on moneylending in 1970. He defended the programme while pointing out that it was impossible to apply the journalistic standards of newspapers to television journalism.

'In television, the mechanism quite often dominates the person who is making the programme,' he told the inquiry. He also repeated his view that there was no such thing as total 'objectivity' in reporting because of attitudes derived from background and training. But journalists must always strive for 'fairness'.

Journalists who worked under him found him to be fair and sympathetic to personal problems, but carelessness or lack of effort could provoke an outburst. He admitted to having a short fuse on occasions but said he did not hold grudges.

In July 1974, Douglas Gageby retired as editor following the setting up some months earlier of the Irish Times Trust and the buying out of the existing director shareholders, of which he was one. This netted him £325,000, which was a substantial sum in those days.

Under his editorship, the paper had practically doubled its circulation, recruited talented writers under the guidance of news editor Donal Foley, and reached a healthy financial situation. He was replaced as editor by the late Fergus Pyle.

Retirement at 56 seemed too early for a man who described himself as a 'working animal', but it gave him the opportunity to pursue his favourite relaxations of fishing and reading. He got involved in writing and presenting a six-part television series, 'Heritage of Ireland', produced by Louis Marcus for RTÉ.

In 1977, he was called back to the editorial chair to reverse the slide in circulation of *The Irish Times*, which was in financial trouble as an economic recession had also caused a slump in advertising. The situation was not helped by the burden of debt which the buyout of the shareholders in better times placed on the newspaper.

The worsening situation in Northern Ireland dominated much of Douglas Gageby's second term as editor. After his second retirement in 1986, he revealed in interviews a passionate commitment to eventual

Irish unity and increasing impatience with both unionist intransigence and Southern turning away from Northern Ireland.

He saw the 1985 Anglo-Irish Agreement, giving Dublin a right of consultation in Northern Ireland affairs, as 'the biggest political happening in my lifetime', he told Deirdre Purcell in a *Sunday Tribune* interview in 1987.

'From the unionists being king—"oh, we can do anything here"— suddenly they're out,' is the way he described the new situation, while paying tribute to the SDLP constitutional approach.

He later lavished praise on SDLP leader John Hume as a worthy successor to one of his own heroes, Thomas Davis, for his efforts to achieve a peaceful reconciliation of nationalists and unionists. But he was also critical of what he saw as a lack of generosity by people and politicians in the South towards reconciliation, citing the rejection of divorce in the first referendum in 1986.

He called himself something of a 'romantic nationalist' and when unveiling a plaque in Belfast commemorating the founding of the United Irishmen in the city in 1791, he said they were 'not failed revolutionaries—they were realists. They had in common the spirit of Wolfe Tone's dictum of the name of Irishman replacing that of Protestant, Catholic or Dissenter.'

In 1999, he brought to fruition a project he had long planned, a biography of his late father-in-law, Seán Lester, covering his career as an international public servant. He saw the task as reclaiming the story of a great public servant for Ireland 'but most of all I wanted to write about how a fellow from Carrickfergus, the son of a grocer, arrived at Geneva and Danzig via the Dungannon clubs.'

He toyed with the idea of owning his own newspaper and told one interviewer that in 1987 he tried to buy the *Belfast News Letter*, the principal unionist newspaper in Northern Ireland. He denied a report that John Hume was arranging financial backing from the US.

True to his insistence that even in retirement 'I'm still a journalist, I'll die a journalist,' Douglas Gageby for years wrote the anonymous 'In Time's Eye' nature item on the editorial page of *The Irish Times*, signed 'Y'. Through all seasons, it revealed his deep love for the natural world and sharp eye for its wonders.

He was the recipient of honorary degrees from the National University of Ireland and Trinity College. In 1994, he won the A.T. Cross Hall of Fame award for his contribution to Irish journalism.

His wife Dorothy, whom he married in 1944, predeceased him in September 2002, and he is survived by his daughters, Susan, a judge of the Supreme Court, and Sally; and sons, John, who works in financial services, and Patrick, a senior counsel; 12 grandchildren, and one great-grandchild.

He died on Thursday evening and his private family funeral service on Saturday in Mount Jerome was presided over by an old friend, the Rev. Terence McCaughey.

Douglas Gageby: born September 29th, 1918; died June 24th, 2004.

INDEX